Reckoning with Rebellion

Frontiers of the American South

UNIVERSITY PRESS OF FLORIDA

Florida A&M University, Tallahassee
Florida Atlantic University, Boca Raton
Florida Gulf Coast University, Ft. Myers
Florida International University, Miami
Florida State University, Tallahassee
New College of Florida, Sarasota
University of Central Florida, Orlando
University of Florida, Gainesville
University of North Florida, Jacksonville
University of South Florida, Tampa
University of West Florida, Pensacola

RECKONING WITH REBELLION

WAR AND SOVEREIGNTY IN THE NINETEENTH CENTURY

AARON SHEEHAN-DEAN

University Press of Florida
Gainesville · Tallahassee · Tampa · Boca Raton
Pensacola · Orlando · Miami · Jacksonville · Ft. Myers · Sarasota

Published in the United States of America

25 24 23 22 21 20 6 5 4 3 2 1

Library of Congress Cataloging-in-Publication Data
Names: Sheehan-Dean, Aaron Charles, author.
Title: Reckoning with rebellion : war and sovereignty in the nineteenth century / Aaron Sheehan-Dean.
Other titles: Frontiers of the American South.
Description: Gainesville : University Press of Florida, 2020. | Series: Frontiers of the American South | Includes bibliographical references and index.
Identifiers: LCCN 2019054516 (print) | LCCN 2019054517 (ebook) | ISBN 9780813066424 (hardback) | ISBN 9780813057514 (adobe pdf)
Subjects: LCSH: United States—History—Civil War, 1861–1865. | India—History—Sepoy Rebellion, 1857–1858. | China—History—Taiping Rebellion, 1850–1864.
Classification: LCC E468 .S355 2020 (print) | LCC E468 (ebook) | DDC 973.7—dc23
LC record available at https://lccn.loc.gov/2019054516
LC ebook record available at https://lccn.loc.gov/2019054517

The University Press of Florida is the scholarly publishing agency for the State University System of Florida, comprising Florida A&M University, Florida Atlantic University, Florida Gulf Coast University, Florida International University, Florida State University, New College of Florida, University of Central Florida, University of Florida, University of North Florida, University of South Florida, and University of West Florida.

University Press of Florida
2046 NE Waldo Road
Suite 2100
Gainesville, FL 32609
http://upress.ufl.edu

For Jon

CONTENTS

FIGURES

FOREWORD

Reckoning with Rebellion: War and Sovereignty in the Nineteenth Century is the second volume appearing in the Frontiers of the American South series. Our purpose in this series is to explore topics that push our understanding of what makes (and has made) the American South. Further, Frontiers of the American South seeks different thematic approaches and new views about the historical meaning of the South, how it evolved over time, and the relevance of this evolution for our own time.

Reckoning with Rebellion expands the boundaries of the history of the Civil War and Reconstruction by considering the international implications of rebellion and war, including how varying views on war, rebellion, and nation-building formed a context for warfare on the American continent. Using examples of the 1857 Indian Rebellion, China's Taiping Rebellion, and the 1863 Polish Insurrection, Aaron Sheehan-Dean probes mid-nineteenth-century ideas about the nature of war. American military men were keenly aware of the warfare abroad, and the conversations they had were shaped by conversations across the globe. With separate discussions of insurgency, legitimacy, and sovereignty's relationship to power and nation-building, Sheehan-Dean seeks to connect the Civil War with a much wider international context. Indeed, he argues that the Civil War itself cannot be properly understood without foregrounding it in a global and broader temporal framework.

* * *

Meredith Babb and Sian Hunter of the University Press of Florida have been a part of this series since its inception and have provided indispensable assistance in helping us navigate book publishing. Both Meredith and Sian are exceptional editors, and we have greatly benefited from their skill.

The preparation of this volume involved efforts by a variety of people. Above all, Aaron Sheehan-Dean took time from his busy scholarly and professional life to produce this volume. The Milbauer Program in Southern History, at the University of Florida, has profited from the enthusiasm of graduate students Aurélia Aubert, Madison Cates, Anthony Donaldson, Meagan Frenzer, Lauren Kimbell, and David Meltsner, who helped bring this volume to fruition.

William A. Link, Series Editor
Gainesville, Florida
August 2019

ACKNOWLEDGMENTS

Although the ideas in this book began percolating some time ago, it was Bill Link's invitation to deliver the Milbauer lectures that helped propel me into real work on the topic. Bill has long been a mentor, colleague, and friend. I am honored to be among the many people in our field who have benefited from his wisdom, generosity, and good humor. He was also a great host in Gainesville. Aurélia Aubert arranged my visit and all of the details with grace and professionalism and was a fun dinner guest. I was fortunate to speak with the smart U.S. history graduate students who offered several good ideas in our conversation before the seminar. During the talks, I benefited from the questions and ideas raised by several people. My thanks go to Jon Sensbach and especially to the crew who attended dinner the second night, where they patiently answered my questions about nineteenth-century Europe: Sheryl Kroen, Norman Goda, and Mitchell Hart.

I am fortunate to work with such a knowledgeable and helpful community at Louisiana State University. Colleagues in a variety of fields have fielded my queries as I blundered into their domains. I am grateful for their patience and help for this interloper, especially Sue Marchand, Asiya Alam, Margherita Zanasi, Steve Andes, and Leslie Tuttle. During a particularly helpful afternoon, the Works-in-Progress Seminar at LSU—Meredith Veldman, Brendan Karch, Jason Wolfe, Zevi Gutfreund, Margherita, and Leslie—gave me excellent feedback on chapter 3. Brendan earned special thanks for recommending so many helpful sources on Poland. Two classes of students, one at the University of North Florida and another at LSU, gamely participated in a course on war and nationalism in the nineteenth century that I had little business teaching. Nonetheless, they raised questions and ideas that helped improve this book and they have my thanks. My deep thanks to Zhenman Ye, who, only moments after arriving at LSU, read the whole manuscript and offered astute comments and prevented several spelling and linguistic errors. I am eager to see how her own research on the Taiping and American Civil War evolves.

I presented a very early version of some of this material at the Transnational Significance of the American Civil War conference at Friedrich-Schiller University in Jena, Germany, in 2011. I am grateful to Jörg Nagler and Märcus Graser, the conference organizers, and to all the participants for their comments. I also extend my deep thanks to Johann Neem, long a friend and a model of scholarly excellence. Johann invited me to present part of the manuscript at Western Washington University's History Workshop. I am grateful to the workshop attendees, who provided an invigorating afternoon of feedback and ideas. Johann, as usual, offered valuable insights into the project. Roger Thomson participated in the workshop, sent me additional readings, and did the great favor of reading a later draft of one of the chapters. I appreciate both his insights and his willingness to help.

I have buttonholed people at conferences and in different settings about this project over the years. Because this project has spanned so many locations, I will miss everyone, but my deep thanks to Brian Schoen, Frank Towers, Stephen Platt (who generously answered a cold-call email with helpful direction), Andy Lang, and Adam Smith. Jack Furniss shared his ideas and even found two of the illustrations for this book. I hope to repay the favor someday. Peter Carmichael read the manuscript and offered his unvarnished thoughts. I will always be grateful for his advice and his friendship. Margherita Zanasi read the whole manuscript with a critical eye and so deserves still more thanks. As did Wayne Hsieh, who has suffered through too much of my work but continues to help in many ways. I look forward to seeing his take on some of these issues soon. Greg Downs, too, has reviewed more of my work than seems fair, but he did so here with his usual keen insight and excellent advice. His recommendations, and those of an anonymous reviewer for the press, have made this a much stronger book. Thanks to them both.

Sian Hunter has been a great editor at the University Press of Florida. I appreciate her support and guidance on this project. Eleanor Deumens shepherded the manuscript smoothly through production. Patti Bower provided an excellent copyediting of it. And Mary Puckett has fielded my queries and served as an excellent liaison with the press. I am grateful for their help.

My brother, Jon, has, as always, listened to ideas, asked good questions, and offered sound advice. His range of knowledge and thoughtfulness continue to inspire me. This book is dedicated to him as a small token of repayment for all I have learned from him. Liam and Annie, my children, may not have always thrilled to stories of the Sepoy, but they sustain me with their humor, inquisitiveness, and generous spirits. Last, and most of all, I am thankful for my wife, Megan, who continues to support and amaze me. While I was producing words on a page, she built a remarkable garden that bears literal fruit. Her thoughtful, keen eye and love keep me rooted.

INTRODUCTION

HISTORIANS, AND AMERICANS GENERALLY, regard the Civil War as our great national trauma. The war's scale, its terrible fratricidal violence, and its two great outcomes—the preservation of the Union and the destruction of slavery—make it the centerpiece of our history. Yet, as participants in the war knew, it was not the only civil or national conflict occurring at the time. In the years just before secession, on the other side of the globe, Indians rebelled against British control in the event the latter called the Sepoy Mutiny. As Confederates and Federals battled each other in North America, Poles pursued independence from the Russian Empire, and the Taiping Rebellion drove China into a maelstrom of violence. Because the nineteenth century ushered in an era of global communication and news sharing, participants in these wars of national liberation knew about the other conflicts. Beyond mere awareness, people involved in these conflicts understood that commonalities and differences reverberated among them. Events in one, and the ways those events were represented and understood, shaped what happened in the others. When U.S. Secretary of State William Henry Seward sent his first cohort of ambassadors abroad in 1861, he counseled them in language that Indians, Britons, Poles, Russians, and the Chinese might have used. "Do we think we exaggerate our national importance when we claim that any political disaster that should befall us . . . might tend by its influence to disturb and unsettle the existing systems of government in other parts of the world?"[1] This was not a rhetorical question. Seward regarded American influence as global, inevitable, and benevolent. He foresaw the day when people around the world would acknowledge and appreciate American power.

But it was not only American influence that people felt. The other mid-century wars generated their own impact. Americans, including Seward himself, came to understand that the fates of nations were tied together.

Historians create meaning about the human experience from the raw material of the past. In order to make that meaning matter to the lives of contemporary readers, we sometimes pose new questions, such as when historians of the 1960s and 1970s returned to the antebellum era to investigate the experience of slavery anew. Rather than studying slaveholders, who had been thoroughly investigated by an earlier generation of historians, scholars turned their attention on enslaved people. Or we might change the context within which we locate a well-known experience, hoping to illuminate new aspects. This book takes the latter approach. It situates the U.S. Civil War in the context of three (mostly) contemporaneous events. These events—the Indian Rebellion of 1857, the January Uprising of 1863 in Poland, and the Taiping Rebellion (1850–64) in China—serve as points of reference for thinking anew about the American experience. Adopting a global perspective on the Civil War should not replace the domestic framework that most historians have used to understand the conflict. These approaches are complementary rather than contradictory. They enable us, as historians, to illuminate different aspects of the past. A global comparison of this sort necessarily relies on hindsight; to evaluate disparate events in relation to each other, we need to see the whole of each of the events. That said, in much of what follows, I adopt the perspective of observers at the time, who contended with language gaps, great distances, third- and fourth-hand observation, and regular miscommunication and misinterpretation. Much of what nineteenth-century observers thought they knew about contemporaneous rebellions was wrong, but that imprecision does not alter the degree of entanglement. I am also aware of my own rootedness in the English language and in my training as a historian of the U.S. Civil War. I anticipate that specialists in each of the conflicts addressed here will take issue with my analysis and conclusions. Despite that, I hope that this book inspires colleagues and students to undertake deeper studies of how these conflicts relate to one another.

In the middle of the nineteenth century, different peoples rose up, claiming national autonomy. We remember some of these conflicts as rebellions, others as civil wars, and still others as colonial struggles. Despite the differences in terminology, these events shared more than chronological companionship. We know the successes because they live on as independent nations today—most of the states in Central and South America and in Europe, Greece, Italy, and Germany, among others. Lingering among these successes were a host of national failures—political communities that coalesced briefly and then sputtered out. By comparing these failed efforts in India, Poland, China, and North America, we gain a better sense of why these conflicts ended as they did, the role of external forces in producing those ends, and what those ends meant for how we think about the nineteenth century. The people of the era lived connected lives; globalization may not have operated along digital networks, but interdependency manifested itself in economics, politics, and war. Debates about the nature of war, sovereignty, and nationalism, rooted in the struggles of diverse peoples, intersected in the mid-nineteenth century. Participants in the wars felt the consequences immediately, and we continue to live with their legacy today.

I am a historian of the U.S. Civil War, so I began this project with the intent of better understanding that conflict. My inspiration came from recognizing that the war's participants observed and wrote about foreign conflicts, and I followed their lead in my research. My source base is mostly English-language newspapers, public records, and private writing from Americans and British sources. I also consulted sources from the foreign conflicts, some translated and some created by English-speaking observers. This foundation allows me to write primarily about Western perspectives on the events considered here. I also consulted the secondary literature on each conflict and in global histories of the period. Always aware of the limits of my training, knowledge, and skills, I have nonetheless worked to understand and evaluate the episodes on their own terms. I hope the ideas proposed here are of interest to these parts of the scholarly community in addition to my Civil War friends.

The analysis that follows considers a set of wars that overlapped in time with the U.S. Civil War or occurred close enough to influence how the war's participants perceived their own experiences through a comparative lens. The key events are the 1857 Indian Rebellion, China's Taiping Rebellion, and the 1863 Polish Insurrection. Of necessity, I also discuss the established powers in these conflicts—respectively, Britain, Qing dynasty China, and Russia. This study analyzes the public conversations about the nature of war. Rather than advancing a clear chain of cause and effect among the midcentury rebellions, I identify the circumstantial connections among them. I hope that readers accustomed to military and political histories of war will see the value of intellectual and cultural histories. People fight wars with a variety of technologies; alongside weapons, tactics, and national ideologies are the ideas that participants bring to the conflict. What might surprise some readers is that Americans were not thinking only about the North American experience as they fought the Civil War—they knew and discussed a variety of global examples. Those voices were part of their conversation about how to manage the war; they should also be a part of ours. When officers and soldiers in the field described policies or reacted to conditions on the ground history, religion, and personal knowledge shaped their reaction. Further, like most modern wars, part of the Civil War was fought in print, as both sides characterized their conduct and that of their enemy. This process of justification and demonization relied upon comparison. Although analogies are notoriously difficult to apply to military conflicts, commentators on both sides charged in, marshaling historical and contemporary examples to promote their cause and denigrate their opponents.

In the aggregate, this book explains Confederate defeat not by looking at the battlefield, as important as this was. I agree with Confederate general George Pickett, who said "the Yankees had something to do with" Union victory, but I also think the American experience of civil war shares important structural similarities with other peoples' nation-building attempts. Compared to other histories, this book emphasizes structure over contingency. In other words, I argue that the global conversation about who could make war and how they could fight mattered to the outcome and meaning of the U.S. Civil War. I do not dispute the importance of unforeseen events or the serendipitous conclusions of battles. Structural forces exist alongside contingent ones; the course of history does not respond only to one form of causation.[2] The first chapter focuses on the manner of fighting—what it means to fight as an insurgent—and how this rebounded against those struggling to establish their national autonomy. The second chapter addresses the problem of legitimacy by considering the ways that foreign powers understood and discussed the midcentury conflicts and how these conceptions shaped their willingness to intervene. The last chapter uses these cases to reconsider how we think about state power in the nineteenth century; it investigates the relationship between sovereignty and power. Rather than seeing the century as the moment when modern nation-states supplanted archaic empires, we see not just the uneasy coexistence of these state forms but the habits they shared as well.

Historians typically approach the U.S. Civil War as a domestic conflict and regard the war's parameters and outcomes as a result of what occurred in North America alone. There are good reasons for this. Northern and Southern people understandably saw their fate as dependent upon national armies, but they did not wear blinders to events outside of their borders. Historians have noted this in studies that compare the experience of U.S. nation-building in the nineteenth century to the cases of Italy and Germany.[3] The wars I highlight here are not typically invoked in histories of the Civil War. This is a curious omission. These conflicts were contemporaneous (or nearly so) with the American one, and Americans used them as reference points throughout the war. Part of the reason that historians have spent less time with these cases is that they derived from different impulses than the North American experience. The Indian troops who led a rebellion against the British Empire wanted to restore Indian control over their continent, the Polish revolutionaries likewise wanted to reestablish the dominant political and economic position they occupied before the Partition of their country. The Taiping sought to supplant the Manchu-controlled Qing Dynasty and build a new Christian order. Confederates sought to conserve the social and economic order that they believed Lincoln's election jeopardized. The Sepoy were driven by anger, Poles by nostalgia, the Taiping by resentment, and Confederates by anxiety. Regardless of these differences and the variety of cultural, economic, and ideological attitudes held by inhabitants, a comparison of these cases remains valuable, first and foremost, because the participants themselves made the comparisons, and second, because such a comparison reveals a surprising degree of convergence in the experiences of diverse peoples in the nineteenth century.

In the chapters that follow, I emphasize different aspects of each of these conflicts, but a little general background may help readers. Traditional accounts of the Indian Rebellion of 1857 emphasize the contingent nature of its origin. By the mid-nineteenth century, the British relied on Indian men, both Hindu and Muslim, to staff their colonial armies. In early 1857, these soldiers, called Sepoys, heard rumors that a new musket cartridge was greased with a combination of pork and beef fat to enable it to slide down the musket's muzzle. Soldiers tore cartridge packets with their teeth before pouring the contents down the barrel, so, for both Hindus and Muslims, putting this object in their mouths would have entailed violating religious proscriptions. Rather than touch the offending substance, soldiers mutinied and refused to obey their British officers. In fact, Sepoy troops and their civilian supporters drew upon a deep well of objections to British control of their world. Since the mid-eighteenth century when the British East India Company established trade contacts with merchants along the east coast of India, the British had intervened more and more directly in the lives of people in this region. By the early nineteenth century, the East India Company had established, through military intervention, a British colony. In addition to the cultural difference of British officials, Indians objected that imperial policy stunted trade and industry in the region, created an unproductive and unequal agrarian policy, heightened social and religious discontent, and created administrative burdens for ordinary citizens and especially the Sepoys themselves.

Rural communities in southern China likewise objected to the control exerted over their region by the Qing dynasty. The Qing seized power in the mid-seventeenth century and led a century of expansion. But internal and external threats challenged the regime by the early nineteenth century. Rural people were angry about lack of development and an agricultural economy straining to feed over 400 million people in the empire. The dynastic system extended and exacerbated an increasingly large gap between the living conditions of the rich and poor in China. The British, who led European efforts to achieve access to the Chinese market, flooded the country with opium, which generated serious social and political tensions within the empire in the early nineteenth century. The Taiping Rebellion was one of several large-scale uprisings that these problems generated for the Qing in the mid-nineteenth century.

In Poland, the January Uprising of 1863 happened contemporaneously with the American conflict; witnessed a discrete cultural group asserting its national autonomy against a larger, longer-established state; and compelled that established state to use emancipation as a war policy. This was the not the first effort at Polish independence. After the Partition of Poland in 1795, which divided Polish lands between Prussian, Austrian, and Russian control, many Polish elites moved to western Europe (especially France and England), where they nurtured dreams of resuscitating Poland even as they assimilated into their host nations.[4] In 1831 Poles launched an independence effort, but this ended in failure and the exile of still more people. These elites (or, in many cases, their grandchildren) returned to Poland in 1863 to lead another rebellion. Russia controlled the lion's share of Polish territory, so Polish leaders targeted its control of the region.[5]

Scholars have explained these episodes in different ways. The Indian and Polish movements are usually regarded as decolonization or protonational struggles, and the Taiping conflict is characterized as a rebellion. Only the U.S. conflict is considered a civil war. What unites these wars are the efforts of people to assert sovereignty over territory. They sought political, economic, and cultural autonomy within a territorial space they considered their own. In North America, Confederates used the language of republicanism and self-government inherited from the western European philosophical tradition. Poles shared some of this background, although the Partition of the Polish-Lithuanian Commonwealth in 1795 positioned them more clearly within an imperial system akin to what the Indians experienced. Neither the Indians nor the Taiping relied on the West's revolutionary language, although elites in each country knew that history. These differences have led scholars to treat each conflict in its own regional context, and that has yielded important insights into their nature. Considering these conflicts together disrupts the domestic narratives around which they are built but I hope produces insights of its own.

In fact, I argue that we cannot understand the U.S. Civil War without understanding the Sepoy and Taiping and Polish rebellions because the participants used those rebellions as referents. Global histories are not a choice but a necessity if we are to understand how people came to use the concepts that they deployed and that we study. Those modes of reference and analogy made a difference by shaping the way that the United States and the Confederacy presented themselves to the world and even made their own decisions. What was legitimate, what was likely to succeed, what was a sign of desperation, what was a violation of norms—these were all generated through comparisons with historical and contemporary experience.

In all these conflicts, people tried to remake their political communities to better meet their interests, defined broadly to include ideology and culture as well as material conditions. Given the chronological overlap of these conflicts and the shared vocabulary they adopted, I believe the similarities and differences are worth exploring. My inspiration comes from two impulses. First, I aim to help globalize the Civil War—that is, to expand the framework for interpreting it in space. Second, I aim to contextualize the conflict more fully in the nineteenth century, that is, to expand the framework for interpreting the war in time. These shifts in perspective help us see both the commonalities and the differences between the American experience and others around the world. The wars of the midcentury were interdependent not just because they drew on common international situations or ideas but also because the fighting of each war influenced the fighting of the next ones in ways that went far beyond technological innovations or the development of tactical or strategic principles.

With a few important exceptions, Civil War historians emphasize the domestic forces that that shaped the fighting or the outcomes of the Civil War. Bringing global processes into the conversation runs counter to military historians' emphasis on contingency. I hope to disarm Civil War historians whose preference for contingent and domestic explanatory systems tends to reify the war's exceptional nature. In particular, the U.S. Civil War becomes part of a domestic history of nation-building, and the other rebellions are filed under imperial or colonial history. Historian Paul Kramer has framed this problem: "traditional historiography often starkly opposes empires and nation-states . . . as periods (the 'age of empires' giving way to an 'age of nation states'). In fact, the intersections of empire, nation, and state were and are intensely complex and variable." Although Kramer focuses mostly on the twentieth century and the relations between nations and empires within it, his conclusions bear on the nineteenth-century conflicts discussed here. "Moving beyond the opposition of empire and nation-state," Kramer writes, "requires thinking about the boundaries of U.S. state power in ways that place the politics of sovereignty at the center of inquiry."[6]

The effort to globalize the history of the U.S. Civil War and to blur the boundary between nation and empire complicates political historians' emphasis on understanding how the war revised American democracy and constitutional order.[7] Outside the halls of academia, the durable legacy of American exceptionalism still allows us to call this topic "the Civil War" and expect everyone to intuit the missing qualifier "American." Even in the new writing on the global dimensions of the Civil War, the United States often remains the pivot around which other events move. To be sure, some Europeans, especially liberal reformers, took inspiration from northern victory in the war.[8] Other Europeans, especially powerful conservatives, applied new practices and policies precisely to avoid the liberalizing dimensions of the American conflict or because they read other lessons from the war's course and conclusion. At the same time, some Americans took inspiration from events in Europe or elsewhere. In short, there was no single fulcrum point. The problem of recognizing the reciprocal influence of ideas and events does not tax historians of capitalism or liberalism or any of the many other historically important processes that shaped the nineteenth century because those were so obviously global in their origins and practice. But the truth is that the central issues of the U.S. Civil War—the subdivision of political authority, the reification of and challenge to a culture of racial supremacy, the nature of national organization, and acceptable ways of fighting military conflicts—were all experienced by other people. These other encounters generated a legacy that Americans could not ignore. In many cases, the opposite held true.

To be fair, some historians have evaluated the U.S. conflict in a broader framework. An older tradition of diplomatic history, which produced a wealth of insights around the role played by Britain and France, has been complemented by the appreciation of "public diplomacy," the more diffuse process by which broad populations set the norms for how countries should interact with each other (although these have tended to focus on the same northwestern European actors).[9] A newer generation of historians has incorporated the methods of global history to stretch the geographic boundaries for the era.[10] We can now see how the earlier processes of emancipation in the British and French West Indies influenced how Americans approached the experience and how the American experience shaped subsequent emancipation campaigns in Cuba and Brazil. Unlike many of these scholars, I make no claims to methodological consistency in what follows. At times I adopt the strategies of comparative historians who juxtaposed events in order to identify similarities and differences. At other points I embody the approach of transnational historians who regard national boundaries as concealing some of the key processes by which the modern world took shape. At still others my approach resembles those global historians who respect the power of nation-states but regard them as much more deeply entangled than an earlier generation of historians.

Domestic-focused narratives of the Civil War possess an important strength—they clearly explain cause and effect. For example, Sherman's capture of Atlanta in September 1864 helped reelect Abraham Lincoln and continue the war with emancipation intact.[11] Or: the political opposition of recalcitrant governors in the South weakened Jefferson Davis's ability to organize and supply Confederate armies. These framings reflect the influence of military and political history at the foundation of the modern historical discipline. The history of ideas works differently because attitudes shift slowly and unevenly. Pursuing a global history of ideas complicates the search for cause and effect even more.[12] One solution to this problem has been for historians to emphasize great revolutionary moments when ideas shifted the course of world history. In particular, historians express enthusiasm for those ideas that propel politics toward liberal ends. Eric Hobsbawm, for instance, argued that the 1848 revolutions had "a great deal in common, not least the fact that they occurred almost simultaneously, that their fates were intertwined, and that they all possessed a common mood and style, a curious romantic-utopian atmosphere and a similar rhetoric." Perhaps most importantly, "they were, in fact or immediate anticipation, social revolutions of the labouring poor."[13]

The recent turn toward global history had accelerated this tendency among historians to identify connections among disparate events but usually of a certain caliber and purpose. Janet Polasky's recent survey of the "call to liberty in the Atlantic world" emerges more as an argument for globalization itself—the interconnectedness of the late-eighteenth-century Atlantic world—although she focuses on the transmission of "revolutionary" ideas among the people in the Atlantic world. How did it happen? "Men and women, black and white, charted journeys following the revolutionary currents that felled monarchs and drowned the privileged," Polasky writes.[14] This emancipatory spirit expanded through print: "revolution traveled at the end of the eighteen century because pamphlets and newspapers, novels and letters, and even rumors had legs."[15] Jonathan Israel offers an even more optimistic vision, as the spirit of the American Revolution rippled out across the globe. He poses his thesis as a question: were "Condorcet and Jefferson . . . right in closely linking the futures of America and Europe, as well as the rest of the world, on the basis of democracy, liberty, and universal and equal human rights?"—and the narrative offers a clear affirmative answer.[16] In another recent work,

Richard Stites argues that "the principal insurrectionary impulse" shared among the four would-be nation builders he chronicles in 1820s Europe (in Spain, Naples, Greece, and Russia) "combined an ideological outlook, liberalism, and personalized spirit."[17]

The work of Hobsbawm, Polasky, Israel, and Stites is impressive and inspiring. I tell a different story than they do, both in terms of the structural similarities in their explanations and in their shared interpretive framework. These historians see ideas moving in one direction, not necessarily from the West out to the world but from reforming republics to retrograde empires. And except for Hobsbawm, whose materialist orientation ensured a more skeptical view of power, these historians emphasize the progressive and democratic currents that flowed across the Atlantic. My reading of the midcentury failures instead suggests an awkward mix of liberalism and conservatism. It may be easy for us to imagine a Victorian world bifurcated between liberal and reactionary regimes and ideologies, but the evidence suggests that diverse people interwove liberal and conservative ideas as they pursued nationhood and the associated imperatives to state power. In short, nationalists used whatever tools were handy. If anything, Northerners in the United States had an advantage because they tapped into a global strain of imperial rhetoric that was ascendant at the moment. In the second half of the twentieth century, this grew more challenging when the rhetoric of decolonization ascended, but in the mid-nineteenth century, British, Russian, and Qing China all shared a vocabulary that reinforced central power.

Coming after the age of revolutionary state creation described by Polasky, Israel, and others, participants in the midcentury wars framed their experiences in terms of the pursuit of sovereignty. People in different places tried to establish control over space. They sought autonomy, although the powers they battled to achieve it and their relations with those powers varied. Considered from the other side, established powers around the world—the British, Russian, Chinese, and Americans—faced insurrectionary movements and responded in similar ways. Abraham Lincoln's question to Congress on July 4, 1861, captured the problem of the era: Lincoln asked whether "a government of necessity be too strong for the liberties of its own people, or too weak to maintain its own existence."[18] This conundrum emerged as the key challenge for democratic republics, something James Madison had anticipated when he said, "You must first enable the government to control the governed; and in the next place oblige it to control itself."[19] Heads of empire rarely worried about whether their governments were too strong and never posed this question publicly, as Lincoln did, but overpowering strength generated its own antithesis. Charles Maier, in explaining the success of modern states (beginning in the mid-nineteenth century), asserts that "the idea of sovereignty thus emerged with a dual thrust. Looking 'inward,' sovereignty was defined as the prince's governmental supremacy within the territorial unit. . . . Looking 'outward' . . . sovereignty was defined as the international independence sanctioned by the Treaties of Westphalia or recognition by other states more generally."[20] Historians have spent more time exploring the international contest over the boundaries of state power than on the internal dynamics of sovereignty. Benedict Anderson and other theorists have identified nationalism as the modern force that compels people into respect for the authority of their state.[21] But the process of building domestic sovereignty was less cultural and soft power than Anderson and others assert. The mid-nineteenth-century rebellions demonstrate how many people used formal, violent resistance to challenge the legitimacy of the states within which they resided and how those states responded with coercion and violence of their own.

Confederates did not lose the Civil War because of what happened in India or Poland, or vice versa, but the history of this era reveals a deep degree of entanglement. Similar events followed similar patterns although separated in time and space. They even responded to each other. In the mid-nineteenth century, this influence was felt most fully when powerful nations offered or withheld their support for insurgents, but it also operated in a more subtle fashion. The discussions about sovereignty, authority, and rebellion that preoccupied literate observers in the nineteenth century created a global conversation that shaped the experiences of people engaged in widely different enterprises. The Confederates hoping to preserve a slave society suffered under the term "rebel" just like the Taiping trying to displace the Qing. When a leading Chinese diplomat talked with the wife of the American ambassador in 1863, he drew a parallel between the threat each nation faced. "We see you are *just like us*," he explained.[22] The ambassador's wife was shocked but also pleased by the analogy because she recognized its rhetorical utility in the civil war back home in North America.

India, Poland, China, and the American South did not share ideology, religion, political structures, or economic beliefs, but their experiences were nonetheless interdependent. People in these places followed events around the world. They drew flattering comparisons between themselves and foreign powers in order to elicit support or sympathy, and they drew invidious comparisons between their enemies and other foreigners in order to do the same. This interdependency suggests a smaller world than we usually associate with the nineteenth century before the advent of modernity's great global contraction. It also returns the U.S. Civil War from the realm of national fetish to one among many global events that shaped the contours of that modernity.

1

WHAT KIND OF WAR IS THIS?

Insurgencies and the Challenge of Legitimacy in War

WHEN HISTORIANS OF NATIONALISM consider the role of war in determining which aspiring nations established themselves, they usually focus on war's role as a unifier. Citizens rally to the flag, and society anneals in the face of suffering and sacrifice. Even military defeat can drive this process when people build a narrative of tragedy that inspires devotion. This phenomenon was not the only connection between wars and nation-building. In the nineteenth century, some wars worked better than others. The challenge for insurgent forces was to gain the broad consent of the people and make insurrection appear respectable and just. People who waged guerrilla campaigns, in whole or in part, complicated their task of nation-building. Rebels in India, China, Poland, and the American South all waged irregular campaigns, and this cost them valuable support. Some insurgents regarded guerrilla war as their only option, but in an age of rule-based warfare this choice carried the risk of alienating popular support even if such tactics possessed military value. For the most part, nineteenth-century Westerners regarded guerrilla warfare as a descent into savagery by people who showed themselves as unworthy of statehood.

The most important signs of respectable military practice were to fight as a regular army with uniformed soldiers who targeted only enemy combatants and observed the laws of war. The more would-be nation-builders deviated from this ideal, the more difficult it became for them to establish independence. In most of the failed national movements of the century, insurgents resorted, in whole or in part, to irregular warfare and doomed their causes. Guerrilla fighting could achieve meaningful strategic objectives and could generate internal support, but it came with at least four high costs. The first was strictly military. In almost every instance, irregular war generated a ferocious counterinsurgency strategy from the dominant power, which often proved impossible to overcome. The second concerned civilian support for the insurgents. Because guerrilla fighting produced more violent and destructive conflicts and because irregular fighters frequently resorted to simple criminality, this form of warfare could alienate the would-be insurgents' civilian supporters. Third, irregular war-making alienated foreign observers, especially Europeans who had collectively forged the laws of war within the Christian just war tradition. This estrangement ensured that insurgents fought alone, making their task more difficult still.

It may sound like these elements were merely parallel processes, but they had a kind of spooky entanglement; events in one place shaped how people responded to similar events in another. Many of the century's national failures adopted irregular strategies, so such conduct became associated with illegitimacy and defeat. This may sound like blaming the chicken for the egg, but by midcentury a chronology and even a sort of typology could be seen. Whatever renown guerrillas earned from their eponymous incarnation as Napoleon's opponents in Spain and Russia began to fade. The irregular violence of the Indian Rebellion of 1857, the guerrilla campaigns against Russian soldiers in Poland, and the decimation levied on southern China in the Taiping Rebellion all tarnished the image of irregular insurgents. Confederates joined this club of infamy in 1861, and they did themselves no favors. The fourth cost of irregular warfare, then, concerns the associations and connotations it generated. The strategic liabilities and the moral stigma that accompanied guerrilla warfare tarnished the people that engaged in it.

Thinking about War

War was not the same across the globe. Some definitions are in order, to make sense of comparing forms of warfare among people with different cultural attitudes toward violence and authority. As historian Carol Reardon has recently shown, military theory remained fluid in nineteenth-century America. Early in the century, Antoine-Henri Jomini and other European thinkers began subjecting military action to scientific analysis, but their writing had little impact on the nature of military operations during the U.S. Civil War. Reardon concludes that "the mechanistic approach that Jomini and other writers of his time had inherited from the Military Enlightenment had given their writings a highly institutional and impersonal tone."[1] The linear and routinized instructions derived from these works offered little help in designing strategies or tactics in a conflict with the size, scale, and complexity of the U.S. Civil War.

In considering irregular warfare, Jomini himself admitted the possibility of what he called "national wars" but hoped never to see one. A national war was one "waged against a united people, or a great majority of them, filled with a noble ardor and determined to sustain their independence: then every step is disputed, the army holds only its camp-ground, its supplies can only be obtained at the point of the sword, and its convoys are everywhere threatened or captured."[2] Although this characterization of guerrilla war overstates the level of resistance that Union troops encountered as they moved through the American South, it does indicate the possible ways in which irregulars could slow down the advance of regular armies, which white Southerners most certainly did. Jomini offered no counsel about how to respond. "As a soldier, preferring loyal and chivalrous warfare to organized assassination," Jomini wrote, "I acknowledge my prejudices are in favor of the good old times when the French and English Guards courteously invited each other to fire first . . . to the frightful epoch when priests, women, and children throughout Spain plotted the murder of isolated soldiers."[3]

Another example of the willful blindness of midcentury military planners toward the course that wars would soon assume can be seen in the writings of Henry W. Halleck, who would later serve as a major general in the Union army and, for almost two years, Lincoln's general-in-chief. In 1846, Halleck published *Elements of Military Art and Science,* which included chapters on strategy, tactics, fortifications, logistics, and army organization but almost nothing about how to combat irregular warfare.[4] Perhaps authors hoped that theories of war could prevent guerrillas by ignoring them. D. H. Mahan, an instructor at West Point for nearly fifty years, addressed *petite guerre* in his writing. He sanctioned surprise attacks and ambushes in some contexts.[5] Not every battle needed to be ranks of infantry facing off against each other. But even where commanders deployed soldiers into smaller units or in more ad hoc formations, Mahan presumed that soldiers were meeting a regular enemy. He did not approve using such tactics against noncombatants, and the bulk of his advice assumed traditional engagements between uniformed soldiers.

Jomini's near-peer, Carl von Clausewitz, offered a more direct assessment of the role of irregulars in warfare. Americans did not read English-language translations of Clausewitz's *On War* until 1874, but Europeans were familiar with his writings from the 1830s. Clausewitz devoted a short chapter to what he called "the people in arms," which corresponded roughly with unorganized popular resistance to an invading army. He offered no moral endorsement or critique of the behavior; his interest was in discerning its effectiveness as a form of war. As a Prussian who personally observed Napoleon's march across Europe, it is little surprise that Clausewitz was "a major proponent of guerrilla warfare."[6] As one of his sharpest readers explains, one of Clausewitz's fundamental beliefs was in the strength of defensive rather than offensive war. He regarded guerrilla conflict as an additional and effective form of defensive warfare because it tied down an invading army, Napoleon crossing Prussia into Russia in 1814, for instance.[7]

European observers who read Clausewitz thus might have anticipated that white Southerners or Poles would resort to irregular resistance, though not at a conflict's opening. As two historians observe about the modern form of guerrilla war that took shape with Spanish resistance to Napoleon: "Spanish resistance was marked by a fact that has been too frequently overlooked: Spaniards used irregular tactics only after their regular forces had collapsed. Guerrilla strategy was not the preferred strategy; it was the only strategy that remained available. Moreover, it did not succeed until a British army entered Spain from Portugal. In Spain, as throughout history, guerrilla warfare was the weapon of the militarily weak."[8] Because of the necessity of gaining foreign recognition and of retaining the support of their own citizens, few insurgents admitted weakness. This was most true in North America, where any sign of weakness contradicted the perception of absolute mastery upon which the slave society rested.[9] Confederates entered the war optimistically, anticipating victory and expecting that the importance of cotton would bring European recognition quickly.[10] In other words, most political leaders, especially those invested in diplomacy and the maintenance of the international order, did not evaluate war solely from the standpoint of efficiency, as Clausewitz sought to do. His goal, he admitted, was to "consider a general insurrection as simply another means of war."[11] For political leaders, in contrast, the shared emphasis on civilized warfare formed a pillar of modern belief.

Historians of guerrilla warfare differ in how they identify the actions of participants in the conflicts under consideration here depending on how they define guerrilla war. Walter Laqueur, one of the pioneers in the study of guerrilla war, evaluates historical examples against a theory of guerrilla conflict. According to Laqueur, "the term 'guerrilla' was originally used to describe military operations carried out by irregulars against the rear of an enemy army or by local inhabitants against an occupying force. . . . Typical guerrilla operations include harassment of the enemy, evasion of decisive battles, cutting lines of communication, carrying out surprise attacks."[12] Because of this definition, Laqueur argues that guerrillas can only operate in rural places; in urban settings, their actions are more properly classified as terrorism. Hewing to this definition, Laqueur argues that "incidents of guerrilla warfare, such as Tantia Topi's raids" occurred in Indian Rebellion, "but this was the exception, not the rule, and many observers, including Marx and Engels, expressed astonishment that guerrilla warfare had not been more widely applied by the insurgents."[13]

Regarding the Polish Rebellion, Lacquer strikes a more equivocal tone. "The three Polish insurrections (1793, 1831, and 1863) were a blend of regular and guerrilla warfare," he writes. "In some measure they were a people's war, but the support of the peasants waned in the course of time."[14] Given their huge disparity in terms of soldiers (Laqueur estimates 1:10 to the Russians), he believes the Poles should have taken to the woods more often. Other scholars of guerrilla warfare rarely consider the conflicts under review here because they are more focused on a typology of guerrillas that applies across time.[15] Robert R. Mackey's book on Civil War guerrillas offers a definition applicable to midcentury conflicts, focused as it is on "irregular warfare" rather than more narrowly on guerrillas. For Mackey, "*irregular warfare* encompasses all forms of conflict—from deep cavalry raids to local bushwhackers—that did *not* involve the main armies of either side."[16] Within the Indian, Chinese, American, and Polish conflicts, these conditions were certainly met.

That said, the dynamics of irregular warfare differed among the four events under review. Three of the conflicts—the Indian and Polish rebellions and the U.S. Civil War—involved militaries that identified with the Christian tradition of just war doctrine. According to European practice, regular soldiers merited the protection of the laws of war when they joined units under the control of established states, wore the appropriate insignia, and adhered to standard behavior at the time, the most important of which was directing military violence toward enemy soldiers rather than noncombatants. In contrast, irregulars fell outside the laws of war by virtue of their composition or their behavior. Guerrillas rarely had official sanction, or uniforms, or established chains of command. But even those who satisfied some or all of these conditions could still be ruled out for failing to distinguish between combatants and noncombatants, for not taking prisoners, or for engaging in maneuvers (such as long-distance killing) that generated no military advantage.

Comparing how the Qing reacted to the Taiping with the parallel process in Western nations demands more context. The Chinese maintained a long tradition of serious intellectual engagement with military ideas and practices, but they arrived at quite different results than Europeans about what was permissible in war. The foundation of Chinese military practice lay in the writings of Sun Tzu, author of *The Art of War*, and the other authors of the "Seven Military Classics," written around 500 BCE.[17] Like many early Western writers on war, Sun Tzu encourages subterfuge, disguise, and ferocity as they are more likely to bring victory. These methods have the potential to generate unintended casualties, although Sun Tzu never emphasizes killing for its own sake. "Subjugating the enemy's army without fighting is the true pinnacle of excellence," he proclaims.[18] He believed the best generals can find ways, through maneuver and planning, to win by not fighting. This approach retained the endorsement of West Point in the 1860s, from which D. H. Mahan wrote, "*To do the greatest damage to our enemy with the least exposure to ourselves*, is a military axion lost sight of only by ignorance of the true ends of victory."[19] Sun Tzu concluded, "Thus one who excels at warfare seeks [victory] through the strategic configuration of power (*shih*), not from reliance on men."[20] Even if the line separating legitimate and illegitimate actions might not be distinct, *Art of War* makes clear there is no gain from simple killing.

Other early Chinese writers and texts complemented and sometimes contradicted Sun Tzu. Another theorist, Mozi, who wrote just after Sun Tzu, articulated the differences between defensive, punitive, and aggressive wars. The latter were never just according to Mohists. Defensive wars were just, and punitive wars (what might be labeled humanitarian interventions today) could sometimes be justified. The Chinese did not use an equivalent to the Christian concept of "just" war (instead using righteous, benevolent, or permissible), but "both early Chinese discussions and the Western just war tradition address the general question of whether war coheres with or can be legitimized by overarching ethical values that govern personal and social life."[21] Another early text on war-making, *The Method of the Ssu-am Fa,* instructed: "When you see their [enemy's] elderly or very young, return them without harming them. Even if you encounter adults, unless they engage you in combat, do not treat them as enemies."[22] This admonition, like similar ones within the European just war tradition, may have been the exception rather than the rule.

As Europeans found ways to integrate Christianity's clear prohibition on taking life with the security and diplomatic needs of early modern states, so too Chinese thinkers found ways to reconcile what they regarded as pressing military needs with their philosophies of war.[23] The Qing, like previous Chinese dynasties, controlled an extensive and sophisticated bureaucracy, including a large and elaborate military. According to historian Joanna Waley-Cohen, "an intense focus on military affairs was one of the Qing state's most distinctive characteristics. Beyond the actual conduct of war, this focus materialized most notably in a wide-ranging campaign intended to propel military success, and the martial values that underpinned it, onto the centre stage of cultural life."[24] The Qing came to power partly on a formidable new military framework called the Banner system.[25] Although historians usually emphasize the bureaucratic and organizational innovations of the Banner system, Qing conquest also included quite spectacular violence. After capturing a city, Yangzhou, "much of the population was deliberately killed and survivors raped and murdered by unruly Chinese soldiers in Qing employ."[26] This event in 1645 was only a year after the official date for the dynasty's origin, which gave such violence the cast of legitimacy.

The Taiping knew this history and must have considered it as they devised their rules for military conduct, which reflected long-standing Chinese practices. The most problematic of these, from the perspective of Western observers in China during the rebellion, was the failure of soldiers to contain violence to combatants. Civilians were routinely subjected to lethal violence through sieges or executions after a city had been captured. Enemy soldiers rarely received protection as prisoners and were instead routinely killed after battles. The issue for scholars is not whether the Chinese had philosophical and practical guides for how to conduct warfare—they clearly did—but how the advice from those sources aligned with Western expectations in the nineteenth century, a uniquely restrained interval in European warfare between the total violence of the religious wars of the seventeenth century and the horrors to come from aerial bombardment in the twentieth. In both the Chinese and Indian cases, the insurgent troops, Taiping and Sepoy, embodied the nations they hoped to establish and maintained regular command structures, but they also perceived the distinction between combatants and noncombatants differently than Western soldiers. As Europeans saw it, these armies, already composed of people regarded as cultural inferiors, operated much closer to the irregular side of the spectrum. British and other observers publicized evidence of these practices in order to deter foreign support for both movements.[27]

Unlike the Taiping, who lost support from the West because they did not observe the distinction between combatants and noncombatants, European and American criticism of the Poles concerned their manner of fighting. The Polish rebels organized a mostly ad hoc army that functioned irregularly. Although they challenged the Russian army in a traditional way in the conflict's opening weeks, it quickly became apparent that they did not have the resources or manpower to conduct regular warfare against the Russians. As one of the leading American news encyclopedias noted, after March 1863, "they had to confine themselves exclusively to guerrilla warfare."[28] European reporting, reprinted in American newspapers, emphasized the irregularity of Polish operations from the beginning. Writing in January 1863, a Warsaw correspondent of the Berlin *National Zeitung* described the destruction of telegraph lines and railways in the country. "The insurgents seem to be about to carry on a guerrilla warfare."[29] A British correspondent reported in April that "the revolt expanded into a guerrilla war."[30] Polish combatants took recourse in attacks on Russian soldiers when they were in barracks or isolated spots around the country.

These attacks took on a more indiscriminate character over time and generated concern in the West about the fitness of Poles as a civilized people. Even many earnest Confederates recognized that to fight as guerrillas was to give up their claim to nationhood. After the fall of Vicksburg and the loss at Gettysburg, the *Raleigh (North Carolina) Standard* proclaimed that "to resist [Union armies by] guerrilla warfare is most probably to be conquered." They did not admit to being "whipped . . . but we may be overcome by mere physical force. Such was the fate of Poland, Hungary, and Ireland. It is no disgrace to a people to be overpowered by mere brute force if they resist manfully and desperately."[31] The implication here—that to continue fighting by irregular methods even when they were effectively conquered would be unwise if not unmanly—underlay American impressions of Indian, Chinese, and Polish fighting.

Guerrillas at War

In North America, the Confederacy created a regular army, organized the same way as the regular U.S. Army, that observed most of the laws of war (the important exception was their treatment of black Union soldiers).[32] But the Confederacy also hosted a body of combatants that organized irregularly and that adhered to none of the standard practices in battle. The Confederacy fought both a regular war and an irregular war against the United States.[33] They fielded massive regular armies that adhered (in most cases) to the laws of war. And they fielded irregular fighters in every Confederate and several Union states. Irregular fighters, though much smaller in numbers than regular soldiers, exercised an outsized influence. In the regions from which the Confederate Army withdrew (and this was eventually much of the South), guerrillas represented the peoples' resistance to Union occupation. Small groups of irregulars drew support from and carried the hopes of a large number of noncombatants.

Union Army officers knew all too well the role of guerrillas. In the war with Mexico in the 1840s (a training ground for many officers who later served in the Civil War), U.S. troops encountered ground level resistance from Mexicans, especially once they occupied towns along the path of their invasion toward Mexico City. Irregular attacks on U.S. soldiers generated a ferocious counter response. The U.S. secretary of war himself "explained that 'the guerrilla system is hardly recognized as a legitimate mode of warfare, and should be met with the utmost allowable severity.'" Soldiers were happy to comply; they "burned villages, killed civilians arbitrarily, and meted out vengeance anywhere they saw fit."[34] The problem confronted by Union troops in the Civil War was on an even greater scale. The *Official Records of the War of the Rebellion* contains thousands of references to the problems posed by irregulars, bushwhackers, "bad men," and any of the other dozen euphemisms for guerrilla fighters used by the war's participants. As historian Daniel Sutherland demonstrates in his comprehensive survey, "it is impossible to understand the Civil War without appreciating the scope and impact of the guerrilla conflict."[35] Whatever the numbers, the Confederacy's guerrilla war was visible for all to see, and the nearly inevitable result was that all the problems that irregular warfare caused for others around the world plagued the Confederacy as well.

The Confederate government maintained an ambivalent relationship with guerrillas. Some Southerners identified themselves with the legacy of Lt. Col. Francis Marion, known as the "Swamp Fox" for his effective use of irregular tactics against British forces in South Carolina during the American Revolution. Robert E. Lee and other West Pointers opposed irregular warfare and promoted regular military service instead. Even an officer like Maj. Gen. Thomas Rosser, who made his fame on daring cavalry raids that superficially resembled the irregular warfare of genuine guerrillas, opposed their use. Writing to Lee, Rosser observed the "many irregular bodies of troops . . . occupy this country and are known as partisans . . . they are a nuisance and an evil to the service. Without discipline, order, or organization, they roam broadcast over the country, a band of thieves, stealing, pillaging, plundering, and doing every manner of mischief and crime. They are a terror to the citizens and an injury to the cause." Despite Rosser's admiration for the bravery of some of the guerrillas, he remained convinced that "such organization, as a rule, are detrimental to the best interests of the army at large."[36]

Nonetheless, guerrillas proliferated throughout the Confederacy and in several Union states. Although by their very nature guerrillas operated outside the regular military hierarchy, their persistence owed something to President Jefferson Davis's refusal to reject them. In 1862 the Confederate Congress passed the Partisan Ranger Act, which was supposed to enable Confederates to organize irregular fighters and bring them within the control of the regular army. Although most of the official Partisan Ranger units operated under loose oversight from Richmond and observed the laws of war, dozens of irregular units never formalized their relations. Lee, for his part, wanted the Partisan Ranger Act repealed. "I regard the whole system as an unmixed evil," he wrote. "No good has resulted from it at all commensurate with its bad effects."[37]

Despite this, Davis regarded the legislation as casting a cloak of legitimacy over the South's many guerrilla units. As a result, in his private correspondence, Davis celebrated the actions of irregulars and in public speeches he condemned the Union's antiguerrilla policies as though they applied to regular soldiers or Confederate civilians. In an address to the Confederate Congress, Davis condemned the Union's "unjust war" against innocent Southerners, in which "expeditions organized for the sole purpose of sacking cities, consigning them to the flames, killing the unarmed inhabitants and inflicting horrible outrages on the women and children are some of the constantly recurring atrocities of the invader."[38] As Davis well knew, Union troops had burned several small towns along the Mississippi River but only after guerrilla attacks on Union shipping and repeated warnings that locals would be held responsible for such actions. The only "inhabitants" deliberately killed by Union soldiers were those engaged in irregular warfare. In their ambivalence, Confederates revealed the dilemmas of insurgents trying to build a nation-state. They appreciated that irregular fighters slowed down Union troops and required the North to widely distribute its forces, but they also knew that nations were built through regular engagements among uniformed soldiers on bona fide battlefields.

Europeans observed the irregular aspects of the Confederate war effort. As early as July 1861 the *Cork Examiner* in Ireland, along with other papers around the United Kingdom, reported on the role played by "guerrilla detachments of the rebels" in the conflict.[39] The most infamous Confederate guerrillas, like William Quantrill and Bloody Bill Anderson, were known in English newspapers, just as they were in the North.[40] British visitors and diplomats likewise monitored the role that guerrillas played. William Stuart, who served as the British charge d'affaires in the second half of 1862, alerted the foreign secretary, Lord John Russell: "The activity of the guerrilla bands in the West appears to be on the increase, and they have extended their depredations to the Free States, causing considerable alarm."[41] The British knew the history of guerrilla warfare in North America. They had faced it during the Revolution, and many believed it was responsible for their downfall. Knowing this legacy, the *London Times* asked "why, with these traditions, the people of the South did not from the first adopt so obvious a system." "The truth is," they wrote, "no country adopts it willingly; all prefer the pomp of regular warfare."[42] The *Times* here echoed Clausewitz's characterization of guerrilla methods as a last resort of the weak.

The Confederates' use of guerrillas created real difficulties for the Union, although not in the way its perpetrators imagined. One of President Lincoln's chief challenges was to fight the war in the least destructive way. Because he intended to reunify the nation, he did not want to alienate Southerners in the process of reestablishing state loyalty. As a result,

Union Army commanders observed the laws of war when they fought the Confederate Army. Injured men were treated as noncombatants, surrenders were allowed, and prisoners were publicly recorded and confined. None of these ameliorating elements applied when Union forces encountered Southern guerrillas. Instead, Northern soldiers adopted increasingly harsh techniques to counter the irregular threat. In modern terms, the Confederate insurgency generated a ferocious counterinsurgency. U.S. soldiers pursued suspected guerrillas with a relish and vengeance that did not reflect their behavior in battles with uniformed enemies. They created special guerrilla-hunting units with wide latitude in regions plagued with irregular warfare.[43] Most importantly, commanders availed themselves of the right of summary justice—drumhead trials held out of doors, which usually ended with the execution of the accused. It took two years for the Union to organize effective strategies against the guerrillas, but once they did, such actions brought Union troops into intimate and punishing contact with Southern civilians, as those people living along the Mississippi River could attest. Whatever its effect on noncombatants, the Union's counterinsurgency strategy hastened Confederate defeat. As Daniel Sutherland, the leading scholar on guerrilla warfare in the U.S. Civil War, concludes, "Rebel irregulars helped their nation lose the war."[44]

Northerners knew how far they could go, how aggressively they could react to the irregular dimensions of Confederate resistance, because they had a recent model. In 1857 Indian troops of the British Empire launched a movement that evolved into what historians today regard as a protonational independence movement, what one historian of India calls the "formative violence of their national history."[45] British military officials and the government regarded the event as a mutiny, but even opposition politicians at the time saw that something much larger was happening. My purpose here is not to debate the causes and motives of the revolt, an important concern for both Indian and British historians. Instead, I want to explore how Indians fought and how the British responded because this dynamic informed how Americans behaved in suppressing the formative violence of their own national history.

Fighting was confined to northern India and was fiercest wherever Sepoy troops, nearly all of whom rebelled, were stationed. The rebels and their supporters organized themselves and prepared for a future state without the British. This was not an effective effort, particularly in terms of an apparatus that could pay for the conflict, but it suggests a vision beyond simply the expulsion of the colonizers.[46] Nonetheless, from the beginning, Indians fought a highly irregular war. Indian troops outnumbered European ones by a factor of five.[47] As soon as Indian soldiers abandoned their posts, reports circulated of attacks on the homes and families of British officials. In some smaller communities, European residents were run off; in many others they suffered worse fates. In other words, when Indian soldiers deployed lethal violence, they did not distinguish between regular combatants and noncombatants.[48] They fought irregularly. The most infamous incident occurred in Kanpur after its surrender, when two hundred women and children were killed and their bodies dumped into a well.[49]

Americans did not regard the event as a legitimate rebellion deserving their sympathy or support. A typical framing came from the *New Englander and Yale Review*: "The East India Company were raising, on apparently secure foundations, a political structure which promised, someday, to rival those of the enlightened nations of Europe. By slow degrees the Christian civilization of the West was leavening the debased myriads of Hindus." But then it turned out that "the whole foundation of the political fabric was found to be worthless . . . and the whole tottered on the brink of destruction. The impending doom was indeed averted, yet, not till furious anarchy had glutted itself with the blood of hundreds of brave men, gentle women, and innocent babes, the thought of whose sufferings and death curdles the blood."[50] Not a war, then, or even a rebellion but simple anarchy of the sort perpetrated by savage people.

Americans inherited this perspective on the conflict from British papers and pamphlets, all filled with salacious reporting and fantasies of revenge.[51] In the summer of 1857 British newspapers overflowed with reporting about the "Indian Mutiny" or the "Bengal Mutiny." A typical article condemned that Sepoy troops had not just revolted "but breathed the bloodiest vengeance against their English commanders, violating women and young girls, and then subjecting them to cruelties more atrocious and unnatural than ever were invented by Roman emperors, Tartar conquerors, or Spanish priests." The paper had a ready explanation—"the Asiatic, in a state of desperation, is a remorseless fatalist, and his propensities tempt him to run a muck of slaughter until overtaken by the doom which he sullenly anticipates."[52] In this reading, Indians, even those enlisted in British forces, would revert to uncivilized behavior without firm control. "On the terrible deeds of the Sepoys," one minister wrote, "their treachery, their murder of their officers, their savage cruelty to helpless women and children, their brutal licentiousness, their setting free the inmates of the prisons . . . on all this we have no heart to dwell [because readers know it already]. It makes one of the darkest pages in the history of our race."[53] Even liberals in the United States stood squarely behind Britain in the conflict. No less a personage than Thaddeus Stevens, a leading radical Republican, referred to the Indian conflict early in the U.S. Civil War to remind the British of their duty. As Stevens recalled, "the insurrection in India embraced many more people than ours, many of them well trained to arms; yet what nation ever thought of recognizing their *de facto* existence, or treating them as a Power?"[54]

When British soldiers recaptured Kanpur, they came upon the infamous well. "Perhaps it would be correct to say," writes an Indian scholar, "that the fate of the rebels all over India was decided at this moment."[55] Furious at Sepoys over what they regarded as a betrayal of their obligation to the Crown and horrified by the killing of civilians, white British Army soldiers responded in kind. When the army captured rebel soldiers, especially officers, they were executed, often in gruesome ways, most famously by being tied to the mouths of cannon, which were then discharged. The British prime minister, Lord Palmerston, "had applauded the idea of razing [Delhi] to the ground, and a former governor-general, Ellenborough, could fling out coarse threats to 'emasculate all the mutineers and to call Delhi Eunuchabad.'"[56] The British justified their conduct as revenge for what had been done to European noncombatants. As one historian notes, "if the natives killed European civilians—and therefore perpetrated unpardonable excesses in waging war against unarmed innocents—the British did the same."[57] According to another, in response to the killing of women and children, "tens of thousands of soldiers and village guerrillas were hanged, shot, or blown from guns."[58] Within a year, the British counterinsurgency had defeated the rebels and restored Crown control. Victory came with thousands of Indian noncombatant deaths, most true innocents.

In the U.S. Civil War, Northerners justified their own conduct by comparing it to what they viewed as Britain's egregious behavior in the rebellion. When the *Atlantic Monthly* explained how the rebels should be treated, it did so by reminding readers of the 1857 conflict. "The Sepoy Rebellion had some features in common with our own," the editors wrote. "It was inaugurated by premeditated military treachery. It seized upon a large quantity of Government munitions of war. It only asked 'to be let alone.'"[59] The journal made clear they were not defending Sepoy atrocities. "But toward the recaptured rebels there was used a course for which the only precedent, so far as we know, was furnished by the highly civilized guardian, the Dey of Algiers. These prisoners of war were in cold blood tied to the muzzles of cannon and blown into fragments. . . . Wholesale plunder and devastation of the chief city of the revolt followed."[60] Their conclusion demonstrated the rhetorical utility of British actions to Americans. "We have thus established what we believe is called by theologians a *catena* [a chain] of precedents, coming down from the days of the Commonwealth to our own time. . . . And we next propose to ask the question, how far it may be desirable to be bound by such indisputable authority."[61] The answer was that rebels against lawful authority could receive mercy or punishment as determined by the situation and the rightful authority.

Northerners used British behavior in India as a shield against criticism, especially when it came from pro-Confederate British conservatives. When the English criticized Northern war practices, Northern writers hurled back an indictment of the treatment of Indian rebels by the British. "The slicing of Sepoys and burning of Begums was the mildest amusement with which the elastic English mind occupied itself during what is facetiously termed the 'rebellion in India,'" the *New York Times* noted in 1862. "It is rather refreshing to see the pious and philanthropic John Bull turn from roasting a Rajah, the glow of the ruddy embers mingling with one of honest indignation and mantling his broad prairie of face, to chide the North American savage for sinking stone fleets in the entrance of Southern harbors."[62] This was an allusion to a plan in the North to sink stone-filled ships at the mouths of Southern ports in order to blockade them (something that Confederates tried as well, although that did not generate much British comment). The plan proved infeasible in any event, but the British expressed great indignation over the idea, which they considered an affront to the principle of free trade.[63] Their denunciations of this "act of hostility to the whole human race" carried their imaginations abroad. Seeking to condemn what they regarded as the irony of "*high-professing puritans who threaten to murder in cold blood*," they reminded readers that "we do not in Europe, when we take a city, cut the throats of all the women and children, as the Taiping have done in China."[64]

For many Northerners, British actions in India both invalidated British criticism of U.S. policies and showed, in contrast, how gentle U.S. practices actually were. Angry over British criticism of U.S. conduct, the *New York Evangelist* asked "whether we have deserved rebukes on that account, and especially *from England,* is a question."[65] The long account of Sepoy executions that followed made clear the *Evangelist* did not think so.[66] In early 1862 *Harper's Weekly* republished an account from the London *Illustrated Times* that showed the execution of Indian soldiers during the 1857 rebellion. As all Americans seemed to know, the British had summarily executed hundreds of rebels.[67] "The circumstances of the case bear some analogy to those which are recurring at the present time in our Southern States," *Harper's* noted.[68] After a long reprint of William Howard Russell's accounts of the executions and other atrocities, the journal closed with the caustic observation that "in connection with the British protests against the Stone Blockade, on the ground of humanity, these reminiscences are instructive."[69]

British critique of the Stone Fleet aroused a particularly strong comparative streak in American voices. Those with long memories would have recalled British plans to create a stone blockade of the French port of Boulogne early in the Napoleonic Wars. The plan came to naught (although it cost the government £16,000, a considerable sum at the time), but the objections raised among opposition politicians in Britain concerned its efficacy alone; the question of morality did not enter the conversation.[70] Hypocrisy aside, many Americans expressed greater outrage that the British would critique their attempt to blockade Confederate ports. *Vanity Fair* weighed in, incredulous that the *London Times* regarded the plan as "among the crimes which have disgraced the history of mankind, it would be difficult to find one more atrocious than this." The editors regarded the criticism as "flatulent humbug" because the British had treated Sepoys far worse, blowing them "from the cannon's mouth by order of the ministers of the government of a Christian Woman."[71] While U.S. Army commanders executed many Civil War guerrillas, they never blew them from the mouths of cannon. They also arrested and imprisoned many suspected bushwhackers rather than killing them. This bolstered Northern claims to a fair response to the guerrilla threat, which they regarded as more intractable problem than the short-lived Indian Rebellion. Alongside a general comparison of British and U.S. war policies, Northerners mounted a robust defense of their treatment of prisoners of

Figure 1. The Northern press used the British experience in India as a way to deflect British criticism of the United States during the Civil War. *Harper's Weekly*, February 15, 1862, "'British Civilization.' How the English Treat Prisoners of War—Blowing Sepoys from Guns in India, 1857." Image courtesy of the Internet Archive.

war as a way to demonstrate their civilizational bona fides. In this case, British actions against Indian prisoners offered Northerners an effective way to position themselves ahead of Europe's leading humanitarians.[72]

Northerners made the same criticism of British actions in China as well. Britain behaved with bewildering inconsistency through the Taiping Rebellion, sometimes attacking the imperial government and the rebels at the same moment. British soldiers of fortune and regular army officers also engaged in widely reported atrocities that were repeated by domestic critics of the war. Northerners were quick to seize on this news. "O JOHN BULL! JOHN BULL! . . . You great beer-swilling Hogshead of Hypocrisies! Now you pray, and then you plunder—now you pity and then you pillage—now you mourn and then you massacre—now you blubber the Black Man, and then you disembowel the Yellow Man," screamed *Vanity Fair*. Given the Brits' global reputation for bloodthirstiness, Americans refused to be lectured to by them.[73]

Even Confederates, apparently unconcerned with the irony of their position, supported the British response to the irregular, often deadly violence of the Indian war. The *Richmond Daily Dispatch*, although it did not assert any real British right to India, supported them in the conflict as an act of "compassion for those miseries of humanity which followed in the train of the Sepoy revolt, and admiration of the courage and constancy of a hand-full of English soldiers in deadly conflict with innumerable foes."[74] That is, in the face of irregular violence waged by an uncivilized opponent, strong countermeasures were necessary and proper. In this respect, Southerners' commitment to a conservative social order demanded they respect British actions even if such a posture discouraged global support for wars of national liberation, like the one they were waging.

Confederates publicized Northern atrocities in order to turn the tables and discourage foreign support of the United States by linking it with the worst of past conduct. The Union's counterinsurgency strategy, which sanctioned lethal violence although rarely against civilians, was a prime target. In 1862 Confederates protested the execution of ten prisoners by Union general John McNeil in response to the killing of a Unionist civilian who had given intelligence to Northern troops. The event found few defenders in Washington, although Lincoln never cashiered McNeil. London's *Daily Telegraph*, a reliably pro-Confederate journal, fulminated: "The hideous and fiendish massacre in cold blood of ten Confederate prisoners, by order of the Federal General M'Neil, eclipses in horror as atrocity the news of which, seven years since, shook this country to its centre, excited in every English breast a feeling of the deepest indignation and abhorrence towards the perpetrators of the crime, and scandalized the whole of Western Europe."[75] The reference here was to the Hango Massacre in the Crimean War, when Russians killed a number of British seamen. Despite the *Telegraph*'s best efforts (and they made a good effort—McNeil turned up repeatedly, and readers knew the hideous figure of Benjamin "Beast" Butler intimately), its goal of reframing Confederates as the true victims did not take hold in Britain.

In fact, Liberal Britons recognized that if the United Kingdom faced an equivalent crisis on their own soil, it would respond with the same vigor as the United States did. The reformer John Bright asked an audience, "Let us suppose that an insurgent army had been so near to London that you could see its outposts from every suburb in this city, what then do you think would have been the regard of the Government of Great Britain for personal liberty, if it interfered with the necessities, and, as they might think, the salvation of the State?"[76] He went on to recollect, as a member of Parliament, that when habeas corpus was suspended in Ireland in 1848, Liverpool representatives came to Parliament not to protest for civil liberties (as British conservatives did in response to Lincoln's suspension of habeas corpus) but to ask that it be extended to their city to quash any pro-Irish sympathies. The U.S. counterinsurgency received no rebuke from John Bright.

A similar dynamic prevailed in Poland. Newspapers that had chronicled Poland's preinsurrection riots and protests in 1861 in detail reduced coverage in 1862 but then renewed their focus as widespread violence broke out in the country in 1863.[77] The *New York Times* began to note the guerrilla attacks made on Russian forces, sometimes through covert and hence unjust methods.[78] This was countered by letters and reports filed by Polish-born Americans, who emphasized the long suffering of the Polish nation. Southerners, ordinarily a group that did not speak loudly on behalf of foreign revolutionary movements, could not resist the opportunity to point out the parallels in these events and the irony that Northerners were failing to support the brave Poles. "Had this Polish insurrection broken out two years and a half ago, every northern rostrum would have thundered with plaudits to the gallant Poles," declaimed the *Petersburg (Virginia) Daily Express*.[79] But even as the paper mocked the depth of Northerners' commitment to their stated values, it made no real move to endorse the Polish cause. For white Southerners, the dangers of endorsing a movement that embraced significant land tenure reform (as the Polish insurrection leaders eventually advocated) overruled the strategic gains of linking independence causes around the globe.

Lacking an organized army (the Polish resistance drew artisans, workers, intellectuals, students, and peasants, none with much formal military training), Poles fought as insurgents against the Russians.[80] Guerrilla units sought out detachments of Russian soldiers, whom they targeted at vulnerable points. Like the Confederacy, which used the same tactics against Union troops, Poles had little chance of defeating Russian forces outright but could compel a peace if they secured the support of most European nations.[81] Predictably, Polish guerrilla efforts provoked a violent response from Russian units, violence that was often directed widely against both guerrillas and the communities that supported them. As one historian notes, "the Russian army took over in Poland as the Tsar gave General Feodor Berg full powers, while in Lithuania the governor-general Mikhail Mraview, a Decembrist-turned-reactionary, fully earned his epithet, the 'hangman of Vilna.'"[82]

Russians leaders rejected the idea that Poles possessed a nationality that merited its own nation. As a former Russian diplomat to China explained to his American counterpart, Anson Burlingame: "the reason [the conflict continues] is that the whole time fresh bands are organized in Galicia and go over the frontier to join those who are in Poland." He blamed the French for underwriting this process. No doubt, the minister and Burlingame had discussed their respective rebellions while in China; the Russian possessed the same resigned attitude toward the war's violence: "perhaps the winter will put an end to this dreadful war; if not I cannot foresee how and when the question will finish."[83]

European observers cataloged the breadth of atrocities that Russians committed in their counterinsurgency campaign. As one English writer argued, "Even when the Russian generals are humane, well-meaning men, they cannot control the troops under them, embittered by a guerrilla war and constantly drunk. Burning alive, burying alive, flogging, are among the horrors of the present campaign that relieve the ordinary incidents of violation and massacre."[84] London's *Telegraph* concurred: "Finding rebellion to wax hotter from day to day, and seeing but little chance of immediate victory, the Czar and his enlightened brother thought it indispensable to unchain the beast wrapt up in every Russian soldier's heart. . . . With all his rascally appetites, legalised by an obliging sovereign, the love of robbery and carnage are fast becoming his primary incentives in the strife."[85] British politicians used more restrained language but offered the same cynical reading of Russian character. In the House of Lords, a minister observed, "That same spirit of injustice and oppression which had been too manifest in the proceedings of Russia for the last fifty years, had made her assume the character of an exterminator, and plunged her into measures of the most violent and outrageous severity."[86] Americans, even when they accepted Russian's right to assert control over Poland, found their methods extreme. The precedent, one paper noted, "can only be found in the bloodiest days of the French Revolution."[87]

The Confederate propagandist Henry Hotze co-opted this discourse to equate Russian excesses and Sepoy atrocities with Northern behavior. "The soldiers and officers of the Czar appear to combine all the savage ferocity of the insurgent Sepoys with the cold-blooded cruelty which has branded with infamy the Northern heroes, Turchin, Butler, and M'Neil."[88] Probably as the Poles intended, this Russian overreaction generated sympathy among the French and English in particular.[89] But it never tipped the balance of U.S. support decisively toward the insurgents. Instead, Northerners artfully sought ways to maintain a theoretical support for the Polish nation and the goal of Polish autonomy even as they favored established power to the chaos of insurgencies and sanctioned harsh reprisals against irregulars. Northerners made direct use of the Polish example, criticizing the South for its reliance on irregular combatants by reference to Poles' use of guerrilla tactics. "The very mode of warfare adopted by the [Polish] insurgents demonstrates that the great body of the people are not engaged in the insurrection," the *New York Times* wrote in late 1863. "The guerrilla system answers in certain circumstances; but when a nation rises to strike for its rights, it is not generally in petty bands, and from inaccessible fastnesses, that it carries on the contest."[90]

The Confederacy, dependent in many regions upon guerrilla units, had long defended their use despite the international opprobrium they engendered. Although Southern papers failed to directly endorse the Polish resistance, throughout 1863 they chronicled Russian abuses against Polish forces and civilians in great detail, more so than in Northern papers.[91] Their favorite sport was comparing Lincoln and Tsar Alexander II. "It is natural that brutes should sympathize," editorialized one Richmond paper, "and that Abe and Alexander should form a 'Holy Alliance' against civilization. They are both engaged in the congenial task of destroying a brave people, and both rule over a race of abject slaves. Nowhere on earth, save in Russia, can the Yankees find sympathizers, far less aiders and abettors."[92] The diplomatic collusion between the two powers only served, as Confederates saw it, to reinforce the underlying similarities between the two brutal regimes.

French conservatives, many sympathetic to the Confederacy, regarded both American actions against the Confederates and Russian actions against the Polish as of a piece. An article in the semiofficial *Patrie* (which carried the loose sanction of the emperor) spelled out the connection. "An analogy was drawn between the situation in the United States and that in Russia. In both countries, the 'sacred precepts of humanity' were trampled under foot in a succession of massacres and pillages. A number of atrocities by Federal troops were mentioned and compared with conditions in Poland." The French authors believed "the existence of the Union, as well as the integrity of the Russian Empire, can not be maintained except by frightful massacres." Rather than approve these measures, the authors called on Lincoln and the tsar to release their insurgent regions.[93]

In the U.S. Civil War and in the Indian and Polish rebellions, the question of how each side defined legitimate belligerents created a sense of alienation between combatants that produced unnecessary bloodshed. Dominant powers—the United States and the British and Russian Empires—rejected the idea that insurgents could fight irregularly. Once they did, those forces ceased to be protected by the regular laws of war. According to one scholar, in the Indian Rebellion, the words "surrender" and "prisoner" were not "in the lexicon of the Mutiny's battles. The Mutiny was a war of extermination."[94] Conditions never deteriorated to this nadir in the American or Polish cases, but irregulars in these conflicts received no mercy. The cultural experience of soldiering—the bravery and discipline required—connected Confederate and American troops, but it did not extend to either Southern guerrillas or to Sepoy or Polish rebels.

The situation in China at midcentury was even worse. There a rebellion in the south, referred to as the Taiping (or Heavenly Kingdom of Peace, a name that turned out to be woefully inappropriate), opposed the ruling Qing dynasty. The bloodiest civil war ever, and the deadliest military conflict of the century, the Taiping Rebellion consumed at least 20 million lives.[95] The scale of the Taiping Rebellion generated tremendous suffering across the southern half of the country. At times the Taiping used their claims to Christian authority to justify a particularly deadly treatment of their enemy. As a proclamation of the Eastern king Yang announced: "We have received heaven's decree to kill all monsters and to save the men of the world and make them happy. . . . Now, the Tartar monster, Hëen-Fung [the emperor of China] was originally a Tartar slave, and a natural enemy of China; he, moreover, turns men into monsters, and makes them worship false gods and oppose the true God, and thus rebel against the August Supreme Ruler of heaven; they must therefore be exterminated."[96] "Tartar" was a pejorative label used by the Chinese Han people to designate the Mongols and other nomadic groups in North China. Likewise, Taiping leaders used the term to insult the Manchurian-descended Qing emperor and degrade him as a barbarian.

With the current access to Chinese-language sources, historians today can see that the Taiping fought in a way consistent with Sun Tzu's emphasis on deception, feints, and tactical advantage. A recent summary explains: "The style of fighting practiced by the Taiping . . . utilize[d] indirect, protracted campaigns of maneuver to gain control of key towns and positions."[97] At the time, however, most Western observers regarded the Taiping as fighting like guerrillas. Two French authors penned the earliest European-language history of the conflict. According to them, "the tactics of the insurgents consisted in feigning flight, and thus drawing their enemy into ambuscades, where they slaughtered them without mercy."[98] Ambushes and surprise attacks were legitimate tactics, but Qing forces, in response, refused to recognize Taiping forces as legitimate soldiers and as a result did not take prisoners. The Taiping responded in kind—after the battle for Nanjing, they killed most of the population and let their bodies float down the river.[99] The result was that all soldiers in the conflict faced the threat of dying on the field or being executed once captured.[100]

A report from two British officials noted that the Taiping's "progress has been marked by devastation and desolation. Houses have been plundered and burnt, lives ruthlessly sacrificed, property confiscated, women ill-used."[101] French chronicles reported the same: "One of the savage hordes massacred at least one hundred thousand people in the town of Ning-Tcheou . . . men, women, old people, children, all were killed with lance blows."[102] Americans were even more critical of the behavior of the Taiping than the British, whose missionaries and intelligence officers labored to counteract the military's diehard opposition to the insurgents.

Anson Burlingame, Lincoln's minister to China, reported to Secretary of State Seward after the 1861–62 Taiping assault on Shanghai that the rebels were "the very incarnation of destruction. The smoke of the fires of the burning houses and villages has been ascending in every direction for more than a week. They take a place, 'loot' it, kill the old and the young, and force the strong men to join them to wear their mark in such a way as never to be able to return to their old allegiance."[103] This was not the path to nationhood.

Although the Taiping organized and outfitted armies, Westerners perceived them as rarely observing the laws of war, and the Qing, defending their empire against a group they considered criminal traitors, wielded a heavy hand in return.[104] As one historian of the conflict notes, "as the war dragged on, the fighting became increasingly predatory, unpredictable, and chaotic. It also turned vicious as both sides called for annihilation of their enemies in ever more absolute terms."[105] This was true of Qing responses to rebellions earlier in the nineteenth century, for which "the cornerstone of [their] counterinsurgency effort was a draconian scorched-earth policy."[106] Western observers, reflecting their preference for established rule, gave the Qing wide latitude in their efforts to suppress the rebellion. "The Imperialists even exceeded the T'aip'ings in savage and murderous vengeance," one wrote, "though in their train of course travelled the prestige of the governing power, and the hope of settled rule."[107] In Jiangxi Province, where a stretch of the Yangtze that had been contested between imperial and rebel troops for five years, the fighting was particularly destructive. As one historian reports, "for long stretches it was hard to tell that there had ever been a normal pattern of human life. Cities were emptied; houses been stripped of wood to their window frames to make cooking fires for the passing armies."[108] An American sailor in Shanghai witnessed the recapture of the city by imperial forces. "Since the fall of the city," he observed, "they have been unceasing in their work of slaughter, taking the lives of every male rebel able to walk along and ornamenting the city walls with hundreds of their heads."[109]

The Qing government instituted vicious reprisals against Taiping after their takeover of Nanjing in 1864, a Chinese equivalent to the counterinsurgency waged by U.S. commanders around the South, although taken to much deadlier ends. "The government's targets included not just the partisans themselves but also the relatives—however innocent—of every known member of the Taiping movement out to the furthest branches of their family tree."[110] Tens of thousands were executed under this rule in Canton. An American missionary in Shanghai after it was recaptured by imperial troops described their behavior: "Owing to the constant plundering carried on by the Imperial men in every direction around, the people can hardly get rice or any thing they need, without having it taken from them by this pirate gang and in not a few instances their heads go too. A premium being offered for every rebel's head, they sometimes catch one having rice, & say he was taking it to the city for the rebels."[111] This mode of warfare did little to endear regular people to the imperial side but it made clear the price of supporting the rebellion. No Western observer at the time labeled this an antiguerrilla or counterinsurgency strategy, but the parallels, in behavior and outcomes, are easy to see.

The Politics of Guerrilla War

Insurgencies generated unintended political as well as military repercussions. To succeed, insurgencies must retain the support of the people they claim to represent. Because irregular fighting implicates civilians in the process of war—as the domestic supply line that feeds, supplies, protects, and guides guerrillas—they unleash unpredictable waves of violence, in the form of counterinsurgencies, that threaten all noncombatants. The result is that irregular wars run the risk of alienating the populace they are supposed to protect. In the Confederacy, guerrillas flourished in the absence of regular U.S. forces and in the more remote parts of the Confederacy—Appalachia, Missouri, Arkansas, and so on—the very places that Unionist support already ran high. Many white Southerners thrilled to reports that guerrillas had organized and resisted Union forces. For these people, irregular fighters offered hope and so merited support. In other parts of the South, the violence and destruction stirred by irregular war could embolden those communities in their resistance to the Confederacy, as it did in northern Alabama and southwestern Virginia. As both places spiraled out of control in 1864, the Confederacy had to devote regular troops to suppressing dissent among white Southern civilians who could have been their supporters.[112]

In north-central Virginia, cavalry leader John Singleton Mosby enforced a bright line among his men—they deployed irregular violence against Union soldiers, not Unionist civilians.[113] As a result, the people of this region supported Mosby through the war. But Mosby was the exception in the Confederate guerrilla tradition. Especially along the contested border between the Union and Confederacy, the violence of guerrillas and their enemies drew civilians into a lethal morass. As one historian has recently observed, "the sudden fusion of racial and guerrilla violence in Kentucky resulted in internecine misery that Missouri had already suffered for years. Residents witnessed public roadside executions, 'awful agonized crushing scenes of woe,' as one woman related . . . 'horrors of these times no language can paint.'"[114] In Arkansas, newspapers warned civilians that guerrillas' appetite for "murder and robbery" meant they must all be on the alert, and the papers called on local men to prepare for service against them. As a result of the situation, "hundreds more civilians simply fled the region altogether."[115]

As bad as the nineteenth century seemed, irregular warfare proliferated in the twentieth century. Guerrilla fighters mobilized against the Nazis in World War II, the British in Malaysia, and the French and Americans in Vietnam. Researchers followed, and the result, especially after the recent asymmetrical wars in Iraq and Afghanistan, is a more robust body of military doctrine about how regular armies should respond to irregular threats. David Kilcullen, one of the most thoughtful of this new cadre of military theorists, sees two options for confronting insurgencies that use local guerrillas to fight. Although Kilcullen writes primarily about the current threat landscape, his analysis offers useful ways to think about the nineteenth-century struggles under discussion here. Dominant powers can seek to destroy guerrilla networks in an "enemy-centric" fashion. The Union pursued this approach when they mobilized guerrilla-hunting squads in western Virginia to track down irregular combatants.[116]

The other strategy, what Kilcullen calls a

> classical counter-insurgency . . . focuses on the population, seeking to protect it from harm by—or interaction with—the insurgent, competing with the insurgent for influence and control at the grassroots level. Its basic assumption is that insurgency is a mass social phenomenon, that the enemy rides and manipulates a social wave consisting of genuine popular grievances, and that dealing with this broader social and political dynamism while gaining time for

> targeted measures to work by applying a series of tailored, full-spectrum security measures, is the most promising path to ultimately resolve the problem.[117]

The Union also adopted this approach. In occupied parts of the South, they appointed provost marshals, who administered the regions with an eye to security and also to cultivating Unionist sympathies among the civilian population. Qing forces mostly sought to destroy Taiping and their supporters, but the British and Russians, like the Union, adopted a more classic counterinsurgency strategy. The East India Company had already built alliances with local elites, and the British exploited these during the conflict to gain intelligence and turn local populations against the Sepoy.

In Poland the Russians exploited class tensions and land distribution as a way to address the "popular grievances" the Poles hoped to kindle into a full blaze. They succeeded. Class divisions that elites hoped to bridge in the early days of the rebellion deterred support for the nationalist movement. Historian Timothy Snyder blames this on the rebellion's leaders, who "were no longer early modern patriots, keen to restore a gentry republic; but they were not yet modern nationalists, fully prepared to define the nation as the people."[118] The failure of peasants to support the uprising happened partly because they were not ideologically aligned with the rebellion's organizers, partly because of insecurity created by the Russian response to guerrilla war, and partly because, in 1861, Tsar Alexander II abolished serfdom in Russian lands, a reform that Polish landholders, who led the rebellion, initially opposed. The tsar's intent was that the new peasants would receive land as well as freedom, but the details of how to accomplish this bedeviled Russia for years. Serfs received land but had to make "redemption payments" to the treasury, which violated their sense that, having worked the land for years, they owned it. Russian emancipation weakened the Polish rebellion, but, as one historian notes "like most compromises in Russia, the 1861 Emancipation Statutes were received with great displeasure by those affected."[119]

Serfs saw little change in their status for two years, but in 1863 the tsar accelerated the transition to free labor. As a European historian observes, "the Tsar . . . outbid the Polish revolutionaries by offering Lithuanian, Belarussian, Ukrainian, and then Polish peasants outright ownership of their land, without redemption payments."[120] Equally problematic in Poland was the decentralized nature of irregular war, which made it an awkward tool to unify a people. Irregulars fought local wars, sometimes with an eye to a larger strategy, but just as often without one. A recent history of Europe describes "more than 1,200 small-scale military engagements fought across Poland, Lithuania, Belarus, and the Ukraine," during the mid-nineteenth century in which "groups of nationalist guerrillas attacked Russian garrisons and troops."[121] A historian of the U.S. Civil War reaches a similar conclusion: "The inability of political and military leaders to exploit the benefits of guerrilla warfare splintered a national bid for independence into a hundred local wars for survival."[122] This approach dispersed and localized state power—not an effective path to nationhood. The result was something like scattering small magnets on a table covered with metal filings. The filings pull together, but each cluster is weak and isolated. Confronted with a stronger pull—in the case of the U.S. Civil War, the Union's military and political authority—such local resistance collapses quickly.

Something like this occurred along the lower Mississippi River in 1862 after the Union Navy captured New Orleans. Threatened by Union gunboats but attracted by the Union's promise of lucrative sugar and cotton sales, planters in Mississippi and Louisiana signed a loyalty oath to the Union.[123] Part of the motive here was no doubt the order and security promised by Northern troops instead of the guerrilla conflict called up by Louisiana governor Thomas Moore. The guerrilla war quickly overflowed its banks and impacted local Confederates as well. The only alternative was for those Confederates to appeal to the Union commander in the region. One citizen began his letter to a Union general with a pledge: "I assure you that the universal sense of the people here is bitterly opposed to this system of irregular warfare." This confession was entirely self interested. His own neighbors were subject to marauding guerrillas, and he did not want the Union punishing civilians for irregular attacks. "No doubt the Federal officers, exasperated by the harassing of these irregular squads, entertain the connection that they are upheld & maintained by the popular feeling and favors. I assure you, that such is not the fact; the reverse is true."[124] The letter writer refused to take the loyalty oath but did note that he had retired from Confederate military service and did not intend to rejoin. In this case, as in many others, the guerrilla war weakened the broader Confederate war effort.

The same popular disaffection manifested in parts of China against the Taiping. Although the genesis of the Taiping movement came from rural areas in southern China, once organized, the Taiping targeted major cities. From these, they hoped to control trade and generate the revenue needed to sustain the movement. Philip Kuhn, a leading scholar of the movement, explains the result of Taiping capture of walled cities. "It was a symbol also of the alienation of the Taipings from their social environment. The rebels were outsiders from the first. Their violent pilgrimage began with their expulsion from their homes and ended with their establishment of new homes in strange territories."[125]

The violence directed against ordinary communities by the Taiping also worked at cross purposes with their goal of generating support to displace the Qing dynasty. One scholar has chronicled the experiences of a particularly intense episode of popular resistance to the Taiping, in Shaoxing prefecture, Zhejiang. Taiping soldiers had wrought havoc in the countryside. Trying to collect the taxes they customarily imposed on conquered regions, the Taiping were driven back by a local militia under the command of Bao Lisheng. Eventually commanding an army of several thousand men, Bao issued an indictment of Taiping abuses to stir support for his army. "They kill people's parents, violate people's wives and daughters, plunder people's property, and burn people's homes. Wherever they go it is like locusts. There are no survivors." The solution he proposed was equally severe: "Let village join with village; let county unite with county. March together with us, killing bandits as we go."[126] Refugees flooded into the villages and some joined the army. The Taiping gathered more forces, at least one hundred thousand, and initiated a siege of the village where Bao's army, by then numbering at least twenty-two thousand, resided.[127] The Taiping starved the villages out, resulting in tens of thousands dead. Bao's army did not hold back the Taiping, and it may have represented a more organized response to the destruction meted out by them, but the people of Shaoxing were not the only ones to resist the Taiping.[128] As William T. Rowe, one of the leading modern historians of the Qing, explains, "actions of the Taiping such as desecrating temples, lineage halls, and grave sites, as well as recruiting poor farmers to attack and kill their landlords or richer neighbors, profoundly alienated the literati, especially those of higher rank and status."[129]

A similar process of civilian alienation occurred in India, where the irregular violence and looting of the Sepoy soured would-be friends of the rebellion. An early and prominent supporter of the rebellion, Maulvi Muhammad Baqar, who edited a prominent Urdu paper, complained that "the population [of Delhi] is greatly harassed and sick of the pillaging and plundering."[130] This comment came within weeks of the rebellion's start. Faith in the Sepoy could erode quickly. The British were counting on this process. Shortly after the rebellion began, Lord John Russell proclaimed in Parliament that "it is not likely that the [Indian] military would be immediately obedient to the civil power, or that the civil power would be able to restrain the excesses of the military. Many must be disgusted by the plunder which will take place. Those who are engaged in trade and commerce at Delhi and other towns will find that the rule of licentious soldiery is oppressive and injurious to their lives and peaceful possessions."[131]

The liabilities of guerrilla war can also be seen by comparing the deterioration of public support for irregular insurgencies to examples where public support for regular insurgencies increased. In historical folklore known to generations of Italian school students, Giuseppe Garibaldi initiated the campaign for an independent Italy when he arrived with one thousand men from northern Italy on the shores of Sicily. Garibaldi's effort was decidedly irregular in its opening movement. He organized his men with the intent of preventing the annexation of Nice by France, which had been approved by Garibaldi's Piedmontese government. He moved south when a working-class revolt in Palermo presented a greater possibility of success.[132] Despite constant critique from Western powers, which referred to his men as "banditti," Garibaldi's campaign evolved into a regular war as he moved up Italy's peninsula and merged his army with that of Victor Emmanuel, the lawful ruler of the Piedmont. This brought the insurgency into the rules and practices of regular warfare and eased the way for Prussians and others to recognize Italy as a modern unified state. Garibaldi was implementing a process described by his fellow nation-builder, Giuseppe Mazzini, who had written, as far back as 1832, "Guerrilla warfare can be seen as the first stage of a national war. Guerrilla bands should therefore be so organized as to prepare the way for, and facilitate by their action, the formation of a national army."[133] Mazzini's advice—nearly the opposite of Clausewitz's observation that weak states resorted to guerrilla strategies when regular war failed—was not followed by participants in the failed national movements of midcentury.

The third liability of irregular war was potentially as costly as the second. If irregular warfare held the potential to alienate a local population, it was virtually guaranteed to estrange foreign observers. Following the

Congress of Paris in 1815, the major European powers pursued a balance of power politics. When assessing how to respond to insurgencies or other map-shifting events, the dominant powers focused on self-interest and strategy—would intervening further their economic and security interest? But these same powers also assessed the manner of resistance among would-be nations, and those assessments played a role in the decision to intervene. As one historian writes of the late eighteenth century, "for many people, Europe's respect for the international rule of law was an important part of what it meant to live in a modern, enlightened age."[134] In the Indian, Polish, Chinese, and Confederate cases, insurgents' resort to irregular warfare marked them as premodern and unenlightened.

The Taiping did their best to garner British favor by presenting themselves as the modern, Christian, restrained force. They killed imperial forces wherever they encountered them but worked hard to protect British and French missionaries and civilians. Their goal, as a recent history summarizes it, was to "establish a modern military, American-style (and Christian) schools, and an industrial economy."[135] This effort failed. Although British missionaries admired the sincerity of the Taiping's desire to spread Christianity in the country, military officials (in the country to ensure its markets were open to British trade) took a much more skeptical view. They watched the military conduct of both sides and grew increasingly critical of the Taiping's tactics. Frederick W. A. Bruce, the British minister to China, emerged as the most vigorous opponent of the Taiping, and he exerted independent control over British military actions in the region. Bruce regarded the Taiping leader as "an ignorant fanatic, if not an imposter." According to Bruce, "the bulk of his adherents are drawn from the dangerous classes of China; the result is rule of the sword in its worst form."[136] In order to subvert this outcome (although his main concern was harm to foreigners and the disruption of trade rather than the lives of Chinese civilians), he ordered a British military defense of Shanghai in 1860. When the Taiping attacked the city, the British were thus able to regard it as an attack on the empire and to formally abandon the neutrality they had never really observed in the first place.

A similar process played out in the North American case. Although British conservatives were loath to admit it, guerrillas played an important but counterproductive role in the Confederate national effort. The *London Telegraph* offered a history of the term and then contextualized it for the 1860s:

> We generally speak of a Guerrilla as a person fighting in a more or less righteous cause, but in partisan warfare. The Guerrilla, as we understand him, is subject to no regular discipline, and acknowledges no chiefs saves those of his own choice. . . . This is the Guerrilla who, with the addition of an addiction to blasphemy and whisky-bibbing, is to this day, flourishing in Florida, in Tennessee, in Virginia, and in many other portions, too numerous to mention, of the Distracted States of America. . . . It is a deteriorative as well as a diminutive.[137]

Coming from a newspaper that flattered the Confederacy and encouraged the British government to intervene on its behalf this was a serious indictment.

Because guerrillas used hit-and-run methods rather than conventional military tactics, they could not secure the control of space that was so important in the nineteenth century. The world's established powers pointed to their control of territory as evidence of their sovereignty, and they expected insurgents to demonstrate the same capacity if they merited support. In 1861 the Confederate States of America claimed a territory larger than continental Europe—nearly three-quarter-million square miles with a three-thousand-mile coastline. They did not have the manpower to defend this much land, and the Union cleverly exploited this weakness by establishing its own authority in Confederate states. Adam Gurowski, an expert in European history and political philosophy, identified this as the Southern nation's chief weakness. "A new nation to be in position to beg a recognition must at least exist in geographical conditions, must be able to show at least approximatively positive geographical boundaries," he wrote. "Certain sovereigns and despots of Europe, certain rotten aristocracies and corrupt, dishonored, mercantile classes may overflow with sympathies for traitors and for slaveholders, and hatred of freemen; but the Governments are no fools and know well what is possible and impossible, what is feasible and what is not." Despite his ancestral ties to Poland, he saw this as their key failure as well: "Poland is no more, and the principal cause of her non-recognition now-a-days is because old Poland has no longer positive, geographical, well-established frontiers. This is one from among the reasons why the South cannot be recognized."[138]

If insurgents could not claim sovereignty on the basis of their control of space, upon what could they base such a claim? Nineteenth-century rebels fought for land and simultaneously pursued other markers of modernity. They issued public statements asserting their autonomy; they used new media, especially pamphlets and newspapers, to promote their cause; and they adopted the language of successful modern nation-states. A key part of this language, as it concerned a peoples' fitness for inclusion in the family of nations, was respect for the laws of war. Fighting irregularly, even if insurgents believed it was necessary to establish or retain control of territory, weakened the claim a people might make to autonomy.

If we consider the midcentury rebellions together, similar patterns of action and counteraction are visible: (1) rebels who fought irregularly invited disproportionately destructive counterinsurgencies; (2) these counterinsurgencies weakened popular support for rebels; and (3) guerrilla campaigns inhibited foreign recognition of rebels. This structural similarity might be of only passing interest, but the elements above coalesced in real time, usually to the detriment of insurgents. Many of the national failures used irregular strategies, which linked such behavior with illegitimacy and defeat in the popular imagination. This framing suggests the chicken and egg problem—did failure tarnish global opinion about guerrilla warfare or did using guerrillas cause failure? The historical (and not simply coy) answer to this question seems to be yes. Few observers parsed the causal relationship, but by the 1860s a general association had been established between would-be nations and the use of irregular war.

Foreign powers never explained conclusively that they failed to support certain insurgents based on how their mode of fighting was characterized, but the evidence, if only circumstantial, seems clear nonetheless. Northerners believed the language and analogies they used mattered. They worked hard to paint Confederates as Sepoys or Poles or Taipings. "The Chinese and the *Sepoys* have become the chosen models of Southern men," announced the *New York Herald* in the wake of the Fort Pillow Massacre.[139] Northerners were so convinced of the correctness of the analogy that they used the language in their private correspondence. Union general C. C. Washburn, writing to Gen. Ulysses Grant's chief of staff in Memphis after the Fort Pillow Massacre, proclaimed that he would not "spare the monsters engaging in a transaction that renders the Sepoy a humane being and Nana-Sahib a clever gentleman."[140] S. R. Curtis wrote to the loyal residents of Kansas City, explaining that the "outrages committed on the unarmed and unoffending people of this department would disgrace savage or Sepoy warfare."[141]

Northern newspapers trumpeted the connection. Headlines continually blared evidence of Confederate guerrilla misdeeds. Irregular war was made infamous through the use of global examples. Chief among these for Northerners was Nana Sahib, well known as the Indian leader who approved of the murder of women and children in Kanpur during the rebellion. In the opening moments of the American Civil War, the *Daily Cleveland Herald* pronounced Jefferson Davis to be the "the Nona Sahib of the Southern Sepoy Mutiny."[142] The *Independent*, a Kansas newspaper noted in the wake of the Lawrence massacre by the guerrilla leader William Quantrill, that Quantrill's "atrocities rival those of Nana Sahib or the Taepings."[143] This was not the only paper to make the comparison.[144] The purpose here, explicitly stated in some papers, was to make the treason of the Confederates as odious as possible. "In this struggle," one author wrote, "it must be seen and felt to be the triumph of honor over dishonor, of magnanimity over infamy, of truth over a lie, of right over wrong, of freedom over slavery, of God and righteousness over the devil and sin." Accomplishing this rhetorical feat required recognizing that, compared to the Confederates, "Nana Sahib was a rebel with a cause."[145]

The language of metaphor and analogy could be conveyed in image as well as text. The New York journal *Vanity Fair* published a series of cartoons in which Confederates generally and Jefferson Davis in particular were represented as Sepoys. In one image, Davis, the "celebrated Sepoy juggler and acrobat," balances on a lit cannonball rolling along a tightrope strung between the American capitol and "treason."[146] In another, Davis and his vice president, Alexander Stephens, are advertised as the "Sepoy Brothers, wonderful jugglers," but their show would only appear for "a short time."[147]

The purpose of these and all the other Sepoy references in the Northern press was to connect the Southern Confederacy with the unjust rebellion of Indians in 1857. The point was made most explicitly when *Vanity Fair* ran a satirical ad calling on all those who "earnestly sympathize with the humane and benevolent conduct, in India, of Nena Sahib" to donate for the erection of a monument in his honor.[148] Subscribers were encouraged to send money to Howell Cobb, whom the journal misidentified as the Confederate treasury secretary. If the Confederacy planned to pursue

VANITY FAIR.
LET US ALONE
CONFEDERATE
TO RICHMOND
IN A POSITION TO BE RECOGNISED.
THE CELEBRATED SEPOY JUGGLER AND ACROBAT, JEFF DAVIS, IN HIS DANGEROUS GLOBE FEAT

Figure 2. Northern newspapers drew on recent memories of the Indian Rebellion of 1857 to identify Confederates as "Sepoys" as a way to cast their cause as illegitimate and bloodthirsty. "In a Position to Be Recognised," *Vanity Fair*, August 24, 1861. Image courtesy of Making of America Project, University of Michigan.

Figure 3. Casting Confederate president Jefferson Davis and vice president Alexander Stephens as the "Sepoy Brothers," *Vanity Fair* predicted that Southern secession would end as quickly as the Indian Rebellion had. "Mind Your Eye!" *Vanity Fair*, August 10, 1861. Image courtesy of Making of America Project, University of Michigan.

the same "Holy Work" as that of the Indian Rebellion, people around the world knew what to expect.

The connections and similarities among these conflicts tells us something about why some national rebellions like Italy's succeeded, and others like the Indians', Poles', and Taiping's failed. Similar to these other would-be nation-builders, the Confederates lost partly because they fought a guerrilla war. Insurgents seeking to separate themselves from established states faced great difficulties. Those people who adopted irregular methods of fighting complicated their task still more. They did so partly because the wars of the mid-nineteenth century occurred in an increasingly globalized world and one whose leading members regarded regular military practice as a necessary precondition for entry into that world. Americans knew about British suppression of the Sepoy Rebellion when Southern states seceded. Russians and the Qing observed the U.S. response to secession and meted out violence against their own rebels in harmony. The great powers of the nineteenth century did not collude about the best ways to suppress rebellion but they shared the same practices nonetheless, effective ones in a world of sovereign states determined to maintain their authority.

2

ALL WARS ARE WORLD WARS

Foreign Imagination and the Fate of Nations

GLOBAL HISTORY DID NOT BEGIN with the creation of the Internet. In what sounds like a modern reflection on our global village, the *Atlantic Monthly* observed in 1861, "there cannot be a Russian War, or a Sepoy mutiny, or an Anglo-French invasion of China, or an emancipation of the serfs of Russia, without the effect thereof being sensibly experienced on the shores of Superior or the banks of the Sacramento; and the civil war that is raging in the United States promises to produce permanent consequences to the inhabitants of Central India and of Central Africa. The wars, floods, plagues, and famines of the farthest east bear upon the people of the remotest West. The Oregon flows in sympathy with the Ganges."[1] Eric Hobsbawm, an early proponent of what we now call global history, said something similar. About the mid-nineteenth century, he wrote, "History from now on became world history."[2]

Despite Hobsbawm's status as a premier interpreter of the modern world, many historians have resisted his confident declaration about how to structure their narratives. There are good reasons for this. Amid dramatic events, people search for explanations that speak directly to their personal experience. Vietnam veteran Tobias Wolff wrote, "In a world where the most consequential things happen by chance, or from unfathomable causes, you don't look to reason for help. You consort with mysteries. You encourage yourself with charms, omens, rites of propitiation."[3] Military and political historians, whose emphasis on contingency helps capture history's dynamism, satisfy this need as well. Likewise, histories written with a domestic focus resonate with current political demands. They provide a usable and relevant past. At the same time, they can obscure other narratives that provide equally important insights into how history works. Intellectual and cultural histories rely on the words and actions left by historical actors to identify habits of mind that might be less obvious in the heat of events but that nonetheless shape outcomes.

Thinking about Rebellion

During the U.S. Civil War, many of the war's participants knew enough about the global history of military conflicts to think in terms of comparisons and analogies. In fact, it was almost impossible to think in terms that did not draw on historical or comparative examples. The result was an intellectual entanglement that boosted or diminished the cause of various participants in the century's great conflicts. It would be too much to claim that language alone determined the fate of nations, but the boundaries of possible action were shaped by rhetoric. In particular, the question of whether foreign powers would intervene in civil or national conflicts in other countries hinged, in part, on how they thought about the people concerned. Did they make up a genuine nation? Was their recourse to war legitimate? Was the sovereignty they asserted something to be respected or ignored? The act of framing these questions and of offering answers immersed participants in the roiling sea of words and concepts associated with war, violence, nationalism, and sovereignty.

Sometimes people crafted language with great precision. Participants in the U.S. Civil War and other national conflicts drew on global analogies in order to justify themselves or condemn their rivals. And sometimes language operated unconsciously—repeated references to "rebels" as opposed to "criminals" or "outlaws" could confer some degree of legitimacy on a cause, even one the writer opposed. Historians have long known that in the major military episodes of the nineteenth century, the disposition of foreign countries toward the participants played key roles in the outcomes. We have rightly focused on the role national interest played in the decision to recognize or support a given insurgent or established power. Intervention, as it was called then, depended upon the advantages to be gained. But alongside that material explanation existed an intellectual framework that also shaped what happened. A key question shadowing the decision to intervene was whether the group merited support. This chapter explores the process by which Western Europeans and Americans conceptualized and explained the legitimacy of participants in conflicts around the world in the nineteenth century and whether those conceptions demanded they intervene or ignore the conflict.

We know the outcomes of many of these stories. In the 1820s liberal Europeans flocked to Greece to support an independence struggle against the Ottoman Empire. When the British brutally suppressed a nationalist rebellion in India, no one intervened. In the middle of the century, Western nations professed support for the Polish bid for autonomy from Russia but sent few fighters and offered no real diplomatic aid. In the United States, Lincoln and Seward celebrated their diplomatic coup in keeping Britain and France from recognizing the Confederacy. At the same time, Europeans intervened in the Taiping Rebellion and helped determine the outcome.

Foreign involvement took one of two forms. In some cases, outside states intervened and enabled one group to succeed. This practice usually redounded to the benefit of established powers; in rare cases, insurgents received support. And in other cases, outside states refused to intervene, usually enabling the dominant power to succeed. I will discuss some of the most famous instances of each possible outcome, but first I want to address the ways that people represented themselves and the language that outsiders used to characterize these conflicts.

In an ideal world, and in the realm of political philosophy, the issue of what constitutes a legitimate polity can be determined impartially, without regard to the advantage or disadvantage that might accrue to communities that recognize it. By the mid-nineteenth century, the political theory of statecraft, what some scholars aspirationally called the "law of nations," was well established. In the seventeenth century, Hugo Grotius, a Dutch jurist, codified many of the prevailing sentiments. In writing about nations and war, Grotius articulated a framework by which people could assess which conflicts were "just" and merited respect and support and which were not. Grotius only sanctioned what we would call today defensive war. "There is no other *reasonable* Cause of making War," he wrote, "but an *Injury* received."[4] As a Christian, Grotius took pains to explain the legitimate conditions under which a sovereign could initiate a conflict. "The Law of Nations has established a certain Manner of making War; so that those Wars which are conformable to it, have, by the Rules of that Law, certain peculiar Effects: When arises that Distinction which we shall hereafter make use of, between a *solemn War*, which is also called Just (that is, regular and compleat), and a *War not solemn*."[5]

Grotius only sanctioned solemn or just conflict. Despite his immersion in the monarchical world of early modern Europe, he made room for war by "subjects against their superiors" in language that seemed to anticipate the claims made by nineteenth-century insurgents. "This is allowed by all good Men," Grotius wrote, "that if the civil Powers command any Thing contrary to the Law of Nature, or the Commands of God, they are not to be obeyed."[6] Later generations of thinkers regarded Grotius's work as the foundation upon which they elaborated the rules for how nations could claim sovereignty in the modern world. Emer de Vattel, a Swiss writer, adapted Grotius's instructions for the eighteenth century. "The right of employing force, or making war," Vattel wrote, "belong to nations no farther than is necessary for their own defence and for the maintenance of their rights."[7]

In the end, theory did not determine the fate of insurgents petitioning for recognition. Nations were not granted recognition based solely on whether they satisfied the principles laid out by Grotius or Vattel. But neither was the decision a strictly strategic or cynical question of power. Because Western Europeans were the very ones who had created the jurisprudential culture that led to Grotius and Vattel, they obligated themselves publicly to at least nominal acknowledgment of an impartial system for assessing legitimacy among would-be nations. Because of this preference for formal patterns, those potential nations that presented themselves to the world in terms of existing statecraft culture stood the greatest chance of being acknowledged.[8] This chapter first explores the issue of how participants framed their story in order to convince others of their legitimacy. Then it turns to the question of how others interpreted these framings.

Military conflicts are understood through analogies—"it's a new Cold War," "the conflict risks becoming another Vietnam," and, more relevant for nineteenth-century purposes, "Southern secession is like the Sepoy Mutiny." Analogical reasoning can carry sanction, support, or scorn. When Northerners associated one event (the secession of the Southern states from the Union) with another (the rebellion of Indian people against the British Empire), they hoped the failure of the latter would stain the former. The association carried more expectation than observation. Nineteenth-century people understood the slippery nature of metaphor and chose their analogies with care, hoping to shift public opinion in their favor by linking their opponents with the most disreputable examples from the past. Military actors used global examples selected to shape impressions of their cause by associating their own conduct with the best of the world and the best of the past. The practice continues today. The ramifications of civil wars circulate around the globe. Nineteenth-century ghosts do not stay put, nor do twentieth century ones. The ubiquity of Che Guevara's face on T-shirts has exported a symbol of the Cuban Revolution around the world. Confederate battle flags showed up on the jeans worn by British punks in the 1980s and until recently appeared in the stands of soccer games in Cork, Ireland. These are trivial examples, but they suggest a modern commercial analogue to the dispersal of global examples that framed how people understood war in the nineteenth century.

Participants in the midcentury wars possessed a global view of their conflicts. The enormous Northern pamphlet literature, which gathered the ideas of ministers, military and political officials, and public thinkers, framed the U.S. Civil War in terms of other wars. "We can now see plainly enough," Presbyterian George L. Prentiss noted in 1862,

> that the age which at Waterloo seemed to be bidding adieu to the sword, was itself pregnant with the elements of titanic strife. The revolutionary storms which swept over Europe in 1848 . . . the Eastern [Crimean] war, the Indian revolt, the wars in China, the Italian struggle, and now our own civil war, have demonstrated, one after the other, that the occupation of the peace society is for the present gone, and that a long time must elapse before spears will be turned into pruning-hooks. So far from learning war no more, never did the nations study it with greater diligence.[9]

That study, as this speaker revealed, inescapably happened in a global framework.

Insurgents and established powers both crafted rhetoric that derived from their culture. It could not be otherwise, of course, given the demands that language itself imposes on its users. As a result, no hard and fast hierarchy of labels existed across the various communities under consideration here. But within the English-speaking world, the sources reveal that certain terms stuck to certain insurgents and that those terms often carried connotations that shaped how people thought about the events. In considering the Italians fighting under Garibaldi, British newspapers refer to them as "banditti," an exoticized and foreign bandit. Better than "criminal," perhaps, but hardly a convincing basis from which to establish a modern state. "Insurgent" often operated as a vaguely neutral term that designated a minority party fighting a larger more established community. "Rebel" politicized any discussion because it could identify the participants with a radical political orientation. As historian David Armitage observes in his study of civil war, "this problem of naming becomes particularly acute when political ideas are at stake. We frame these terms to persuade our friends and to combat our enemies."[10]

In America the terms carried more complex baggage. Beginning in the secession movement and extending throughout the war, Confederates identified themselves with the American Revolution, but they did so in order to link themselves to a noble past rather than as an endorsement of the political meaning of the Revolution.[11] Indeed, none other than Robert E. Lee bemoaned to his son in January 1861 that "secession is nothing but revolution."[12] To combat this perspective, they labored to impress upon themselves and the world the conservative nature of their movement. In the words of historian Anne Rubin, they "rewrote the history of the United States with their own distinctive slant."[13] American insurgents rejected the designation of rebels. "Americans recognized that independence," Eliga Gould argued, "was a condition that required the consent of other governments, not something that they could achieve unilaterally (or solely on their own terms)." This was especially true, Gould continues, because of the "Union's origins in what the English historian Edward Gibbon called the 'criminal enterprise' of rebellion. In *Common Sense*, Thomas Paine warned that as long as 'we profess ourselves the subjects of Britain, we must, in the eyes of foreign nations, be considered as rebels.' For Europe's rules to recognize a band of outlaws who were, by their own admission, at a war with their lawful king would be 'dangerous to *their peace*,' wrote Paine."[14]

Whether they proudly proclaimed or awkwardly concealed their status as rebels, people at the time used particular words to seek advantage, to position themselves in relation to others. But like every user of language, it controlled them as much as they controlled it. A political scientist recently explained how "sticky words" create problems for their users. He argues that "the power of rhetoric to shape and transmit political ideas through arguments is not unrestrained. Past arguments used by political actors in particular ways may limit the choice of future arguments available to them."[15] The poet Kay Ryan offers her own take on this idea in a poem titled "Bait Goat," in which she writes,

> There is a
> distance where
> magnets pull,
> we feel, having
> held them
> back. Likewise
> there is a
> distance where
> words attract.[16]

Nineteenth-century insurgents knew this, too, and Confederate rebels perhaps most of all. According to this concept, certain words attract others and limit the speaker's range of action. Words like "secession," "nation," and "independence" trapped Confederates in a web of patriotic rhetoric associated with the American Revolution and its promise of liberal democracy. They wanted autonomy but not reform. Most Confederates imagined a more hierarchical and conservative nation than the one they left.[17] On the other hand, established powers faced their own challenges from sticky words. Denouncing an independence movement in the United States left Northerners ill equipped to support one in Russia. Or as a worried Adam Gurowski noted in 1862, "As independence is to-day the watchword in Europe, so the cause of the rebels acquires a plausible justification."[18]

Rebels Abroad

Because of this reality, we need to understand both what people intended in their use of language and what transpired outside their control. How did "rebel" resonate in 1860s America? In 1848 Americans celebrated reports of republican revolutions in western and central Europe, but those ventures ended in failure.[19] By 1860 most Americans seemed positively allergic to foreign revolution, which they feared would infect the body politic, upsetting the progress of the preceding decades. As historian Adam Smith notes, "for many Americans . . . events in Europe [in the 1850s] rekindled the horrors of undisciplined violence that had stalked the

American imagination since the twin Reigns of Terror in the 1790s—in Jacobin France and the racial apocalypse (as it was imagined) of Haiti."[20]

At the broadest level, the global language of war and nation-building offered tools to differentiate a civil war from a revolution, a rebellion, or simple banditry. Comparative events created the lens through which Americans understood their own nation, and most Americans, North and South, associated secession and civil war with unstable republics. The political conflicts of the 1850s over slavery and its expansion into the western territories generated anxiety that demanded a foil for the virtuous republic. In the 1840s and 1850s, Americans seized upon a local example: Mexico. To their eyes, Mexico represented the perils of instability, and Americans defined themselves in opposition to the political failures of their neighbor to the south.[21] Although they celebrated the national movements that liberated Spain's colonies across Central and South America, Americans expressed little faith in the ability of Mexicans to govern themselves.

Numerous challenges faced the young nation after its independence in 1821. Despite the success Mexicans experienced throwing off Spanish rule, the independent nation did not possess a strong sense of cultural or political unity. Would-be Mexican nationalists confronted serious challenges. The Spanish colonial legacy bequeathed a divided, elite-driven politics. The Catholic Church leveraged its economic and cultural power to weaken reform movements. And would-be reformers disputed among themselves about the best shape for their postcolonial republic. Above those domestic cleavages hovered the menace of the United States, culminating in the humiliating conquest of Mexico in 1847.

Conservatives and Liberals struggled through the middle decades of the century to fashion a stable and prosperous Mexico. As one historian notes, for the central state, "the high level of provincial independence that had prevailed during the colonial period had been exacerbated by the violent, decade-long independence struggle, and several regions in the new republic were strenuously disinclined to cooperate with any central government."[22] The result was decades of political instability: riots, coups, and regional independence movements.[23] Benito Juárez, who led the Liberals through this era, pursued national unity to propel Mexico forward. As a historian of Mexico explains, the Liberals' "aim was the integration of all corporate entities and ethno-linguistic groups into one common civic identity in a nation-state governed in accordance with the principles of sovereignty of the people, equality before the law, representation according to population, and the supremacy of the civil power."[24]

White Americans resorted to an easier explanation for Mexico's instability: the country's mixed-race population was incapable of self-government and its Indian population too prone to rebellion.[25] Americans cheered and then assisted the breakaway province of Texas in its independence bid in the 1830s, but they condemned the Caste War of the Yucatán, the largest and most successful of the regional secessionist movements that wracked the country in the 1840s. Launched by inhabitants of the Yucatán Peninsula, largely indigenous Mayan farmers, and led by a group of often antagonistic local elites, the war produced a generation of dispossession and death across the region. Americans offered little aid to the Mayan rebels, content to regard the latest secessionist effort in Mexico as evidence of their wisdom in annexing Texas. "The Indians were still ravaging the country with fire and sword," wrote an Alabama newspaper in a typical summary of how Americans understood the event.[26] Even a journal as liberal as the *National Anti-Slavery Standard* could not avoid the lesson: "During this period, the Republic has been distracted, not only by the civil war which displaced Bustamente and elevated Santa Anna to power, but also by the insurrection in the Yucatán, and the long civil war which ensued in that quarter."[27] Some Americans felt an interest in the conflict and sent resources to help counter the rebel threat, and a handful fought as soldiers against the insurgents around Merida, on the northwestern corner of the peninsula.[28] But in general, Americans blamed the civil discord, which destroyed trade, communities, and families, on the political incapacity of Mexicans themselves.

Americans also expressed contempt for a federal state, which the Mexicans claimed to possess, that could not maintain territorial sovereignty. In 1848 the *Baltimore Sun* reprinted an article from the *Merida Union* that "shows the inhabitants consider that nothing can save them from utter extinction but the protecting hand of some foreign power, to obtain which they are willing to sacrifice even their nationality."[29] This was a false report, but the notion of voluntarily abandoning one's nationality conjured a cowardice among the people and a gross incapacity on the part of Mexico City. Americans would have been horrified to learn that this was precisely how some British observers characterized secession in 1861. As Hugh Dubrulle shows, "the mere fact of secession seemed to indicate [to Britons] that something was profoundly deficient in American national feeling."[30] The London *Times* explained the matter with precision: "If a nation is to be defined as a community which desires to live under one Government, then the United States before secession were certainly not a nation."[31] Worse still, the rebels in the Yucatán were consistently characterized by American newspapers as "Indians," a political community that should not have been able to challenge Mexico City's authority.

As the major port city on the Gulf of Mexico, New Orleans received first word of events in the conflict, and the *Picayune* filed regular reports about the conflict that were reprinted in newspapers across the United States. The *Picayune*'s editors expressed concern that what began as what they called an "insurrection" was transforming into a "caste war," meaning a war between the races, something quite ominous to Louisiana slaveowners.[32] The insurgents in the Yucatán sought primarily to be left alone and never pursued a strategy of positive organization oriented toward the global community.[33] The result was a long conflict defined by persistent attacks and counterattacks on noncombatant communities and the depopulation of a large swath of the peninsula. As a large-scale insurgency next door to the United States, the Caste War of the Yucatán cast a shadow on its neighbors. In the context of the approaching U.S. Civil War, the conflict increased the sense among Americans that civil wars befouled weak states and demanded a firm response. As a popular lecturer in the North prophesied in 1860, if the United States was not careful, "it might yet succumb, as had its neighbor, to 'the worst of all wars, the maddest and most insane of all the sinful follies of which civilized men can be capable . . . Civil War.'"[34]

Commentators ascribed the same moral weakness and attendant dilemmas to China, where the Taiping Rebellion flowered in the 1850s. Since 1644, when ethnic Manchus from the north organized a new military coalition, the Qing dynasty ruled China. At its height, the polyglot empire encompassed 400 million people over a vast space of western Asia. As a successor to preceding dynasties, the Qing inherited an imperial system that derived tax revenue, conscripts, and goods from the provinces. They also inherited the resentments of people from the hinterlands who initiated rebellions throughout the first half of the century. Westerners recognized that the Chinese possessed a much more robust state than the Mexicans, but the scale of the empire and the degree of central authority claimed by the Qing spurred secessionist movements that threatened the whole. Rather than a self-governing republic whose structural integrity derived from the voluntary allegiance of loyal men, China seemed to possess the atavistic elements of older European empires. According to an Ohio newspaper, "the popular judgment has been that rebellion was chronic among the Chinese people."[35] Instead of interpreting this condition as reflecting a desire for liberty among the Chinese, as Western observers did when Latin American colonies threw off Spain's yoke, they condemned the Qing for failing to exercise proper authority over their dependents.

When reports of the Taiping Rebellion reached American shores, observers feared that it "indicates a prolonged civil war, which in China is attended with indescribable horrors."[36] Beyond the problems that accompanied war among savage people, Americans saw in China many of the problems they identified in Mexico. In their view, the Manchus were an incompetent and corrupt ruling class who alienated the people. Several years into the conflict, the *Boston Daily Advertiser* offered what amounted to established American wisdom on the subject: "Of one thing all must be satisfied, viz: that the government that could let a country sink into the state China is now in, is unworthy the name of a government—unworthy any support."[37] This perspective, cynically organized around which regime was likely to offer the most trade access, reflected ignorance about how regime change worked in China. Chinese people approached the question of governance and succession differently than did Westerners. Rather than the divine right of kings or the process of electoral turnover in the new republican framework, Chinese embraced the "concept of a 'Mandate of Heaven' (*tianming*) [which] bestowed instant legitimacy upon successful rebel leaders." Within this system, dynasties exercised authority until a challenger displaced them, often through war. As China scholar Elizabeth Perry explains, "in Imperial China, one who managed to wrest the throne by force thereby gained Confucian sanction for his rule: as the proverb put it bluntly, 'He who succeeds is a king or marquis; he who fails is an outlaw.'"[38] The Taiping were the largest but not the only regional challenge to the authority of China's central state in the early nineteenth century. In fact, the Qing defeated all the insurgents and reformed the state, which continued into the twentieth century.[39] Americans misinterpreted the integrity and durability of the early nineteenth-century Chinese state. As historian of China Stephen Platt observes, in 1838, Qing China was "powerful, prosperous, dominant, and above all envied."[40]

Europeans coveted that prosperity. In particular, they sought access to what they regarded as China's vast consumer market. In the 1830s the British leveraged their naval superiority to force their way into China. During the Opium Wars (1839–1842; 1856–1860), they forced treaties on the Qing that promised access. When the Taiping Rebellion began in 1851, the British were still wringing concessions from Qing officials, complicating their ability to respond to the internal threat. As another China scholar notes, "the Opium War brought into the open feelings of anti-Manchuism among the Chinese that had festered under the surface for two centuries."[41] Although the British commanded the military forces that subjected China to new trade rules, all Westerners benefited. In the wake of the Second Opium War, American businessmen increased their investments in the China trade. For them, the threat of civil war in China was that it complicated their efforts to trade there. As one American trader complained to the U.S. commissioner to China, "in two essential points at least the Chinese government has failed to perform all the stipulations of the treaty of Wang-Hia. It has failed not only to protect us from the encroachments of those who are in rebellion against the government, but has taken no effective measure to secure us from the attacks of its own soldiery; and merchandise, in its transit to and from this place, has been stopped and duties levied upon it in the interior."[42]

If the Qing weakness had only been political, it might not have shaped foreign affairs to such a degree. That said, the economic concerns driving American attitudes helped the Qing at the expense of the Taiping. Grotius's rules offered little help to the insurgents. Whatever their faults, the Qing had signed trade treaties and seemed willing to expand foreign access to domestic markets. The Taiping seemed sympathetic to Western ideas, but they were an unknown quantity and American traders preferred the stability and order promised by the Qing to the uncertainty presaged by the insurgents. This position reflected the long-standing antipathy of most merchants toward rebellion and war, which disrupted markets and commerce. Philip Kuhn explains, "The British fear was not that the Taipings would take a hostile stance towards foreign trade or even towards foreign treaty rights, but rather that their supposed inability to establish effective government would throw the country and its commerce into chaos."[43]

Northern newspapers emphasized the destruction and incivility of the Taiping insurgents, which led readers to see the movement as less political and more an orgy of violence. The *San Francisco Bulletin* led the way with much of the national coverage, emphasizing the sacking of cities and the disruption of trade occasioned by Taiping military actions. "The Taiping Rebellion," the paper concluded, "continued to be a devastating scourge."[44] California papers increased their emphasis on Taiping depravity once the U.S. Civil War began. "The Hongkong papers are filled with accounts of rebel atrocities at the capture of Ningpo," one observed in 1862. "A complete panic had visited all classes of the native community, and everybody—high and low, rich and poor, man and woman, young and old—who could get away, fled from the city as from a place doomed to destruction. After the rebels had settled themselves in the city they began the work of destruction—sacking, firing, and murdering."[45] Missionary newspapers, which might have supported the insurgents, given their desire to foster Christianity in China, more often seem to have regarded them as idolaters. A report in the *Missionary Herald* could have been lifted straight from the anti-Chinese *Bulletin*: "Taiping, the banditti, which caused no little trouble to the authorities in these two provinces, being unworthy the name of a party, their main object, as fully proved by their depredations and piracies, being plunder."[46] The U.S. minister to China in the 1850s echoed this language, describing the Taiping as "a handful of insurgents, whose origin was a band of robbers in the interior."[47] Other papers referred to the Taiping as "rebels," "insurgents," and "marauders."[48] Northerners only rarely referred to the rebellion as a civil war, instead deploying the same terms of derision they used to describe Confederates.

American attitudes toward the Taiping Rebellion were not inevitable. In the event, most Americans criticized the Qing for fostering an environment in which the Taiping flourished; that is, they interpreted the rebellion as evidence of Chinese weakness. But instability did not always signal a weak nation. This same judgment, for instance, did not apply to France, which experienced four major political shocks between 1789 and 1871. The French Revolution in 1789 divided Americans, some of whom, like Thomas Jefferson, lauded the movement against monarchy and toward constitutional rights as resonant with the American Revolution, while others condemned the turn toward violence and destruction during the Terror as emblematic of the dangers of unchecked democracy. Napoleon's ascendancy reassured conservatives that order would prevail, but his military advance across Europe alarmed many. The July Revolution of 1830 brought popular sovereignty to France but retained a king on the throne. In 1848 France, like other western European countries, was seized by political tumult when a popular movement overthrew the king and created the Second Republic. This, too, failed to take. Louis Napoleon Bonaparte was elected president, but within three years he dissolved parliament and declared the Second French Empire. The century retained its capacity to surprise when Parisians launched a quasi-independence movement in 1871 with the creation of the Paris Commune.

Today historians view this sequence as France's tumultuous but linear movement toward a democratic republic. At the time this benevolent outcome was less certain. Nonetheless, western European and American observers at the time did not criticize the various French monarchical regimes that fell to popular insurgencies as weak and ineffective. Instead, they lauded the liberal reformers who launched efforts to curtail the rights of kings. The contradictions in designating some people (Enlightenment-inspired Frenchmen) as "rebels" and others (Indian subjects or Chinese peasants) as "marauders" or "guerrillas" points to an underlying tension in the conceptual frameworks of the period. When the midcentury rebellions are viewed together, what stands out most clearly is the role of race in shaping European attitudes. At the most basic level, racism informed the ways that Western observers responded to sovereignty struggles in the mid-nineteenth century. As historian Cemil Aydin has argued, "especially in the second half of the nineteenth century, [European rulers] mobilized notions of national and racial greatness, imperial glory, and Christian values in bolstering imperial power."[49] This was certainly true for white Americans reporting and commenting on the efforts of Mayan people to attain independence on the Yucatán Peninsula. Americans extended little of the respect or support to Mexican or Indian or Chinese insurgents that they did to French or Italian or German rebels who pursued similar goals. Most Americans at the time did not regard this as inconsistent—they believed that a people's fitness for self-rule hinged on cultural factors every bit as much as political claims.

The ironies of this attitude surfaced throughout the era. Dark-skinned insurgents, at home or abroad, could be portrayed as either rapacious and destructive or weak and effeminate and sometimes both at once. In the U.S. Civil War, Confederates received the same inconsistent treatment. In some reporting Northerners portrayed them as savage opponents eager to disembowel their enemies and fashion jewelry from the bones.[50] On the other hand, when Jefferson Davis was captured by Union troops in southern Georgia in April 1865, he was covered in a blanket. Northern cartoonists transformed this into his wife's shawl and sometimes her dress in a transparent bid to emasculate the Confederate chief. Latent in this conversation was whether the rebels that the British faced in India or the Russians faced in Poland or the Americans faced in the South were inferior or superior men.

The problems of race appeared most prominently when people of color sought autonomy within existing state systems, especially if they called their actions a revolution. Although Northerners still prized their connection to the rebels of 1776 and their role in building the United States, the efforts of people of color to liberate themselves from colonial rule or slavery tarnished the word "rebellion." The problem of how to characterize military or political resistance by people of color took its original shape for white Americans in the Haitian Revolution and its liberation from the French Empire at the turn of the nineteenth century. At the time the event occurred and for many decades afterward, Frenchmen did not possess an intellectual framework that could identify the efforts of enslaved people on the island as war-making. They believed that enslaved people neither desired nor sought freedom. As one plantation manager remarked just before the rebellion, "I live tranquilly in the midst of them without a single thought of their uprising unless that was fomented by the whites themselves."[51] Because they believed enslaved people incapable of political thought, the French could see only violence. What they proudly called a "Revolution" in France itself, in 1789, mutated into what they regarded as insurrection or rebellion in the West Indies.

Today we know that enslaved people possessed political sensibilities and used these to shape their responses to the uncertainties they confronted in the mid-nineteenth century.[52] As Steven Hahn has written,

> to speak of slaves' politics may seem a contradiction in terms, for the slaves had no standing in the official arenas of either civil or political society. . . . Yet the slaves did express and act according to their individual wills, fashion collective norms and aspirations, contest the authority of the owners on many fronts, build institutions to mobilize their resources and sensibilities, produce leaders who

> wielded significant influence, and, in ways we have still to appreciate fully, press on the official arenas of politics at the local, state, and national levels.[53]

That said, white Southerners at the time refused to acknowledge this capacity, except when they worried about the effect Haiti might have on their supposedly obedient slaves. Throughout the 1790s and for many decades after the event, slaveowners suppressed information about the revolution. This proved mostly in vain. Sailors, soldiers, deserters, pirates, and slaves themselves carried information about Haiti around the Caribbean and Atlantic basins. These stories circulated beyond French boundaries—the Spanish and English expressed great anxiety that slaves in their colonies would catch the spirit. They were right to worry. As historian Julius Scott notes, "by 1793, the continuing rebellion of blacks and people of color in Saint-Domingue provided a rally point for would-be revolutionaries in other areas."[54] By the time of the U.S. Civil War, news had traveled even farther north. "'The result of the insurrection in St. Domingo has long been known among the contrabands of the South,' a chaplain in Port Royal, South Carolina, could observe during the war, and 'the name Toussiant L'Overture has been passed from mouth to mouth, until it has become a secret household word.'"[55]

Black and white Americans did not share a common perspective on the events in Haiti. White Americans absorbed the stories told by white Haitian refugees to their shores. As a result, they usually explained martial resistance to slavery either with recourse to an external hand (mis) guiding enslaved people or demoted it to interpersonal violence and stripped its political content. Today we can see what they denied. Haiti was a "rebellion-turned-revolution," a useful phrase for capturing the historical complexity of what happened on the island of Saint Domingue.[56] What initially appeared to be rebellion by slaves legally bound to their masters transformed into something that altered the island's distribution of wealth and land, restructured the political system, and overturned the racial order. Perhaps even more worrisome to the British and Spanish, the independence of Haiti also upset the imperial order; a revolution indeed.

White Americans' concern about radical black politics continued to grow in the 1820s as multiracial people liberated themselves from Spain in Central and South America.[57] The initial flush of support for Latin

American nations waned as pro-slavery politicians articulated their fears over supporting the new mixed-race republics. John Randolph of Virginia distilled this message to its purest essence. Opposed to a plan by President John Quincy Adams to send American delegates to a hemispheric conference in Panama in 1826, Randolph lamented that Americans would be "willing to take 'their seat in Congress at Panama, beside the native African, their American descendants, the mixed breeds, the Indians, and the half breeds.'"[58] Unlike most white Virginians who tried to valorize the Founders without sanctioning rebellion, Randolph's disdain for the people involved in nation-building extended to the whole process; he repudiated not just Latin American rebels but the founding idea of American independence and its rebel author, Thomas Jefferson.

By using "rebel" to refer to the Taiping or other nineteenth-century insurgents, newspaper editors denied them legitimacy. This was in addition to the more explicit condemnations of Taiping behavior in battle or in occupied cities. Northern papers reprinted reports from European missionaries, diplomats, and military officers, usually treating them as reliable and objective reporting. A correspondent of the *London Times* offered his observations about the Taiping: "'I was disgusted with their disreputable and disorderly appearance. Their pretensions to Christianity are of the shallowest description, and they do not possess even a superficial knowledge of its tenets, much less of its practice.' The results could be seen in their actions. "They are polygamists, opium-smokers, and the only Bible example they seem to follow is that of the Israelites in the conquest of Canaan. The whole country has been laid in ruins by them, the women carried off, the men pressed into their service, and fire and bloodshed mark their track everywhere."[59]

The Taiping sought to counteract European impressions of their regime as a lawless, violent insurgency. Some of the rebellion's leaders knew English and had studied Christianity with Western missionaries. They clearly absorbed more than just spiritual lessons. In an early "manifesto of the right to the throne," Taiping authors assailed the Qing claim to authority. Demonstrating their close reading of Western political language, they offered a defense of their movement grounded in nationalism and self-determination.[60] The Manchu, they wrote, "are descended from an insignificant nation of foreigners" who "seized on our treasure, our lands, and the government of our country." The Taping trumpeted the fact that they had displaced the Qing in many provinces and established a new

Chinese government. "The right to govern consists in possession," they concluded, in a tautological argument that would have found favor in the American North.[61]

Nonetheless, this claim to legitimacy and statehood fell on deaf ears once the Civil War began. In his dispatches regarding China, Secretary of State William Henry Seward avoided using the phrase "civil war" whenever possible, except in the most general terms. Instead, he referred to the Taiping action as a "revolution" or a "rebellion," neither of which he sanctioned.[62] The policy outcome followed naturally, as Seward instructed the U.S. minister to China, Anson Burlingame: "Lend no aid, encouragement, or countenance to sedition or rebellion against the imperial authority."[63] Seward remained consistent. On the day when the U.S. Army captured Richmond in 1865, he spoke to a crowd from a balcony at the War Department. "'What shall I say,' he asked the crowd, 'to the Emperor of China?' He answered his own question: 'I shall thank him, for he never allowed the rebel flag to be raised in any of his ports.'"[64] This was a clear dig at the British and French, who had allowed Confederate ships to access their ports and even helped build Confederate cruisers. Opposing Chinese rebels proved to be both moral and strategically advantageous. The boundaries of language appear more clearly in the rare cases where Americans came to support or at least accept Taiping victory. In late 1857 a report filed by an American missionary, W. P. Martin, was widely reprinted in American newspapers. Martin offered a thorough assessment of the situation after several years of war. In a piece calling on the United States to affirm the Taiping as the rightful rulers of China, it was not coincidental that he declared, "They aim to effect a *revolution* in the highest sense of the word. It was the idea of a new order of things that fired the mind of its prime mover."[65]

English-Speaking Rebels

In the cases of both Mexico's Caste War of the Yucatán and China's Taiping Rebellion, most U.S. observers used the language of rebellion and sedition, which implicitly rejected the legitimacy of insurgent's causes, rather than that of civil war. Northerners deployed the same method in the American conflict. When President Lincoln called up the state militias in April 1861, he referred vaguely to "combinations too powerful to be suppressed by the ordinary course of judicial proceedings."[66] In the coming days, Lincoln used "insurrection" to describe what was happening and by July, with Congress in session, began using "rebellion," his term of choice for the remainder of the conflict. As historian Gaines Foster shows, in both official correspondence and public discussions, Northerners identified the conflict as a rebellion. "Civil War," which recognized some degree of legitimacy on each side, emerged as a compromise term in the postwar period, a way to enable reconciliation by obscuring the origins and even the meaning of the conflict as Northerners at the time understood it.[67] For steadfast Northerners, the stigma of rebellion never subsided—the U.S. government titled its official history of the conflict *The Official Records of the War of the Rebellion*. Given the host of negative associations that the word "rebellion" carried in the 1860s, any use of it by Northerners degraded the cause to which it was applied.

The British observed the same foreign conflicts that Americans did—they were intimately involved in the Taiping Rebellion—and they experienced the same challenges when they sought to conceptualize or explain the American conflict. Their language was no less fraught; every word conjured a host of associations. For Britons considering the U.S. conflict, the decision to describe it as a civil war, a rebellion, a revolution, or something different altogether carried great weight. During the Indian Rebellion and in the years afterward, British papers referred to Sepoys, especially their leaders, as "rebels." They characterized the Taiping the same way. And this language reappeared at the start of the American conflict. "The spirit of disaffection, amounting to actual rebellion, which prevails in South Carolina and the other slaveholding states," is how the *London Morning Post* characterized conditions in January 1861.[68] The editors feared that Buchanan's ineptitude would leave Lincoln in a worse condition still. "The flames of civil war will then have been lighted, and South Carolina, at least, will have to be reconquered by the sword."[69] As their response to the Indian Rebellion indicated, the British believed rebels merited firm treatment to restore order. The *Dundee Courier* was unequivocal: "It has been England's universal rule to acknowledge a *de facto* revolutionary Government whenever it has established its practical independence by incontrovertible proof—then and not sooner." That had not yet occurred in the American case and, as a result, "there can be no question whatever of the constitutional right of President Lincoln to treat the hostile Confederation as a treasonable rebellion, which, so far as it trenches on Federal property and laws, he may resist by force."[70]

The question of what to call the war in Britain drew readers back into debates about the meaning and legacy of the English conflicts of the seventeenth century. This was a contested period with a politicized language. As Robert Zaller explains, "for two hundred years after the event, it was the Civil War to those who remembered it fondly or indifferently, and the Great Rebellion to those who remembered it ill."[71] Historian Christopher Hill, among others, has studied the changing meaning of the word "revolution" and finds that by the 1640s, "already the sense of change, of a significant transformation in personal or political circumstances, is present in the word: revolutions do not always have to be circular."[72] Hill observed the increasing use of the word by people of differing ideological positions in relation to political change through the middle decades of the seventeenth century. Although some conservatives used the word in a way that carried forward its original astronomical meanings to suggest a restoration or return to a first position, it seems to have already absorbed the color of radicalism, as when Oliver Cromwell himself told parliament, "'Let men take heed,' he warned, 'how they call his revolutions, the things of God and his working of things from one period to another.'"[73] In Cromwell's (convenient) view, revolutions came from God and could neither be stopped nor legitimately opposed. Hill concludes that "the idea of revolution as a significant political transformation thus appears to have emerged during the Interregnum."[74] Hill's phrasing here avoids the question of moral judgment. Surely the first generation of people to use the word, coming as it did in the midst of violent upheavals in English society, must have held sharply differing views of the normative value of "revolution" as well as "civil war."

In fact, the Georgian interpretation of the English Civil War, then dominant, emphasized the treachery of the Parliamentary forces in the conflict. Historian Timothy Lang notes, "No one, in the late eighteenth and early nineteenth centuries, was prepared to utter a good word in defense of Cromwell and the Puritans."[75] That said, Cromwell's rebellion did not represent simple banditry. He and his followers sought to institute a new political order, but one outside the sphere of legitimate change. By the middle of the nineteenth century, the connotations of civil war in England were changing. British Reformers and Whigs led the way in this act of reinterpretation. Instead of writing about the 1640s and 1650s as treason, they adopted the language of "civil war," granting some degree of legitimacy to each side and came to recognize Cromwell for the role he played in helping establish constitutional liberty. Some historians even lionized Cromwell, believing that "the Civil War had been, in fact, necessary and justifiable."[76] The apotheosis of this process were Thomas Babington Macaulay's *History of England* and Thomas Carlyle's editing of Cromwell's *Letters and Speeches*, which presented the Civil War as "a desperate struggle between Light and Darkness, God and the Devil."[77]

British historians emphasize the internal forces driving this shift, but some of the impetus for this change in perspectives on their civil war seem to have come from outside Britain. In British discourse the labels of revolution and civil war came unglued from their historical referents in England and functioned instead as general shorthand in which civil wars were acceptable and normal historical processes, and rebellions were abnormal and destructive. They lost their tie to the ideological dimensions of the English experience partly because of the American one. This is one of the ways to account for the language of the *Telegraph*, a leading U.K. paper that trumpeted Confederate victories and maligned Union statesmen and military officers at every chance, and that opened its coverage by asking "can any good come out of this lamentable civil war in America?"[78] This was a paper that, although expressly opposed to slavery, could not regard the Confederacy as "a mere petty 'insurgent.'"[79] Their New York correspondent was happy to quote the Peace Democrat Fernando Wood condemning a civil war founded on "social or moral ideas"—that is, emancipation. Such a conflict was destined to end in failure. According to Wood, "History will repeat itself in this instance as it has in a thousand others—our nature has not changed; men are now as in the days of Robespierre and Cromwell—bloody, treacherous, fanatical, selfish, and unpatriotic."[80] The *Telegraph* was a conservative paper, but they found a way to make peace with civil war, and they seem to have done so partly because of how they interpreted the American one.

Northerners wanted the British to regard the conflict as a minor domestic affair in order to deter interference. Secretary of State Seward explained to the British ambassador, Lord Lyons, "The so-called Confederate States have waged an insurrectionary war against this Government."[81] But Lyons evaluated the conflict differently, explaining to Lord Russell, the British foreign secretary, that "a fierce civil war would seem to be almost inevitable."[82] "After the recital of these immense efforts," Russell observed of the North's war mobilization, "it seems quite inappropriate to speak of 'unlawful combinations.'" He was quoting Lincoln's efforts to rhetorically contain the scope of the rebellion. "Indeed, it cannot be denied that the state of things which exists, is a state of civil war; and there is, as regards neutral nations, no difference between civil war and foreign war."[83] Russell had read Vattel, who recognized that "when a party is formed in a state, who no longer obey the sovereign, and are possessed of sufficient strength to oppose him—or when, in a republic, the nation is divided into two opposite factions, and both sides take up arms—this is called *civil war*."[84] As David Armitage explains, Vattel's innovation was to see that "it followed that if the two independent bodies were now, in effect, two nations, the law of nations should regulate their contentions; a 'civil' war thereby became an international war." This then changed the nature of how foreign governments could respond to the conflict. "Under normal circumstances," writes Armitage, "the integrity of a sovereign state was sacrosanct . . . but in the case of a state split into two 'nations,' other powers could try to restore peace."[85] The question of whether and how they could intervene depended on how they assessed the justness of causes at stake in the war. In the American conflict, competing pressures paralyzed British action, but this was not the case with the Polish or Chinese conflicts, where they derived the authority to intervene from Vattel and the motive from their treasury.

Late in the U.S. Civil War, the *Telegraph*'s editors reflected, "Many years must pass away after a civil war before the partisans of either side can be calm and impartial in their estimate of the enemy. Not until the passions excited by the bitter struggle have worn themselves out, can men recognise and acknowledge that the foe whom they were wont to meet in actual clash of battle was a good and honest citizen fighting for a cause which his conscience approved as just." The paper calculated that at least a century was required for tempers to cool. "We English, whose liberties were gained at sword's point, have surely reached a 'more removed ground' from which we can judge disinterestedly. We think of our own great civil war, and while rejoicing that on Marston Moor and Naseby Field the Puritan Ironsides swept the glittering squadrons of the Cavaliers before them . . . we can still sympathise with the gallants who took horse for the King."[86] The maturity of the *Telegraph*'s perspective on war actually undercut their strategic position, which remained pro-Confederate throughout the war. The English Civil War was not the U.S. Civil War, but a willingness among British thinkers (conservatives included) to accept the necessity of internal conflict as a part of a nation's political development predisposed them to regard the American experience as normal or natural and not one in which they could claim a role. The opposite attitude prevailed among the French. According to a recent assessment by a French historian, Édouard Drouyn de Lhuys, the powerful French head of foreign affairs, "rejected all revolutionary movements. In this case, the principle that guided him was stability and he was therefore instinctively opposed to the South's rebellion; all the more so if the rebellion was likened to the nationalist revolts that were sweeping across Europe, with which he felt no affinity."[87]

The Uses of the Rebellion

Northern newspapers hoped to encourage the French perspective by drawing explicit comparisons among insurgents in order to delegitimize the Confederacy. The Taiping provided one such analogy. The *San Francisco Bulletin* quoted a British paper to establish the comparison and then suggested the necessary conclusion regarding British policy. "There is just now, says the [London] *Times*, a dragon in the path—the Taeping 'land pirate'—who stands between England and her golden apples, and this dragon must be killed by someone." Then the obvious conclusion for a pro-Union paper: "How like in malicious animus, as well as in their pecuniary consequences to England, are the incendiary acts of the great Chinese dragon to the fierce rebel of our Southern States! But John Bull hesitates to touch the one, while he talks of squelching the other with as much as coolness as if the Emperor of China had already sent him a special invitation to do so."[88] The paper continued to malign the British, "the spoiler of nations," for failing to do what was right and proper in the U.S. case when they were so eager to act in China.

The language of global and historical analogies enabled Northerners to explain their conduct to themselves and to foreign parties. They used the example of China as a foil to highlight their benevolence, as they did when comparing themselves to the British response to the Sepoy Rebellion. A Quaker paper explained, "Rebellion against the authorities [in China], as being the most atrocious of sins, is expiated by the most revolting tortures imaginable." After imperial troops seized a city from the Taiping, all the captured soldiers were beheaded. "The heads were all carefully collected, and placed in small wicker cages, to hang from the walls of the city, as an *in terrorem* to all the rebelliously disposed."[89] The implicit comparison was with the presumably generous treatment Confederate prisoners received in Union prisoner-of-war camps. Northerners also used global examples to affirm the natural alliance between those established polities confronted with rebellions. "At the present time Russia and the United States occupy remarkably similar positions," *Harper's Weekly* editorialized. "A portion of the subjects of the Russian empire, residing in Poland, have attempted to secede and set up an independent national existence, just as our Southern slave-owners have tried to secede from the Union and set up a Slave Confederacy; and the Czar, like the Government of the Union, has undertaken to put down the insurrection by force of arms."[90]

Confederates, who aspired to join the nations of the civilized world, did the same. In their efforts to solicit European support, whether rhetorical or material, Confederate diplomats portrayed the North as fighting in ways that violated the laws of war and Confederates as representing the European tradition of civilized military action. By late 1863 Jefferson Davis could barely conceal his frustration with the lack of European support. To the Confederate Congress he asserted, "If [our] conduct [in Pennsylvania] . . . fails to command the respect and sympathy of civilized nations in our day, it cannot fail to be recognized by their less deceived posterity."[91] It did not inspire respect or sympathy then or in posterity. This diplomatic failure reflected the broader failure of Confederate nationalism abroad, which helped doom the new nation. Even South Carolina representative William Porcher Miles recognized this basic fact when he lamented that "foreign nations had evinced no appreciation of our regard and observance of the laws of humanity."[92]

Despite their frustration, Confederate propagandists never relented in their efforts to paint the North in the worst possible light. The Lincoln administration, in this view, existed alongside other infamous regimes, akin to the brutal and illegitimate despots that other insurgents sought to unseat. A Richmond paper was no doubt thrilled to quote a Northern Democrat who situated Lincoln's aspirations to conquer the South in company with other tyrants: "Has Italy forgotten, or did she ever forget and forgive, her subjugation by Austria? Does not the Hungarian, amid the desolation of his country, still watch on the banks of the Danube for the coming of the day when he may strike down the dominion of the Caesars and restore the violated constitution of his country? Has Poland forgotten the wrongs long past, and is she quiet at the feet of the despots of Europe? Has Ireland embraced the English letter with obsequious love?"[93] What united all these tyrannical efforts was a mistaken belief that people—a genuine national people—could be battled into submission.

If Southerners sought to diminish the standing of the North by identifying it with every malign regime they could identify, they took more care with how they self-identified. If any Confederates considered themselves rebels, it was only in imitation of the rebels of 1776, and only then in their guise of throwing off the yoke of tyranny. None of the regrettable rhetoric of "all men are created equal" carried over to the midcentury effort at American state-building, as Confederate vice president Alexander Stephens made clear in his inaugural address.[94] For the most part, Confederates did not consider themselves rebels, and consequently they refused to associate themselves with similar insurgencies around the world, even when the parallels loomed large. Instead, they sought, as Drew Gilpin Faust noted years ago, to hail "the similarities between the Confederacy and other recently established states in order to claim the South's right to international support and recognition."[95] The nations they had in mind were the Dutch Republic, Italy, and Greece. An American observer in China in the 1850s described the grounds upon which the Taiping could resist the Manchus in language that Jefferson Davis would later echo. "I am no advocate of revolutionary principles or outbreaks against constituted authority," he admitted, "but we must always distinguish between the laws of a country and the unrighteous decrees of a tyrant usurper."[96] Despite the shared foundations, Confederates never aligned themselves with the Taiping, Poles, or any other rebel group.

This self-imposed isolation reveals the weird vacuum into which Confederates' conservative revolution exiled them. If the cultural sympathy between British aristocrats and Southern plantation owners was nearly strong enough to compel British recognition of the Confederacy, Russia should have been an even easier sell. Its elite were similarly well educated as well as grounded their power in the exploitation of bondsmen. But Confederates preferred to go it alone. In early January 1863, as reports of the burgeoning Polish rebellion spread, Richmond's leading paper scoffed that "'an extensive anarchical conspiracy' has broken out in Greece, and a 'Chinese Rebellion' is reported in the London News." The authors could not withhold the apparently unironic comment: "The world generally seems to have gone deranged. Satan has certainly been let loose."[97]

Northern readers must have surely whispered "amen" if they read the extract.

From a rhetorical perspective, the Polish effort at national liberation from Russia proved occasionally useful for Confederates. Like Confederates, Poles refused the label of "rebel." As one scholar has noted, "Russians, and particularly those in official positions, nearly always spoke of mutiny (*miatezh*) of 1863; Poles and more liberal Russians referred rather to the insurrection (*powstanie*)." The dynamic with the language of the U.S. conflict bore more than a little similarity. This same historian writes, "Speaking of mutiny, the Russians stressed the traitorous, disloyal action of the Poles. Choosing to speak of insurrection, Poles described instead the just rebellion of oppressed subjects against a despotic power."[98] Given Russia's support of the Union, Confederates promoted the Polish cause if only to heighten the comparison between what they regarded as two dictatorships. Southerners believed the Europeans should do the right thing and liberate Poland from "Russian barbarians" but doubted this would happen. "We have no hope of any such interposition in her behalf. The same selfish and pusillanimous policy which held the free Governments along before still prevails in their councils."[99] In tracking the Polish uprising, Confederate chroniclers took every opportunity to connect Lincoln and the tsar. Compared to the sectional tyrant, Abraham I, "the Emperor of Russia," one paper noted coyly, "is a bona fide glint in war, an open and above-board despot, who never pretended to know the meaning of popular or national rights and who has not crept through obscure and tortuous bye-ways to a tyrant's place and power."[100]

Whether Confederates believed there was any real sympathy between themselves and the Polish movement, by mid-1863 they described the rebellion there as legitimate. "The insurrection in Poland has now become a national rising," one newspaper noted. "The isolated resistance of a few bands of desperate conscripts has developed into a revolution which takes all the strength of Russia to make head against it."[101] The Confederates hoped to shame the Union by exposing the contradiction between their position on self-determination in the 1850s and their wartime posture toward Poland. The Russian minister to the United States, Edouard de Stoeckl, identified the same tension. "'It [the Lincoln government] now flagrantly contradicts its own declarations made during the Hungarian revolution and its actions in the hasty recognition of the Italian kingdom,'" de Stoeckl wrote. "'It finds itself now constrained to recognize in

America what it wanted to deny in Europe: that a government cannot exist without authority and that in order to maintain this authority . . . a display of power is at times indispensable.'"[102] The Richmond papers kept a careful eye on the movement in Britain and France to demand mediation to end the Polish rebellion, no doubt hoping such a step would generate momentum for a similar action in North America. By year's end, laudatory chronicles of Polish heroism and suffering gave way to discouraging reports on the failure of Britain, in particular, to lead on this issue.

Confederates also used historical analogies to shame the United States. They replicated the example offered by British conservatives, comparing the North to Cromwell. In this vision, the North was synonymous with the Puritans, whose "great expositor of their creed, and its most genuine representative, Oliver Cromwell, set the first example in Ireland, whither he conducted an expedition in 1648, and it was cruel and bloody enough to satisfy even Yankee thirst of blood." What followed, in the *Richmond Daily Dispatch*'s column, was a reminder of the horrors of Drogheda, site of an infamous massacre ordered by Cromwell. In a perfect trifecta of villains, the paper put Lincoln, Cromwell, and Tsar Alexander II together:

> But there is a more modern example for the Yankees. . . . We mean the example of Russia. Alexander II is at this moment sending thousands of unhappy Poles to Siberia every week. He is following closely in the footsteps of his father, and will, if he can, depopulate Poland to fill it up with beastly Russians. That is precisely what the Yankee Government designs to do in the South. It means to deport all the white population, and supply its place with negroes, or, what is infinitely worse, with Yankees.[103]

Confederates obstructed their own path to independence. By rejecting the reformist elements (as modest as those were) of other midcentury rebellions, they isolated themselves from the momentum of the era.[104] In contrast, consider how, in many accounts of nation-state development, the energy of liberal reform crosses boundaries and mobilizes disparate actors toward a shared goal. For example, Richard Stites's recent book chronicling the failed European nationalist movements of the 1820s identifies liberalism as the common thread uniting the "four horsemen" at the center of his study. This was a classical liberalism, which opposed "whimsical executive power; irrational, confused, and unfair laws; entrenched privilege of church and nobility; and the drain on the economy

EXTREMES MEET.

Figure 4. This cartoon in the British satirical journal *Punch* conveyed the pro-Confederate argument that Abraham Lincoln and Tsar Alexander II were mutually compatible tyrants. *Punch, Or the London Charivari,* October 24, 1863, "Extremes Meet." Image courtesy of the Internet Archive.

of unproductive populations such as monks and nuns." In response, liberals "touted political freedom as transparency, reason, balance, compromise, and rule of law—abstractions that translated into civil rights, representation, and independent judiciary offering equal justice for all, and a free press."[105] Stites's subjects—the four horsemen of his title—carried liberal constitutions to Spain, Naples, Greece, and Russia in the early 1820s as the means of changing the conservative regimes that ruled their countries. Stites created this braided narrative because "ideas do not spring from nowhere, and it would be imprudent to ignore the powerful liberal or quasi-liberal intellectual currents of the time, for they illustrate not only the structure of information exchange but also the similarities in the sources of revolutionary and political action across countries and individuals."[106] Later, and more hesitantly, he writes about "the principal insurrectionary impulse—if one may use such a sweeping term—[which] combined an ideological outlook, liberalism, and personalized spirit."[107]

Less hesitantly, Stites writes: "Into this broad stream flowed the rivulet of liberal internationalism in the 1820s. Revolts galvanized constitutionalists across Europe. Ideas, like waves emanating from diverse sources in the depths, broke raggedly on faraway shores."[108] It is an appealing vision, but the arc of the moral universe does not bend toward justice on its own—it must be bent. Relying on environmental or biological metaphors often conceals the historical processes that historians are responsible for identifying. The midcentury rebellions possessed disparate ideological origins and expressions from the earlier ones but shared some structural similarities. They did not derive energy from a shared seismic shock like the one that ripples through narratives of liberal success in the nineteenth century. The historical actors in India, Poland, China, and the American South manifested a common desire to rule themselves and articulated that desire with the nearest tool they had on hand—the emerging language of national self-determination. They defined "themselves" in disparate ways—the white Southerners who built the Confederacy drew enslaved black Southerners within their circle, Polish elites did the same for the serfs (soon to be peasants), and the Indians and Taiping wanted to exclude the British and Manchu, respectively. To paraphrase Leo Tolstoy, happy national families are all alike; every failed national family is unhappy in its own way.[109] As Tolstoy showed, the unhappy families can teach us more than the happy ones. The same holds true for nations.

Debates over Intervention

The debates over insurgents' claims to autonomy and the rebuttals offered by established powers might have occupied only the realm of philosophy, but—as Vattel himself observed—"war cannot be just on both sides."[110] It may be hard, he admitted, for outsiders to evaluate the justice of rival claims in a domestic conflict, but that difficulty does not excuse inaction. Because war constitutes the most terrible action that people can take, it remains incumbent on others to assess the causes of conflicts and act in accordance with those beliefs. What were the results of the contest over ideas and language that combatants waged alongside the physical battles? How did the perspectives shaped in the global conversation about sovereignty, autonomy, and statehood determine what actually happened in wars? Historians have been careful to not claim too much when assessing the role of outside powers on domestic conflicts. About the U.S. Civil War, one historian has written that "the neutrality of the great maritime powers of Europe made possible the victory of the Union in the great crisis of the Republic."[111] That is, foreign intervention (or, in the U.S. case, the lack of it) enabled but did not directly cause the war's outcome. The same can be said for many nineteenth-century insurgencies. When assistance was offered, it could mean moral support and diplomatic aid, as happened during the Greek War of Independence from Ottoman rule, one of the few occasions in which outside powers supported an insurgency. Or it could take a direct military form, as happened in the case of the Qing dynasty's resistance to the Taiping rebels, when the more typical reflection of the European preference for the status quo manifested as support for the empire.

In the early nineteenth century, modern-day Greece was a province of the Ottoman Empire. Greek ex-patriots, living in central and southern European cities like Venice, Naples, and Budapest, nurtured a Greek nationalism that harkened back to the glories of antiquity. Although people living in Anatolia, the southern Balkans, or on the peninsula between the Adriatic and the Aegean Seas did not necessarily identify themselves with this cultural project, they responded to the call for liberation from Ottoman rule made by movement leaders. The campaigns for Greek independence in the late 1810s culminated in the War of Independence in 1821. By 1830 Greece had established itself as an independent nation. During the conflict, philhellenes from around western Europe traveled to the region and participated in the military campaigns. These included famous names like Lord Byron, who died on the peninsula in 1824.

Although as fighters these men played a minor role, reports of their participation inspired support in the West. London created a "Greek Committee" that loaned money to the fledgling cause. Greek Committees soliciting both private and public donations followed in France, Hungary, Sweden, Denmark, Spain, and Portugal.[112] The range of countries and ethnicities represented by philhellene fighters was remarkably broad, and their letters home encouraged public support for a Christian enterprise that promised to weaken the world's largest Islamic empire. Even more important than moral support, Britain and Russia (and later France) intervened directly in the conflict, demanding first mediation and later an armistice. As a recent study observes, "the Greeks won . . . by way of foreign intervention." This act "presented a scenario as yet unseen: one or more of the Great Powers taking the part of rebels instead of crushing them."[113] It was a sight rarely seen again; when the Great Powers weighed in, they almost always did so on behalf of established power.

In China, British intervention, this time concealed beneath a rhetoric of impartiality, enabled the ruling Qing dynasty to suppress the Taiping Rebellion. This was an unlikely action because in the middle of the conflict the British forced their way into China on a flimsy pretext and wrought concessionary treaties from the emperor after destroying the forts protecting access to the interior and steaming up nearly to the gates of Beijing. This event humiliated the emperor and distracted his regime from the domestic rebellion they faced.[114] The British returned in 1859 to deliver the ratified trade agreement to the emperor and were repulsed by Chinese forces at the forts guarding the entrance to the grand canal leading to the imperial capital. As historian Stephen Platt notes, "something important had shifted in the course of that day, and the high-spirited swagger of Britain's previous wars in China—the sense among her military that Asia was little more than a playground for their invincible ships—was broken. Replacing it were the bloody taste of humiliation, and a hunger for revenge against the 'inferior race' that had beaten them."[115]

The threat of further interference from Britain was quite real. During the Opium War the Manchus had suffered a humiliating defeat at the hands of a numerically smaller British force. It disrupted trade patterns and imperial control, especially in the south, where the British traders lived. Nonetheless, and despite the embarrassing defeat at the hands of Qing forces, Britain never granted the Taiping the "belligerent rights" that the British granted the Confederacy at the start of the U.S. Civil War. Instead, they maintained support for the Qing in the conflict. The Taiping worked quite hard to leverage their Christian aspirations (which were sincerely held) into respect and support from the British.[116] In some cases this yielded gains. Thomas Taylor Meadows, a British intelligence officer who read and spoke Chinese, compiled detailed updates for the government. In 1851, the year that the Taiping formally declared independence from the ruling Qing dynasty, he wrote, "I deem it advisable to make these remarks because the periodicals of Canton and Hong Kong . . . concur in representing the present disturbances as one might regard the proceedings of a few bands of burglars and robbers in the Scottish highlands."

Meadows saw things differently. "That the Imperial Government considers the affair nothing less than what we would call rebellion, and a very serious rebellion, is made sufficiently plain by the measures it is taking."[117] At the same time, the *Chinese Repository*, a journal published in Canton by an American missionary, referred to the Taiping variously as "insurgents," "riff-raff," "discontented persons," and "outlaws."[118]

Meadows offered one of the most insightful explanations of the predicament faced by the Taiping in their effort to acquire European support. "The misconception that exists among foreigners in China on this subject . . . as to whether the various bodies now in arms against the government are rebels or mere robbers and pirates, forms another example of the thralldom in which language holds us," Meadows explained, "and of the confusion and mischief that may arise of mistaking the meaning of a single word." Foreigners drew the wrong implications from the language of the event. "The word in this case is *tsih*, that applied by the Chinese to the bodies of men just alluded to. Now in the least imperfect of Chinese dictionaries, that of Morrison, this word is explained to mean, *robber* or *bandit*. These English words are, however, but a portion of the meaning of the Chinese one; which is very comprehensive, signifying *all persons who set the authorities at defiance by acquisitive acts of violence*." As Meadows would learn, many different people soon found themselves in this position. "As the object which it is sought to acquire may be a bag of money or may be the empire; it follows that this one word, tsih, is in fact equivalent to the three words, robber, bandit *and rebel*."[119]

By 1852 English-language reporting on the Taiping Rebellion shifted to using "rebels" and "insurgents" in their reporting on China, but these did little to change the moral stature of the combatants.[120] By 1853 the French minister to China, Alphonse de Bourboulon, would write that "whatever doubts may exist about [the revolution's] ultimate success, whatever obstacles the indifference of the masses and the resources of the [Qing] dynasty may yet oppose to the rebellion's triumph, it is clear to me that this revolt is one of formidable character and proportions."[121] Americans adopted the same language, at least in their private writings. The American commissioner to China in the early 1850s, Humphrey Marshall, focused on protecting Americans and their property in the country. He fielded letters from an array of officials, most of whom used the language of rebellion and rebels.[122] Marshall himself bemoaned that, rather than "the restoration of tranquility," he could only see that "the cloud of civil war lowers more darkly than ever over the horizon of China."[123]

This on-the-ground intelligence never shifted the British government's policy and they were the leading Western power in China. One honest assessment from a British observer in the country encouraged modesty because of how little the British understood about the Chinese. "It is a dangerous thing to meddle with the government of a nation counting four hundred million of souls," he wrote, "particularly dangerous, when we have so few men at all acquainted with the language!"[124] Despite the interest of Western missionaries in fostering an indigenous Christian community in China, British policy was determined by what presented the most advantages in terms of future trade.[125] Regardless of their difficulties with the Qing, the British considered them a more reliable partner in future trade agreements than the Taiping. British racial attitudes also played an important role. As historian Beth Lew-Williams observes, "to be deemed civilized, a country had to have a modern bureaucratic state capable of self-defense, basic human rights, Western norms of diplomacy and international law, and legal power over all people within its territory."[126] As Lew-Williams shows, over the nineteenth century, Westerners adopted a perspective framed around the differences between civilized and savage people. British and American observers situated China in the latter category, and this empowered the West to intervene in China itself.

Perhaps most important were the trade agreements reached at the end of the Second Opium War. William T. Rowe summarizes the situation well: "On the diplomatic front, by virtue of the 1858 Treaty of Nanjin and the subsequent Beijing Convention, the West had fulfilled its mission of bringing China into the comity of nations. Ambassadors of foreign nations . . . quickly took up their posts in Beijing."[127] Although the treaties humiliated the dynasty, the action must have facilitated their effort to keep foreigners from helping the Taiping because they already had established relations with China. The importance of treaties and diplomacy to foreign respect for sovereignty was integral to the American Revolution and Western European perspectives in general. As historian Eliga Gould has shown, "in proclaiming their nascent statehood, Americans accepted that their new governments would need to conform to the norms of Europe's colonial powers, especially the norms enshrined in the public law of European treaties and diplomatic customs."[128] Indeed, by 1861 the

Taiping had lost the support of many of the foreign missionaries who had previously served as their strongest supporters.[129] British, French, Russians, and the Americans all sent delegations that treated with the Qing. They professed neutrality but worked to extract trade concessions from the empire in exchange for military support.[130] After 1860 British and French soldiers cooperated with Qing troops in defending imperial cities (principally Shanghai) and in attacks on rebel positions. It was not just Westerners who intervened. The Qing dynasty also accepted a Russian offer to help transport grain from the South to the North in exchange for land concessions.[131] The scholarly consensus on Taiping reflects the received wisdom about the role of European intervention in Greece's independence struggle: "international intervention dealt the Taipings a severe blow."[132]

Nonintervention allowed European powers to play just as decisive a role in conflicts with less risk. Major powers could deny support to insurgencies, and those efforts would fail. Sometimes the difference in a war is the dog that does not bark, the event that does not happen. In India, no country came to the aid of the Sepoy because no one wanted British ire turned on them and because Europeans with colonial holdings (or those who hoped to obtain them) appreciated the precedent established by British suppression of the rebellion. In Poland, during 1863, despite an initial wave of rhetorical support for Polish insurrectionaries, England and France shifted their professed neutrality slowly and put only light pressure on the Russians. Far fewer freedom-fighters trekked east than in Lord Byron's day.

The British, in particular, considered the Russians rivals for power and supported threats to the regime in the hopes of weakening it. In the early 1830s they supported the first Polish uprising against Russia, albeit from the security of western Europe. That movement began among Polish officers at the Russian Military Academy in Warsaw, who drove out the Russian-appointed grand duke and established a provisional government. Russia broke the resistance and dispersed some twenty thousand of the Polish fighters to western Europe, where "associations of Friends of Poland were set up in London, Nottingham, Birmingham, Hull, Leeds, Glasgow, and Edinburgh to organize support for the Polish cause."[133] Thirty years later this history established a precedent for British support of the Poles but not enough to overcome the risks of a new war with Russia.

The London *Telegraph* reassured its readers in 1863 that the Poles did not expect British troops to fly to their aid or even to help with arms sales. Instead they wanted moral support. "What the Poles have been asking and are still asking, and what they seek to obtain to-day . . . is merely sympathy—not sympathy solely *sentimental* and *commiserating, but sympathy* of a grave, a solemn, and a warning character—sympathy that shall be a solemn verdict of condemnation of the atrocities committed by Russia in the Polish provinces." The paper hoped that 1863 would not repeat what occurred in 1831, during a previous Polish uprising against Russia. Then, English "indignation against [Poland's] oppressors took a sentimental and not a violent turn, but one nevertheless quite as destitute of utility. We set the wrongs of the enslaved people to music, sang them in ballads, and ground them upon street organs. We painted Polish women chained to posts, while ferocious Cossacks scourged them with whips. . . . And then, little by little, the interest in Poland began to decrease. . . . The Polish question was voted a bore."[134] Interest remained higher in 1863, but it did not translate into useful assistance. Adam Gurowski, the skeptical Polish expatriate, suffered no illusions about British assistance. "More than forty years of experience satisfied me about England's political honesty. In 1831, Englishmen made speeches, the Russian fought and finally overpowered us."[135]

Even British liberals who believed in the rights of ethnic minorities to establish political autonomy evinced little enthusiasm. "You will have observed the great prominence given of late to the Polish question," the British reformer Richard Cobden wrote to his friend Charles Sumner in the United States. "I do not believe it possible to involve England in a war with Russia for Poland. Nobody here believes in the capacity of the Poles for self-government. They are good fighters, and not very scrupulous as to what flag they fight under, but they are bad citizens."[136] France, partly from religious sympathy, expressed more support but were too far away to pick a fight with Russia while the Prussians stayed neutral. These ambivalent Europeans may have taken succor from the vigor of the U.S. response. In 1864 an essayist recalled the history of failed Polish rebellions "to warn statesmen and nations against involving the world in a general war in a hopeless attempt to reconstruct a civilized and responsible State out of these impracticable materials." Any intervention was bound to fail. "Poland, as a country, had neither a natural unity, a definite locality, nor a settled boundary," the author wrote. "As a nation, it had neither internal cohesion, no object of existence. Its people were serfs, too ignorant to judge and too depressed to have a will in regard to public affairs. Its chiefs were as destitute of true patriotism as they were reckless of moral obligation."[137] The Polish rebellion suffered the same fate as other insurgencies in the nineteenth century—it failed in 1863, and not until another half century had passed would Poles claim their own state.

The most famous case of nonintervention was the U.S. Civil War. Despite strong efforts by Confederates, both France and England remained loyal to the United States. In 1861 Queen Victoria recognized Confederates as belligerents under the laws of war, and this enabled the British to sell them arms but, crucially, did not grant them the status of the independent nation they claimed to be. Nonetheless, the Union expended considerable energy in its European diplomacy to keep Europe neutral.[138] This is the one part of the Civil War's global history that has drawn the attention of scholars. Collectively, they have offered a variety of explanations for what motivated Britain, in particular, to withhold its support for the Confederacy. Howard Jones has shown how Britain calculated its economic self-interest, its national security, and its self-imposed obligation to promote humanitarianism. For many members of the government, these impulses all encouraged the country to mediate a peaceful solution, but the determination of the North and the likelihood of an American attack on any nation that intervened deterred action.[139] Richard Blackett has identified the deep well of support for emancipation and free labor among Britain's working class, an identification that drew them to the Union side.[140] Don Doyle has demonstrated that European liberals supported the North because they saw in its success or failure the future of democracy itself.[141] These authors have offered effective answers to the question of why Britain and France (effectively) sided with the Union rather than the Confederacy. My purpose is not to replace them but to add to the story they tell.

In many respects Confederates built a functioning state, which should have earned European respect. As a generation of historians have shown, most white Southerners supported the new nation for a variety of reasons although never with blind loyalty. Just like the United States, the Confederacy experienced intense class and gender conflict during the war. The collapse of slavery fostered an increasingly violent racial animosity among white Southerners toward black Southerners. Despite all of this, the Confederacy nearly resisted the military pressure of the Union long enough to make itself independent. A critical part of their failure came from the lack of foreign sanction or support, itself largely contingent on the Confederacy's steadfast support of slavery.

The Confederacy failed, partly for the lack of arms and supplies that open support might have promised and partly for the added luster that European recognition would have granted. Confederates recognized this, and although they maintained a veneer of bravado about going it alone, they coveted European recognition. Henry Hotze, an Alabamian, ran a newspaper in England to promote the Confederate cause. Despite a vigorous defense of the naturalness of the Confederacy and the ease with which secession was approved within the South, he also recognized the importance of support: "It is true that few nations have ever succeeded in creating an independent existence when altogether left to their own resources. Infancy, both of a nation and an individual, needs the fostering care of others to ripen into vigorous life."[142] Hotze offered a plethora of contemporary examples, the most important of which were Dutch independence from Spain (aided by "the moral support of all Protestant Europe") and the American Revolution. It was a frank acknowledgment that nation-building required international support not just internal consensus (which the Confederacy also did not possess).

Northerners, meanwhile, worked just as hard to discourage European intervention. Doing so entailed the same process of corralling global analogies. "Here then is the first demand for the dissolution of the Union, the dismemberment of the Government, and the ruin of the nation," lectured Daniel C. Eddy, in a Fast Day service responding to reports of anticipated European mediation in the Civil War. "It comes from selfish hypocritical England, that has its foot on the neck of Ireland, its grasp on the throat of Turkey, and that has India bound to the mouth of its cannon! It comes from France,—-ambitious, mysterious, paradoxical France, that wants to vie with England in dependent colonies, and that is looking through Mexico to 247,453 square miles of glorious territory in Texas. It comes from the ambitious statesmen, the corrupt Governments, the rotten courts, the besotted tyrants, the crumbling thrones of Europe."[143]

The Russians helped in this effort as well. In 1863, with Americans still worried about European intervention, the Russian navy sent a fleet of ships to San Francisco and another one to the Atlantic Coast, including a visit to the Federal Navy Yard in Washington, D.C., that drew visits from members of Congress. The visits to ports along the seaboards drew admiring coverage from national newspapers and journals. Both sides gained from this public but shallow strategic alliance. Some historians have argued that Russia only pursued this policy to protect her ships from a possible blockade imposed by Britain and France over its Polish policy, but Americans read the action in terms of their self-interest. U.S. Secretary of the Navy Gideon Welles celebrated their arrival. "In sending them to this country at this time there is something significant," he wrote. "What will be its effect on France and the French policy we shall learn in due time. It may moderate—it may exasperate. God bless the Russians."[144] Welles instructed naval officers "to show [the Russians] all proper courtesy" during their visit.[145] Whatever the self-interest in Russia's move, the effect bolstered Northern fortunes during the lull in military progress after Gettysburg. Historian Albert Woldman's assessment retains its strength: Russia's "Polish policy was threatening to embroil her in another European war. She needed America's support for nonintervention in the Polish insurrection, as much as Lincoln's government needed Russian support for nonintervention in the rebellion of the Southern States."[146]

British nonintervention can also be explained, in part, by considering how Northerners worked to stigmatize the act of rebellion more generally. Relying on the long-standing discourse in Europe and the United States that disparaged rebellions as illegal or immoral, Americans hoped that impugning the honor of insurgents would discourage foreign recognition of the Confederacy. It seems to have worked. After all the effort by Northern propagandists to malign rebellion wherever it occurred, they must have thrilled to a column in the *London Daily News*: "All wars are deplorable, especially civil wars" wrote an English observer. "But almost every country has been compelled to engage in them at some period of their history, and they have worked out the solution of their difficulties by sacrifices and bloodshed, as the Americans are now doing, purchasing by these means peace and security for the future." This correspondent noted that "during our Indian mutiny the French Press assured us that our efforts to recover our supremacy were quite vain, and that our Sepoy executions and heroic battles were but so many needless cruelties and bootless sacrifices. I do not think we listened with much patience to these opinions, or that we should have been willing to accept the mediation of any one in our quarrel."[147] Lincoln himself could not have phrased it better. Although he would not admit to "Sepoy executions," Lincoln sought, above all else, the recovery of national supremacy and repudiated the idea of mediation.

One smoking gun does not decide a war, and this one was held by a citizen rather than a cabinet minister, but U.S. efforts to stigmatize rebellion ensured that Britons and probably other Europeans paused before endorsing the Confederacy. For established states to intervene in domestic conflicts, they did not need to see a reflection of themselves in one of the participants. The twentieth century contains a dismayingly large number of examples when the United States aligned itself with regimes with which it had little in common. Instead, they needed to *not* see a reflection of their former or future enemies. Part of what enabled Northern victory in the Civil War was its success at making the Confederacy look like ordinary insurgents of the sort against which major states routinely aligned themselves.

Diplomats and foreign correspondents are not encouraged to use their imagination when evaluating foreign conflicts. Decisions to support or oppose a given war are supposed to be based on reason alone, for which we need the most reliable and accurate representations of the conflict. But the mid-nineteenth century experience teaches us there can be no impartial explanation outside of those most contested words: rebellion or civil war. Try as they might to distinguish the uniqueness of their experience, the Sepoy, the Taiping, the Poles, and the Confederates all found themselves ensnared in the same web of global analogies and historical examples. Their fates rested not just on their own abilities but on the experience of other rebels around the globe. The Oregon did not just flow in sympathy with the Ganges; it shaped its course, and vice versa.

3

THE CENTER HOLDS

Authority in the Nineteenth Century

FOR AMERICAN HISTORIANS, the Civil War marks a break between "early" and "modern" U.S. history. This convention offers a useful structure for teaching purposes even as it oversimplifies a complex story. For students, perhaps the most notable feature of this change is leaving behind monarchies and empires for the world of republics and nation-states. But the habits of the colonial period gave way slowly in the nineteenth century. This was not just a question of a transition between eras. Empires and republics coexisted and shared more than a little DNA. They both pursued control over territory, sometimes contiguous and sometimes not. The necessity of power, in this long process, compelled monarchs and presidents alike to suppress rebellions and to consolidate their authority.

C. A. Bayly's history of the birth of the modern world synthesizes a generation of work that identifies the nineteenth century as the transformative era. Bayly argues that the nineteenth century "above all, was the period of the 'internationalization of nationalism,' when the ideas and practices of the nation-state became rooted among the elites in all major world cultures."[1] Bayly's history revolves around political change. As a result, the shape and composition of polities matters a great deal in his narrative. There is much to recommend this approach. Many people created new nations in Europe and the Americas, at least three dozen in this first enthusiastic wave of nation-building. They have proven more durable and more destructive than their founders could have imagined. Most historians—not just Europeanists but Americanists too—see the rise of the nation-state, and liberal republics more specifically, as the defining process of the nineteenth century. Jürgen Osterhammel's recent global history of the century challenges this characterization. In Osterhammel's view, the era should be regarded as more imperial than national.[2] "The nineteenth century," he writes, "was much more an age of empire than, as many European historians continue to believe and to teach, an age of nations and nation-states."[3] Similarly, historian Cemil Aydin refers to the long nineteenth century as the "era of imperial self-strengthening."[4] Global historians see this process continuing well into the twentieth century. The editors of a recent history of the modern world argue that "the period between 1870 and 1945 was characterized by sustained and intensive imperial activity that remapped significant portions of the globe."[5]

The history of mid-nineteenth-century rebellions, successes and failures all, suggests that both empires and nations expanded their reach. The century was not characterized more by national or imperial forms but by both and, undergirding them, by a confidence in central power that possessed territorial aspirations. Better still when these powers could claim to also represent liberal reform in the form of free trade, more equitable access to land, or expanded male suffrage. Given the national reorganization and subdivision in the early twenty-first century—in Central Europe, Southeast Asia, and Saharan Africa, to name just a few—we might no longer regard territorial consolidation as natural, but that was not the view in the mid-nineteenth century when the most successful polities were those that asserted authority over diverse peoples and vast distances. What is more, territorial consolidation was promulgated as a natural part of modernity.[6] This idea discouraged support for insurgents who tried to disrupt or break apart countries and encouraged insurgents who sought to bind places together. In other words, the prevailing suppositions among Westerners about how the world should be organized shaped the outcomes of those struggles. We can see today that those suppositions were neither natural nor inevitable, but participants at the time did not. Representatives of established states condemned secessionist insurgents not just for the immediate and specific harm they caused in a given place but because they resisted the trend of the modern world.

Proponents of this view offered a variety of explanations. The cultural legacy of empire building, from the Romans forward, suggested that great regimes expanded; they did not contract.[7] Strategic realities reinforced this view—dividing weakens a people—and represented a dangerous trend in a hostile world. Power, and the recognition of power by outsiders, came from addition, not subtraction. Inertia played no small role either. In the empires and nations subject to revolts, the institutions of daily life—courts, mail, and media networks, and so on—helped keep places together. But whatever the reality of the power of centralized states to resist dissolution, my concern here is with the idea of central authority. Europeans and Americans applauded themselves for accomplishing it by midcentury and could not imagine a process by which they would reverse the hard work of the previous decades.

Established powers leveraged a powerful sense of their own entitlement to authority, whereas rebellions splintered in multiple ways, offering competing and incompatible conceptions of authority. The preference for centralized power emerged in different parts of the world at the same time. In the previous chapter, I refer to the shift in British historical interpretation of the English Civil War and Cromwell in particular, which occurred in the mid-nineteenth century. A historian of this process has noted that "to establish Cromwell as a model statesman was to legitimate the use of force and the power of the state."[8] This historiographical shift was consonant with the ideological shift in the nineteenth century that regarded force as compatible with liberalism and liberalism as compatible with empire. It prepared Britons to suppress the Sepoy, tolerate the Qing, and stand by while the United States and Russia suppressed their own uprisings. Americans made the same shift, celebrating the growth of the nation as a reward for their virtue and accepting the use of violence against Native people, Mexicans, and others as a necessity in the building of North American civilization.

In the previous chapter, I organize the ideas topically and referred to the various case studies as evidence for my assertions. In this chapter, I explore the history of the different places with an eye to how participants and outsiders viewed the questions of power and sovereignty. I move in chronological order, starting with India and Britain, then the Taiping and Qing in China, then Poland and Russia, and finally the Confederacy and the United States in North America. In each of these cases, insurgents lost wars of independence to polities that leveraged their authority within a world increasingly defined by central states. They did so because those states wielded the tools of war—financial instruments, institutions for mobilizing and organizing manpower and natural resources, and established systems of diplomacy—and because of the emerging preference for large-scale political organization.

This outcome stands in contrast to the revolutionary moment in the late eighteenth and early nineteenth centuries, when independence movements succeeded throughout the Western hemisphere. The new nations birthed in the revolutionary era distinguished themselves from the empires (British, Spanish, or Portuguese) from which they emerged, but the difference between these state forms in the nineteenth century was not always so clear. In the eighteenth century, many people used "empire" descriptively rather than pejoratively as a way to characterize people who controlled their own territory, especially large territories. The term began taking on negative connotations after Napoleon founded the First French Empire in 1804. By the 1850s "the word [imperialism] was used in England to describe the dictatorial form of government practised by the emperor Napoleon III of France."[9] But Britons were building their own empire at the same time (and calling it by that name). Americans watching this process oscillated between critical judgment and admiration. As historian Paul Kramer notes, "this republican anxiety about empire was not hegemonic in the nineteenth century; especially prior to the Civil War, public figures used the term affirmatively to denote a large and impressive domain, often infusing it with a strong whiff of sublimity."[10] This sense must have shaped Thomas Jefferson's enigmatic pronouncement that America would be "an empire of liberty." The pithiest modern definition of empire explains it as "political control over effective sovereignty."[11] The key issue, and the one being fought out in the wars discussed here, was who exercised control over whom? Who gained sovereignty, and who was subject to domination? It is also important to remember that empires shaped the lives of people in the metropole not just the peripheries. Being the subject of an empire was different than being the citizen of a republic. Americans learned this lesson from Edward Gibbon's writing on the fall of the Roman Empire. In the 1840s, the great decade of continental expansion, white Americans expressed more concern about the impact of expansion on the republic itself than on the Native people or Mexicans who came under American power through wars of conquest.

The British Empire

Britons, too, showed little concern for the people, usually people of color, subject to their expanding nineteenth-century empire. The most glaring example of this was the Indian Rebellion of 1857, which remained a problem for British historians for generations. Because few Britons questioned the legitimacy of the empire until after its decline following World War II, any challenges to it in the past were on their face illegitimate. Hence the "Sepoy Mutiny," the term used by British historians for well over a century, which connotes illegitimate resistance to lawful authority. By the 1980s British historians had begun deconstructing the empire and changing their perspective on what happened within it. Eric Stokes wrote in 1986 that "1857 has come to be regarded as the formative violence [of India's] national history, the proof that colonialism had been withstood even unto blood."[12] Achieving this position required rethinking the naturalness of British authority, something hardwired into British imperial rule around the world. In fact, British officers knew at the time that what they witnessed in India derived from real grievances and assumed the character of a genuine national movement rather than an unlawful "mutiny." In April 1858, after the rebellion had been suppressed, a secret letter from the East India House in London to the colony's governor general acknowledged that "we must admit that . . . the hostilities which have been carried on in Oude, have rather the character of legitimate war than that of rebellion."[13] This attitude was never publicly affirmed. British officials, who took control of the colony from the East India Company in 1858, buried the frank assessment contained in this cable. Instead, the British articulated a deep belief in the necessity of their rule over India. In 1858 an English minister celebrated that "it was no undue stretch of imagination to suppose that with order, better government, and established peace, India would teem with her products of industry and of climate . . . and also result in the gradual loosening of terrible and debasing delusions" (i.e., Islam and Hinduism).[14]

In the first chapter, I emphasize the ways that the British sought to delegitimize the Sepoy because of how they fought. British newspapers highlighted their irregular actions—especially the killing of noncombatants—as evidence that the movement was immoral and had to be resisted. But this was not the only arrow in their quiver. In addition to the question of conduct, the British rejected the idea that India could claim independence. Even if Indians had sought autonomy with the most restrained military action, the British would have responded with outrage because such an action challenged the integrity of the empire itself. This attitude was also shared by Americans observing the conflict. "To disperse the rebels, to re-establish English authority, to restore order and peace, are comparatively easy tasks," explained one American journal.[15]

The more difficult challenge was creating a political structure that would enable orderly long-term rule. Neither this journal nor the British contested the core question of whether the British had a right to control India. From the American perspective, like the British one, the superiority of Christian institutions answered the question.

Even Americans who supported democracy failed to support the rebellion. Francis Stockwell, a Boston banker, made detailed observations about the conflict in his diary. After debating the question "Is India justified in the attempt to throw off British rule?" at the Boston Young Men's Christian Association one evening (he argued in the negative), Stockwell, celebrated news that the British had recaptured Delhi. "Though by no means decisive on the war," Stockwell noted, "we consider the fate of Delhi the first indispensable achievement towards a reconquest of the country. The crisis of imminent danger to the British supremacy in India has passed."[16] The Panic of 1857 generated most of Stockwell's anxieties, but he considered the rebellion as "the event of 1857," because it concerned not just 200 million Indians but the "sympathies of all civilization." Stockwell believed that, "as Americans, we are, or we should be, the most deeply interested in noting that progress of liberal ideas, the gradual rise, under old despotisms & monarchies, of the democratic power; the measures which indicate the successive steps won by the advancing party." Rejecting the Sepoys as a "savage, treacherous crew," he saw nothing in 1857 to give him cheer. "Not a single one of interest can be found, & if existing practices indicate truly existing public opinion then the liberal cause looks now to be completely prostrate."[17] The Cromwellian vision of a powerful state directing reform had taken root across the ocean as well.

Americans watching the Indian experience drew a clear lesson about the importance of unitary sovereignty and the power to sustain it. Charles Creighton Hazewell, a prominent American newspaper editor, summarized the conflict's meaning in the *Atlantic Monthly*: "There cannot be two masters of the Indian Empire. The Briton must rule it politically and religiously, or he must be overrun by the treacherous and rebellious Indian. Every instance of servile respect for the caste superstition of the Hindoo subject, can only be attributed by him to fear in his Christian conqueror. It emboldens him for rebellion."[18] Hazewell was not anticipating a similar crisis in North America, but if he were, it is impossible to imagine this loyal son of New England not responding in the same way. As the U.S. Civil War would test, there could be only one master in America as well.

The Indian Rebellion offered additional lessons, although all pointed at the same conclusion. The Sepoy did not project the vision of an alternative state. This failure further impeded their claim for independence. The people living in south-central Asia identified themselves with a variety of religious, linguistic, ethnic, and cultural groups (as well as having different sorts of relationships with the British, a feature that weakened the insurgency). This had a physical parallel, as one historian reports: "From the first, then, rebellion failed to create a liberated area in which support for the rebel regime could become safe as well as legitimate."[19] The result was that the rebellion lacked a leader or alliance that could unite people. Every rebellion faces this challenge; successful ones in the nineteenth century compensated by building something new out of distinct pieces, as happened with the creation of modern Italy and modern Germany. Writing about India, William Dalrymple says, "150 years after the event, scholars are still arguing over the old chestnut of whether 1857 was a mutiny, a peasants' revolt, an urban revolution, or a war of independence. The answer is that it was all of these, and many other things too; it was not one unified movement but many, with widely differing causes, motives, and natures."[20] This offers both a fair description and an important argument that helps us understand the conflict's outcome.

Dalrymple's conclusion could be applied to the Confederacy, with slightly different terminology. The U.S. Civil War was a secessionist war against a federal state, an agrarian revolt against an emerging industrial capitalist order, and a slave rebellion. It was a regular war and an irregular one; it had coastal and riverine dimensions (with their distinctly different natures) and discrete regional theaters: eastern, western, and trans-Mississippi. The diversity of experiences within the South account, in part, for its failure. A recent essay alerts us to the ways that participants acted on their own within the larger conflict. "The local wars," Thavolia Glymph writes, "and enslaved women's struggle to find a path to freedom constitute an inextricable part of the larger struggle whereby slaves authored and implemented their own proclamations of emancipation."[21] That is, enslaved people created an insurgency of their own that drew upon but remained separate from the larger Civil War. The many local wars within the South distracted the Confederate leadership and disrupted their efforts to claim they were building something new and unitary.[22] This would be no Italy.

The Qing Empire

Like the Sepoys in India, the Taiping in China challenged a mighty empire. They manifested more cohesion than the Sepoy, unified as they were by a religious vision, but the established order in China—the Qing dynasty led by Manchus from the north—persevered. Qing officials took every opportunity to remind Western powers that they claimed historical precedent and had opened the country to foreign trade (although not as much as Britain and others wanted). In the West, historians have focused on the cultural dimensions of the struggle, highlighting the role of Christianity in infusing the rebels with a vision of a new world.[23] More recently, Stephen Platt has revived the Taiping insistence that the war was a national one. "The central issue of the war, as Hong Rengan [one of the leaders] framed it, was the liberation of the Chinese people."[24] The Taiping asserted a kind of ethnic solidarity at the base of their movement. "In such a light," Platt writes, "the more nationalistic appeals of the rebels—namely, that they were overthrowing alien rulers in order to restore the Chinese to power—need to be taken more seriously than they have been in the past."[25]

Although U.S. minister to China Anson Burlingame remained loyal to the empire in his public statements, his wife, Jane, distinguished between what she called the "Tartars" and "the Chinese." "The Tartar ladies," she informed her sister, "wear long dresses, while the Chinese ladies wear short dresses, and trousers."[26] An observant woman but still very much an outsider, even Jane Burlingame could see differences between the two people. The Taiping promoted this line of thinking. One of their earliest pamphlets articulated a nationalist interpretation: "We conceive that the empire belongs to the Chinese, and not to the Tartars; the food and raiment found therein belong to the Chinese, and not to the Tartars; the men and women inhabiting this region are subjects and children of the Chinese, and not of the Tartars."[27] Not every historian interprets the conflict in the pseudo-nationalist language used in this pamphlet. Many Chinese disliked the Manchu but did not envision themselves or their polity in terms that are recognizably "nationalistic." Nonetheless, Western observers often interpreted it through the lenses they wore, and in the mid-nineteenth century, national glasses were all the rage.

The Taiping, especially those conversant with Western ways of thinking, took advantage of this perspective. As historian Philip Kuhn explains, "the rebellion was proclaimed to be a national uprising against alien oppressors. The appeal was to national pride in the face of usurpatious rule by China's 'traditional enemies'—the northern barbarians—who had fastened upon China a cruel and corrupt government and befouled her culture with alien uses."[28] Westerners living in China picked up on this message. One visitor explained the Taiping's ultimate failure as deriving partly from this admixture of nationalist politics and religious prophecy. "It was the mixture of the two movements—religious reform and political revolt against magisterial oppression—which probably ruined the enterprise," he explained.[29]

Part of the Taiping critique derived from their sense that the Qing leadership was illegitimate because of their failure to represent the interests of the real people of the country. This was a strategically wise argument to adopt, resonating as it did with emerging European models of republican representation (notwithstanding Europe's dim regard for democracy). In the rare cases where established powers supported insurgent movements against traditional authority, they did so only where clear popular support for the movement was visible (like in Greece's war against the Ottoman Empire).

The British struggled to determine if the Taiping could claim such support. An English language journal in China concluded that "although the men with whom the insurrection originated [the Taiping] are neither esteemed nor liked by their northern brethren, yet any change it is believed must be for the better. . . . This deep feeling of dissatisfaction has been adroitly turned to account by the rebel leaders."[30] Did the British and other outsiders believe the claims of legitimacy on the part of the Taiping? Some missionaries and other reform-minded observers did, arguing that "the Taiping were a rebellion of the Chinese people against the Manchu tyranny, and to stand in their way was to side with the tyrants. . . . The rebels' brand of Christianity might be imperfect or even unpalatable, but they nevertheless had the right to national freedom."[31] One Taiping supporter in Parliament was William Henry Sykes, a Scotsman who formerly headed the East India Company: "The Taiping, he concluded [in a speech to Parliament] were nothing less than 'an insurgent national party, holding one third of China, pledged to the expulsion of the [Manchus], the extinction of idolatry, and the introduction of the Christian religion.'"[32]

An American missionary who had taught the leader of the Taiping Rebellion when he was a student in the 1840s concurred. "Instead of rebelling against the government, with a design of upsetting the dynasty, they seem rather struggling for religious liberty, and *are really upsetting idolatry!* I now sympathise with them in their struggle, and look for important results."[33] If the Taiping had not professed Christianity (their leader asserted that he was the brother of Jesus, God's Heavenly Son), it seems unlikely that missionaries would have sanctioned regime change. The prospect of a Christianized China leading the liberal reform of a heathen empire won them over. A U.S. sailor in Shanghai characterized the Taiping in precisely these terms. "The Reble leader assumed the title Taiping-Wong—'celestial virtue' and professed as his principles the establishment of a liberal government modelled after that of the United States the opening of all China to foreign trade the establishment of the Christian religion and the abolition of Idol-worship the use of tobacco, opium, liquor and other natural vices."[34]

The Qing, who tolerated Christian missionaries in certain places but maintained the regime's Buddhist orientation, fought back. Just as the Russians would do to deter American support for the Poles, China's imperial regime compared the Taiping rebels they faced and the Confederates. In a conversation with Jane Burlingame, one of the imperial rulers, Prince Gong, made the comparison explicit. "By the rebellion of the southern parts of the United States against their government," he explained, "your country is placed very much in the same position that China is, whose seditious subjects are now in revolt against her.'" Burlingame regarded the comparison as a great analogy. "They said, 'We see you are *just like us,*' she wrote to her father, 'You have got a rebellion, and we have got one too—so, *we can* appreciate your case.' I wonder what the 'Southern Chivalry' will say to being put on a par with the 'Taepings!'"[35] Taiping means "heavenly peace," but Burlingame regarded the term as shorthand for illegal rebels or savage warriors, as most Americans did. Like other Northerners, Jane Burlingame was happy to endorse analogies that disparaged the Confederates as just another version of unlawful insurgents menacing established governments around the world. Her husband, the ambassador, seems to have taken the analogy to heart because he used it in his efforts to forestall trade between the Qing and Confederates. A young American merchant in Hankow reported that "Mr. Burlingame by comparing our rebels to the Taipings has succeeded in persuading Prince Kung to close the ports of China to" Confederate ships.[36]

The British consul to China agreed. Frederick Bruce opposed the Taiping even though he hated the Manchus. The Taiping, Bruce wrote, were "'merely a body of men in arms against their legitimate Government,' and in such terms, they were but rebels."[37] In 1855 the American commissioner to China felt compelled to remind American nationals living in the country that the U.S. Congress had extended the laws of the United States over Americans in China. Accordingly, "murder and insurrection or rebellion against the Chinese government, with intent to subvert the same, shall be capital offenses, punishable with death."[38] In other words, just as Americans rejected the right of rebellion from its citizens at home, it did so abroad as well.

Although it is hard to trace a direct cause and effect, Western observers regarded the incapacity of the Taiping as symptomatic of the threat posed by rebellions. By eroding authority, rebels produced more chaotic and less efficient governments. One European in Shanghai reflected on the causes of failure of the Taiping. It had, he believed, "fallen into its dotage before it reached maturity, the Rebel movement was brought to an ignominious end solely through its own inherent weakness. With such chiefs as it possessed, it were a miracle it had even attained its professed objects. . . . Utter ignorance and imbecility were the distinguishing peculiarities of the policy adopted; imbecility with respect to the internal working of a government, ignorance of the relations with foreign nations whose aid would have been success, and whose opposition was certain destruction."[39] Whatever the faults of the Qing—and there were many in Western eyes—they ran a reasonably coherent state.

Equally important, they ran a state that had obligated itself to one of the cardinal virtues of the new liberal order—free trade. America's ambassador, Anson Burlingame, spent many years in China, became one of China's most influential backers, and in 1867 even represented the empire in negotiations with the United States. In a speech after the war, Burlingame drew these elements—a durable and powerful state and one committed to liberal modernity—together. China "has expanded her trade, she has reformed her revenue system, she is changing her military and naval organizations, she has built or established a great school, where modern science and the foreign languages are to be taught," he told a New

York audience. "She has done this under every adverse circumstance. She has done this after a great war, lasting through thirteen years, a war out of which she comes with no national debt."[40] Burlingame's postwar assessment remained consistent with his wartime position that only the Qing could ensure the stability American merchants required.

It is no great insight to argue that inertia exerts as powerful a force in political affairs as it does in physics. Established powers with existing agreements—diplomatic, economic, or security related—had a significant advantage over insurgents seeking to build those ties anew. Humphrey Marshall, U.S. consul to China in the 1850s, had little faith that the Taiping would really convert China to Christianity. As one historian notes, "Instead, he saw the Taipings as a convenient excuse for Europeans, especially the British and the Russians, to carve up the empire into fiefdoms and close it to American trade. Instead of aid to the Taipings, Marshall advocated providing American military, commercial, and diplomatic support to uphold the Qing state."[41] Burlingame, one of Marshall's successors, arrived in Shanghai in late 1861, when the city was under siege by the Taiping. Like other foreign diplomats, he negotiated with them but hoped they did not regard this as actual diplomacy. "It is clear that we cannot recognize the rebels without a violation of our treaty obligations, and I shall, in this most delicate condition of affairs, act with the greatest caution."[42] The ties of diplomacy and trade between the U.S. and the Qing (to say nothing of their useful analogies) weighed in their favor. Adam Gurowski, working within the State Department in 1864, juxtaposed American behavior with the "so-called Christian and European Governments," whose practice was to "treat people of the far East like barbarians—to wrest by brutal force from their governments whatever could be wrested, treading down all, even the most elementary, notions of right, justice and humanity." In contrast, "Burlingame inaugurated the co-operative policy, whose aim is to strengthen the Chinese Government in the exercise of its administrative and judicial power."[43] In this context, the state itself functioned as a kind of technology, a system that both contained and transmitted power. It was more elusive than military weapons but, for nineteenth-century powers, no less important than the fiscal practices that enabled warfare in the first place.

These same questions of material cohesion and regime stability played a central role in the North American struggle. The issue of popular

Figure 5. Sent by Abraham Lincoln in 1861 to China, Burlingame supported the ruling Qing dynasty and secured Chinese support for the Union in return. Anson Burlingame and Chinese diplomats, LC-USZ62–66340. Image courtesy of Library of Congress.

support for the Confederacy preoccupied Lincoln and generations of historians after him. At the war's start, Lincoln and Secretary of State William Seward believed that most white Southerners remained loyal to the Union. They were painfully disillusioned by the next four years of war. The historiographical contest over the degree of support expressed by nonslaveholders for the Confederacy has been long and contentious, but evidence demonstrates that most white Southerners supported the Confederacy.[44] This is not the same thing as asserting that a majority of Southerners stood behind the new nation. Nearly all of the 4 million enslaved people (close to half the Confederacy's total population of 9 million), supported the Union. And within the white South substantial divisions existed.[45] Foreigners looking at the Confederacy saw a divided population because it was divided.

They also saw an inefficient state. The Confederacy could not generate the revenue it needed to sustain itself, and the Confederate Congress set new records for lethargy in a legislature. In 1864 the Confederate government emptied Andersonville prison as Sherman's army marched through the state. The prisoners were sent east to Florence, South Carolina, which had no capacity or personnel to oversee tens of thousands of malnourished and angry Union captives. Instead, the men fled, with thousands walking south hoping to find Sherman's men and others heading north for Knoxville. Confederate inhabitants of South Carolina referred to it as a "Yankee Plague," and the experience of waking up to find escaped prisoners camped in one's barn impressed upon them the incapacity of the Richmond government.[46] Robert E. Lee attracted European respect for his military prowess, but the western Confederacy was a shambles, with its revolving cast of much less competent generals. This was not Taiping-level incapacity, perhaps, but it did not augur well for the permanence of a Southern nation.

The Russian Empire

The relative ease with which Americans refused to recognize the Taiping could not be replicated in the Polish Uprising of 1863. Unlike the Sepoy or the Taiping, the long tradition of a "sentimental legacy" between the United States and Poland encouraged Americans to respect Polish aspirations for freedom.[47] Americans, especially educated elites interested in reform, knew the history of the place because it was one of those global episodes that people followed carefully. Jean-Jacques Rousseau and John Adams both used it in their arguments about the nature of political power.[48] Although the State Department remained circumspect to protect diplomatic relations with Russia, many Northerners argued that Poles possessed a legitimate claim to national identity within the empire. Throughout 1861 the *New York Times*'s reporting focused on the violence committed by tsarist troops, often against innocents—women, children, and clergy.[49] A typical pro-Polish editorial in early 1861 announced that "all classes of all religions had fraternized for the purpose of obtaining peaceable reform." The paper assured readers that the movement's broad support expressed "the impossibility of suppressing the nationality of Poland, the impossibility of repressing the country."[50]

These American supporters viewed the Polish insurrection as part of a general liberal movement toward greater freedom. Henry Ward Beecher, one of the leading reform ministers of New England, urged Northerners to join "the army of freedom," marshaling its ranks in Italy, Poland, and Russia as they marched "upward and onward toward that goal of universal human ambition—personal freedom, personal liberty, and the right to be, to do and to act freely as one pleases."[51] Such supporters carefully distinguished the nature and purpose of rebellion in Poland and the United States. Meeting in New York, the American Ladies' Committee offered the most effective rebuttal to those who tried to connect the two. "Let no one weakly attempt to confound the uprising of [Poland] with the rebellion now raging in the Southern United States," they wrote. "The principles involved in the two cases are so radically different as to stand in utter startling opposition. In Poland the struggle is to restore legitimate authority to its rightful holders—a Government truly Polish; while our revolted States seek to wrest that authority from its legally elected rulers, the President and Congress of the United States. The resurrection of Poland means Union—life. The rebellion means division—death. One means love of country; the other—alas!—hate."[52]

Although Beecher did not speak narrowly about an American nationalism (he concerned himself with the kingdom of God), other writers identified a unified nation as the key mechanism by which Americans would encourage "the goal of universal human ambition." In contrast to Poland, which was a movement toward a cohesion of culturally similar people, one newspaper described "the American rebellion [as] an anomaly in the spirit of the age, not only because it is a movement for Slavery instead of Freedom, but because it seeks a division instead of a union of people of the same blood." The naturalness of blood unity had "wonderfully kept alive a sympathy for Poland all through the European masses; and which makes the absolute resurrection of that dead and buried kingdom not only possible but even probable." Confident of victory, Northerners believed that "the spirit of the age will assert itself here just as positively as it is doing in Europe. The struggle against nationality here, as everywhere, is hopeless. The American people are one people, and it is as fixed as destiny that, come weal or come woe, they will continue to live under one Government."[53]

Northerners framed their response to secession as not just lawful but imperative. Lincoln lauded the Union as "the last best hope of man," by which he meant the only place where democracy persisted. In this formulation, repudiating secession benefited Americans and people around the world. In a sympathetic assessment, historian Thomas Bender writes, "One might fairly argue that Lincoln's fusion of freedom and nation over the course of his presidency strengthened the connection between liberalism and nationalism, while Chancellor Otto von Bismarck's illiberal unification of Germany in 1871 subverted it."[54] Bender's argument sharpens a point made a generation earlier by David Potter, who also cast Lincoln and Bismarck as polar opposites yet took pains to emphasize that "the nineteenth-century conjunction of nationalism and liberalism was by no means inevitable."[55]

Confederates, although loath to affiliate themselves with rebels of any sort, interpreted the Polish experience in a way they hoped would lend legitimacy to their own struggle. According to the *Richmond Daily Dispatch*, "the Poles are a nation of historic renown, struggling for their proper place among the nations with a self-sacrificing patriotism, which years of oppression seem not able to extinguish." They hoped the North would remember the Poles' long memory of their own nationality. "A nation . . . may be conquered, but they cannot be kept down. Though crushed to earth they will rise again and again, and so long as the breath of life remains, will, at every opportunity, assert and re-assert their independence."[56] By war's end, the Confederate press proved willing to at least accept Polish aid, if not see common cause. Richmond papers reported the arrival of a delegation of Polish exiles in the capital. The *Daily South Carolinian* heralded the moment, celebrating "the sons of Poland [who] have ever shed their blood in defense of nations struggling for independence, as the battle fields of Europe and American will testify."[57]

While many Northern commentators respected Polish national aspirations, they also believed that democracy or, indeed, any cooperative and lasting society required an ultimate authority. In this view, Poland's attempts to separate from Russia threatened the unity of the state just as secession corroded American democracy. Southerners may have been dissatisfied with Lincoln's election, but they could seek redress within the system. The North's refusal to accept Southern secession reflected a belief that democracy required losers. As Lincoln phrased it, "there could be no appeal from the ballot to the bullet."[58] Seward, the U.S. secretary of state, was a firm believer in the benevolent and ineluctable expansion of America. For him, this growth was predicated on the integrity and strength of the central government. Seward saw a great sympathy between Russia and America. "Russia, like the United States, is an improving and expanding empire. Its track is eastward, while that of the United States is westward," he wrote in 1861. "Each carries civilization to the new regions it enters, and each finds itself occasionally resisted by states jealous of its prosperity, or alarmed by its aggrandizement."[59] Russians, at least the elite who staffed the diplomatic corps, returned the favor. Edouard de Stoeckl, who served as Russia's minister to the United States in the 1850s, identified America's power in its consolidation. It grieved him "to see the two sections of the country, called by nature herself into the most intimate alliance, engaging in a war without rhyme or reason and without any other possible termination than mutual ruin and destruction. Eighty years of prosperity without equal in history are due to this Union."[60]

Seward put his friendly stance into practice by having the U.S. minister to Russia reassure the tsar that the United States would support them.[61] In May 1863, when France called for international mediation to end the conflict (which would have implicitly recognized a Polish nation), Seward refused to lend support and helped kill intervention.[62] Similarly, when the insurrection erupted in 1863 and Russia mobilized military force to suppress it, Northern papers retreated from their earlier pro-Polish position, usually by criticizing the pro-Poland bias of England

and France. In language that Seward would surely have approved, the *New York Times* explained that "what the Polish revolutionists claim is not political amelioration, but national independence. They demand that the Russian ruler shall submit to a dismemberment of his empire. They will take nothing less. Americans who are fighting against a similar movement, cannot call in question the Emperor's right to resist."[63]

American criticism of western European intervention in the Polish crisis also came to serve as a proxy for keeping Europeans out of the U.S. conflict, which was why Adam Gurowski issued fulsome praise for the Russian foreign minister "Prince Gortschakoff's answer to the demonstration of lying, hypocritical, official diplomatic sympathies made in favor of the Poles by the cabinets of France of England, and of Austria." Gurowski effused, "The Gortschakoff notes are master-pieces for their clear, quiet, but bold and decided exposition and argument."[64] In language that could have been lifted from Northern repudiations of British efforts to mediate the American conflict, critics of "the interventionists" (in Poland) argued that such do-gooders "consigned to oblivion this important fact, that it was an insurrection of the aristocracy and of the democracy of the towns, and that the mass of the peasantry, who constitute in Poland the vast majority of the population, were not only quiescent, but even devoted to Russia."[65] Many Northerners, including Abraham Lincoln, believed the same thing could be said about the Confederacy. Again, popular support became one of the litmus tests for assessing a true nation.

Further, by 1863 the *Times* had circled back to Seward's argument regarding the integrity of empires. "Is it reasonable, for instance, to ask the Czar to grant a general amnesty, a national diet, and a national administration to a people while in open insurrection against his authority? Or is it reasonable to require him to proclaim a suspension of hostilities, while his enemies are waging war on him? How would England have felt had the French Emperor required her, during the Sepoy revolt, to pacify India by withdrawing thence her civil and military officials, and restoring to the Rajahs their old supremacy?"[66] The Russian minister, de Stoeckl, made the same argument in his correspondence with his superiors: "To permit the principle of secession, that is to say, the right of a State to break the federal pact when it decides that it is appropriate to do so, is to render absurd the very idea of a confederation." In language that Lincoln echoed, de Stoeckl asserted that "a government thus constituted would be an utter fallacy." He blamed the South for failing to use the recourse to public opinion and constitutional reform that they had. "To give legal sanction to secession 'would be to pronounce the doom of all governments present and future,' [de Stoeckl] asserted. 'Vigorous action on the part of the government will have a wholesome effect in the loyal States of a reassertion of national supremacy. It is essential that the secessionists be either vanquished or taught a bitter lesson.'"[67]

The *New York Times* also challenged the underlying similarity of the conflicts, just as the American Ladies' Committee had. The London *Times* may have argued that

> the case of Russia and Poland, and the case of the North and the South, are, in its opinion, quite analogous. There are belligerents, and rebellion, and civil war in both cases; yes, and fighting, and devastation, and slaughter; but what further analogy exists between them, it wou'd puzzle even the *Times* man to show. In the one case is a people struggling to regain a nationality of which they were treacherously deprived. In the other some half a score of States are striving to break up a Union to the formation of which their progenitors had freely assented. In the one case there is resistance to oppression; in the other there is no oppression to resist.[68]

American reformers may have recoiled at the comparison, but American and Russian history shared a legacy of using war to build a sovereign state. Building on the traditional boundaries of the ancient Rus, tsars of the eighteenth and nineteenth centuries asserted control, often forcibly, over a host of ethnically and linguistically distinct peoples in Central Asia, the Baltics regions, Poland, and Finland.[69] In many of these cases, Russian practices resembled U.S. campaigns against Indians and Mexicans. They built a state and created sovereignty through war. Tsar Nicholas I, who reigned from 1825 to 1855, regarded the incorporation of Polish lands, in particular, into the Russian Empire as a question of nearly existential importance. Writing to his brother, the tsar asked, "Which of the two should perish, Russia or Poland, since it is evident that one of them must?"[70] Nicholas was trying to manage the process of gradual reforms begun by his predecessor, Alexander I, many of which centered on securing control of Poland and circumventing the growing calls for liberalism in Europe.

Alexander II, who succeeded Nicholas, inherited his father's conservatism but was drawn against his will into greater reforms in a process that would have been familiar to Lincoln. The tsar's perspective was reinforced in the popular media, even by former liberals. One of these, Mikhail Katkov, became the most influential propagandist against the Polish rebellion. He ran two popular newspapers. According to one historian, "Katkov's message was simple: the conflict between Russia and Poland was a struggle for the very existence of the Russian state."[71] Alexander's designee to restore order to Poland, Count M. N. Muraviev, regarded suppression of rebellion as part and parcel of a unified and powerful Russia. "We were faced with the task not only of crushing the open rebellion," he wrote later, but "to do away with the very possibility of continuing the mutiny and, on the other hand, to promote to the greatest extent of our powers the unification of the country with the rest of Russia."[72]

Still other Northerners reconciled themselves to Russian supremacy over Poland because, as a powerful empire, it possessed the strength to implement the liberal reforms needed to build the modern world. During a ceremony honoring the sailors and officers of the Russian Fleet while they harbored in Boston, the city's mayor lauded the connection between the two countries: "Diverse in their political organization and their forms of government, Russia and the United States are both progressive nations, fostering, as time goes on, liberal sentiments and each promoting by rational means the elevation of the great mass of the people."[73] The positive reception of the Russians made its way to the Russian ambassador to China, who expressed to his American peers their "great delight at the reception which his countrymen are receiving in America."[74] Admiral Lessoffsky, of the Russian fleet, expressed excitement because "these serfs, who I regret to say were a short time ago but little more than beasts of burden, have made, of themselves, without support of the government, four thousand schools."[75]

Lessoffsky chose his example wisely—education was precisely the type of liberal reform that Republicans like Boston's mayor supported. The abolitionist journal *Liberator*, which reported on the event, closed with a rapturous quote from scripture: "Loose the bands of wickedness: Undo the heavy burdens: Let the oppressed go free: Break every yoke. *Then* shall thy light break forth as the morning; and thine health shall spring forth speedily; thy righteousness shall go before thee; the glory of the Lord shall be thy reward." They intended this quote, from the Book of

Isiah, to illustrate what would come from an empire of Russia's size enacting liberal reform.[76] Another American observer offered a more specific but no less enthusiastic prediction for Poland:

> Under the new policy of the Emperor, you will be secure of protection against foreign enemies, and domestic turbulence, you will have a religious liberty yourselves, and all your neighbors will have the same. . . . Your serfs will be free, your laborers will have land, your peasants will have justice, your children will have schools, your families will have Bibles, your towns will have newspapers, your trade will have roads and telegraphs, and your land will have Peace, and prosperity will roll in upon you with a tide and a permanence, such as Sarmatia never knew through all its turbulent history.[77]

The danger of having foreign powers support an insurgency or even just call for mediation raised the immediate problem of having military aid or diplomatic support flow to an enemy and reflected a belief among outsiders that the conflict was no longer a domestic concern. Containing popular resistance with domestic force was one of the hallmarks of an established state and had been an integral component of the early American state.[78] No one questioned the right of the U.S. government to suppress the Whiskey Rebellion in 1793. The Southern rebellion was larger in scale, but Northerners did not believe that difference changed the underlying issue. The rebels disrupted the normal relations between states and the federal government and could be lawfully suppressed under the Constitution.[79] Northerners argued that the intervention of a foreign power would contradict the national unity promised by the Constitution, even the very idea of self-government. Northerners were especially incensed by British rumblings about intervention; they had remained steadfast supporters of London's claims of authority over its empire. "After hearing all the various rebukes, counsels, and curtain-lectures addressed to us from the mother-country during the past eighteen months," one Northern lecturer admonished, "would anybody venture to dream that the British Government had ever been anything else but the gentle, impartial, and divinely appointed 'guardian of civilization?' Would anybody believe that it ever had made, or ever could make, the smallest objection to the 'secession' of old Ireland, the Ionian Isles, or the ancient nationalities of India?"[80] Americans pushed back against British complaints about the U.S. failure to support intervention in Poland. The *Hereford Times* offered the clearest explanation, under the heading "American Backing Russia against Poland": "It can never deviate from her policy of non-intervention," the paper wrote, "except in cases of evident necessity."[81] Just as no necessity existed for British intervention in North America, so no necessity existed for European intervention in Poland.

Northerners rejected the notion that they were building another Poland by subjugating the South. "It is often urged by our foreign enemies, and by those in England who merely look at this great struggle as critical observers, that if we succeed in conquering the rebel States, we only create an American 'Ireland' or a 'Poland,'" the *New York Times* wrote. "If this great war were merely a war for territory . . . there would be much force in the objection." But the paper rejected all the grounds on which this claim could be made: the Union was a democracy, not an empire; Northerners and Southerners were of the same race; they shared a common past; the South had dominated the federal government since the nation's founding; and no injury had been done to individual Southerners. "But beside all these grounds of hope for the result of the struggle, we must never forget that all the peasantry and a large portion of the middle class in the South are still really on the side of 'the conquerors'—a thing never true of Poland or Ireland. The four millions slaves—loyalists even unto death—must never be disregarded in considering the possible chances of the future."[82] Emancipation served as a trump card, and its play by Lincoln and Alexander enhanced goodwill between the United States and Russia and blocked efforts by their respective insurgent enemies to mobilize larger armies.[83] Describing serf emancipation, one American editorial noted that "at a single stroke, millions of human beings are set free from an ancient oppression, and endowed with new privilege and rights. Like the Proclamation here, it is of course the death-blow of the revolution, at which it is aimed."[84]

The American Empire?

The relationship between state-building, facilitated by war, and liberal reform, was as complex and unpredictable in the United States as elsewhere. Aside from Republican policies like the Homestead Act and the Land Grant College Act—both designed to uplift the white settlers who would soon fill the continent's interior—Republicans' primary claim as the champions of liberal reform was emancipation. Northerners regarded slavery's end as resonant with both classical liberal ideals of individual liberty and free labor and the nineteenth-century belief in universal rights. But the failure of the state to protect even the basic elements of emancipation—the ability not to be killed during the violence of Reconstruction, for instance—limited the scope of this change. As one historian has observed, "in all too many cases the nationalist feelings and ambitions that had earlier advanced the cause of human freedom and dignity now worked against such aspirations. Sometimes nationalism simply overshadowed liberal commitments; in other cases specific choices favored it over liberalism."[85] That retreat from Reconstruction in turn weakened the state itself. Greg Downs argues that this failure to protect African Americans in the South undercuts claims about whether Republicans built a reliably powerful and sovereign state in the aftermath of the war.[86]

Northerners marshaled emancipation and liberal reform alongside appeals to national unity and raw power to draw a parallel between the U.S. and Polish cases favorable to their cause. The connection did not have to be precise in order to be useful. Lincoln himself revealed that in a letter to Bayard Taylor, who served as secretary of the legation at St. Petersburg. "There are only slight resemblances between Russian serfdom and slavery in the southern states," Lincoln told Taylor, "although they rest on the same basis—property in Man—but the complete success of the scheme of emancipation in Russia has much significance for this nation at the present time."[87] *Harper's Weekly* offered a more strident characterization: "The recent abolition of serfdom in Russia is seen to be an act of profound political sagacity. In the same light the expressed intention of the Southern leaders of our rebellion is sheer fatuity. A republic resting upon slavery is . . . absurd."[88]

It was not just the fact of slavery but the method of ending it that brought the United States closer to Russia in governing spirit. Although Reconstruction witnessed a disgraceful abdication of national authority to protect the lives and property of black people in the South, in the context of the Civil War, the federal state could take credit for emancipation. America's first wave of emancipation happened in the wake of the American Revolution and occurred in a decentralized manner; individual states revised their constitutions to outlaw slavery.[89] Lincoln continued to pursue this method in the first two years of the Civil War, to no avail. His efforts to persuade the Upper South states of Missouri, Kentucky, Maryland, and Delaware to end slavery generated nothing but frustration and compelled him to issue an emancipation edict that he had long denied even rested within his power to issue.[90] Despite all its caveats and limits, the Emancipation Proclamation represented a remarkable federal intervention in what had long been regarded as an area of state authority. Recent studies of the process of emancipation concur in emphasizing the essential role played by the Union Army; the federal army's willingness to provide refuge to enslaved people who ran to freedom helped propel the country toward a policy that few could have foreseen.[91]

Historians of emancipation typically separate the American experience from other Western hemispheric powers because it occurred in the midst of a fratricidal war. In this it resembles the Haitian experience but little else. And yet emancipation in the United States resembled the method in other parts of the hemisphere in the sense that, whatever its course, it derived from the power of a centralized state. Both the British and French empires ended slavery in the West Indies by fiat, in 1833 and 1848, respectively. In both cases, colonial metropoles made decisions that contradicted the preferences of settlers in the peripheries.[92] When Brazilian and Cuban emancipation finally arrived, they, too, enacted gradual processes managed by central states.[93] Regardless of the particular mix of military pressures, political will, and social activism in a given state, ending slavery required the authority and resources of a powerful state.

This lesson was not lost even on white Southerners. The preference for central power could be found even among professed state rights advocates, like Cassius Clay, the U.S. minister to Russia. Clay was a Kentucky Unionist and that even rarer breed, a white Southern abolitionist who hewed to a vision of limited government but strongly supported the United States in the Civil War. In 1863 Clay reported that revolutionaries were trying to incite fear by throwing incendiary bombs into homes in St. Petersburg. His reaction reassured Russians of American support and signaled the alignment behind central authority common among even newcomers to the Republican Party. "The upshot of such a forcible overthrow of the central power would be universal anarchy," Clay wrote, "and the dissolution of the Empire back into petty governments and old-time barbarism. Were I a Russian, I should certainly be on the side of absolutism, and await such progress as came of general enlightenment and slow civilization."[94]

Once they abandoned Poland to its fate, Americans found ready explanations for the outcome. Poland was but one of the many subregional powers unable to maintain its autonomy. For some Americans, this was not a cause for alarm but part of the modern order. It explains why a large body of conservatives—both Democrats and a surprising number of Republicans—supported Russia's claim to sovereign authority. According to this argument, people could and would be subject to authorities they opposed. "The present map of the world shows a hundred instances," one author wrote. "Hungary has been conquered by Austria, the ancient kingdom of Poland has been partitioned and annihilated. Venice has been held for centuries a conquered province of her German aggressors. . . . All India is the conquered dependency of England, as Ireland and Wales are." Extrapolating from this general principle, this thinker saw that in the U.S. conflict, "it is certain there can be no reunion with the rebel States or people but by the thorough subjugation of them. They must be conquered and punished. Their insolence must be rebuked and humbled, and they must be so perfectly chastised that they will not hereafter have the power to rebel against the National Government."[95] Confederates hardly yearned for rebukes, but even they seemed to have recognized the bind they occupied. When the *Daily Richmond Examiner* discussed the Polish exiles who visited the capital in 1864 to pledge support, it hoped Poland would recognize the Confederacy but wondered "if such a thing was possible with a country without a sovereignty."[96]

Alongside this cynical view of the role of power in the world, Northerners made more intellectually responsible arguments for the importance of preserving sovereign authority. Most obviously, Confederate victory would break apart the federal government, perhaps not just divide it but destroy it. Edward Everett, the former Massachusetts governor who shared the Gettysburg stage with Lincoln, encouraged Northerners, "We must remember that the recognition of the Confederacy is the prostration of the government, and the dismemberment of the territory of the United States, over which that government is legally and constitutionally established. Such has rarely, if ever, been the case, at least to anything like the same extent, in the revolutions, the civil wars, and the rebellions of Europe."[97] The great British liberal John Bright agreed. In comparing the War of Independence to the Civil War, Bright regarded the former as legitimate but the present rebellion as unjustified. "Now the question is not the want of representation, because, as is perfectly notorious, the South is not represented, but is represented in excess." Instead, echoing Everett, Bright told his readers, "I want to know whether it has ever been admitted by politicians, or statesmen, of people, that a great nation can be broken up at any time by any particular section of any part of that nation."[98] The result was incompatible with security, peace, or prosperity. "If the thirty-three or thirty-four States of the American Union can break off whenever they like," Bright explained, "I can see nothing but disaster and confusion throughout the whole of that continent. I say that the war, be it successful or not, be it Christian or not, be it wise or not, is a war to sustain the government and to sustain the authority of a great nation."[99] Following one of Bright's speeches on the topic, Mr. Howell, an English bricklayer, proposed a resolution censuring his government for letting go of the Confederate ship *Alabama*. "The attempt of the American slaveowners to break up the Union," Howell explained, "is destructive of the first principles of political society."[100]

The State of the Future

Although nation-states were still aborning at midcentury, many people already regarded the process of nation-building as the inevitable accompaniment of modernity. Attempts to denationalize, to break apart established republics, struck Northerners as both immoral and a violation of the natural order. Charles Drake, in a ruminative pamphlet on the "character, motive, and aim" of the rebellion, rejected the argument that the South had a legitimate claim to rebellion as others in Europe and the world had. "For [Confederates] to kindle the flames of civil war," he argued, "and become murderers of their own kindred and destroyers of their own Constitution, merely to satisfy a lawless craving for a separate nationality, is a manifestation of folly and crime having no approach to a parallel in history, and capable of no explanation but that which brands its authors as the most atrocious of parricides, and consigns them to the lowest depths of infamy."[101] Francis Lieber, the foremost scholar on the law of nations and war in the United States, wrote: "This host threatens to sunder your country and cleave your very history in twain, to deprive you of your rivers which God has given you, to extinguish your nationality, to break down your liberty."[102]

Lieber, a German immigrant and law professor, believed that Confederate victory would not just separate the North and South but would destroy the United States. "We will not hear of it," he pledged. "We live in an age when the word is Nationalization, not De-Nationalization; when fair Italy has risen, like a new-born goddess, out of the foaming waves of the Mediterranean."[103] Like his listeners, Lieber—who wrote widely in Northern newspapers and published a hugely influential pamphlet series—knew the global context and regarded the United States as in its mainstream. Another writer, the prominent abolitionist minister Joshua Leavitt, echoed Lieber in his writings on nationalism, rejecting what he called the "ethnological delusion" that nations could only be composed of single "races." "What a terrible refutation we find in our civil war now raging," he wrote. "To launch a nation into existence upon such a theory, is to go to sea in an egg-shell, or to build a bridge upon cobwebs." Leavitt had perhaps read too much pro-slavery propaganda; he identified "Yankees" and Southerners as separate races but regarded them as bound together. "The evils arising from the mingling of races must be borne with, and alleviated as they may, but the destinies of nations will be governed by other considerations."[104]

Foreigners likewise believe the United States composed one indivisible whole. Richard Lyons, the British minister to the United States, identified America in the vanguard of the movement that Lieber celebrated. "No people," he wrote, "attaches the idea of national greatness to the extent of dominion so strongly as does the American. No people is more ambitious of a national greatness."[105] The Russians, eager to flatter American aspirations, likewise encouraged the Union. Their foreign minister, Alexander Gorchakov, reassured Cassius Clay, "How much we desire to see it emerge promptly, by means which consolidate its power, in founding it upon the Union."[106] Gorchakov articulated his perception of the Union as the source of American strength at the war's beginning, writing to the Russian ambassador to Washington: "It would be deplorable that, after so conclusive an experience, the United States should be hurried into a breach of the solemn compact which, up to this time, has made their power. . . . United they perfect themselves; isolated, they are paralyzed."[107] The Russians, like the Americans, cheered on the effort to build a more powerful state through territorial consolidation.

In their more rhapsodic moments, some Americans cheered the assertions of national power with a zeal that probably alarmed even pro-war Republicans. Celebrating the draft act, the printing of national currency, and the consolidation of the national banking infrastructure, *Harper's* identified these measures as "equivalent to the step which, in republican Rome, was taken whenever the state was deemed in imminent danger, and which history calls the appointment of a Dictator. The President of the United States has, in effect, been created Dictator, with almost supreme power over liberty, property, and life—a power nearly as extensive and as irresponsible as that which is wielded by the Emperors of Russia, France, or China. And this is well. To succeed in a struggle such as we are waging a strong central Government is indispensable."[108] Southern readers must have thrilled to Northerners comparing Lincoln with Tsar Alexander II, Napoleon III, and the Qing emperor. A more measured explanation, but one no less honest about power, was given by Gurowski: "The rebels deserve, to the end of time, many curses from outraged humanity. By their treason they forced upon the free institutions of the North the necessity of curtailing personal liberty and other rights; to make use of despotism for the sake of self-defence."[109]

Even if *Harper's* exaggerated, the journal accurately identified the commonalities among those states that suppressed nationalist rebellions in the mid-nineteenth century. Writing about India, one British historian concluded, "The outcome was to be a conception of empire grounded ever more firmly in notions of Indian 'difference,' and a revitalized conservatism that gave that empire a central place in Britain's vision of itself."[110] The British suffered no crisis of confidence or rethinking of empire. Instead, they regarded the rebellion as evidence that earlier reforms had failed because Indians were fundamentally uncivilized. Indians, Sepoy troops chief among them, should have supported the British but instead betrayed them. The axis of loyalty and betrayal played a similarly foundational role in the American conflict, where analogies to Cain and Abel littered Northern newspapers and where white Southerners regarded the efforts of enslaved African Americans to free themselves as betrayal. As the British home office consolidated power in India and other British colonies, especially Jamaica after the 1865 Morant Bay Rebellion, conservatives in England itself expressed a similar reliance on coercion.[111] The essence of this new attitude appeared in James Fitzjames Stephens's *Liberty, Equality, Fraternity*, published in London in 1873. As a historian notes, "the judicious application of force, wielded by a powerful legislator, was thus in a fundamental sense its own justification. As expressed in the coercive sanctions of law, force was not an evil, Stephens maintained, but a necessary element in the creation of a civilized social order."[112] Postwar Republicans in the United States would have agreed.

During the U.S. Civil War, French liberals, like their British allies, assumed the permanence of the federal state in the United States. "The French," writes one historian, "especially those who supported the North, had little to say about the constitutional question in America. Accustomed to a unitary state, with no question about the location of sovereignty, they had little comprehension of the subtle constitutional arguments to which the United States had become accustomed. The illegality of secession was taken almost for granted by the liberal journals."[113] This was nearly the same for many Northerners. Unity in government and nationality possessed a power akin to a law of nature or logic. "This necessity of union demands of the Government, imperatively demands, that it take whatever step is necessary to its own preservation," explained the *Atlantic Monthly*. "It is as with a ship at sea,—all must pull together, or somebody must go overboard. There can be no such order of things as an *agreed state of mutiny*,—forecastle seceding from cabin, and steerage independent of both."[114]

The metaphors are an obvious clue. Whether Northerners were talking about ships split into pieces, or a body politic torn asunder, or a house divided, they used metaphorical language to imply the inevitability of the Union. They did not dissemble. Northerners believed in a perpetual Union and they sought a language that conveyed it.[115] What they may not have appreciated was the degree to which such language was intelligible by other people living in seemingly different circumstances. What Northerners articulated, and what Confederates resisted in ways that resonated with other global rebels, was a rhetoric that validated centralized states. It was a language deployed by the British in India, by the Russians in Poland, and by the Qing in China. In each case, the political parameters of conflict varied, but in each case, insurgents lost, in part, because they failed to overcome the stigma of rebellion and the increasingly powerful intellectual sanction for central state authority. An unshakeable belief in this concept lay at the core of Northern experience in the Civil War.[116] *Harper's Weekly*, one of the most stalwart explainers of the Union cause, cast the issue in terms of world history. Before France, England, Russia, Spain, and other European powers became true nations, they were composed of local fiefdoms at war with one another. "Nothing is commoner, in ancient history," the paper wrote, "than the rebellions of minorities against the decision of majorities. It is ripened experience and enlarged civilization which alone have taught and enforced the great truth that minorities must yield to majorities, and yield peaceably; and the same great teachers have also taught us that the tendency of civilization is toward the destruction of small and the consolidation of great nationalities." In language that the British, Qing, and Russians all echoed: "in one word, civilization centralizes. Barbarism divides."[117]

Civil War historians have come late to appreciate the cultural and intellectual parameters of the conflict. Given the importance of technological, environmental, political, and economic factors, it is easy to understand why. In trying to account for Union victory or Confederate defeat, there are a plethora of factors to catalog. These forces—the new technologies and tactics, the social dynamics of war-making, the creative state-making in each place—all possessed their own important legacies for the world. The reality of these connections should not blind us to other connections and legacies between the U.S. Civil War and other civil and national conflicts occurring around the globe at the same time.

When we conceptualize the Civil War in exceptional terms, we fail to appreciate the extent to which Confederates were part of a diverse club of nineteenth-century failures. Their experience was not just similar to that of the Sepoy, the Taiping, and the Poles; it was connected to them as well. Those conflicts and the rhetoric that emanated from them shaped the U.S. Civil War, and vice versa. In particular, this chapter emphasizes the ways historians have explained the mid-nineteenth century more generally. For some, this era was defined by the rise of the nation-state, while more recent scholars emphasize the continuing strength of empires. The core issue that all of these studies explain is how people successfully organized durable communities, safe from both internal and external threats. Creating those communities, in every case, required suppressing the preferences or interests of some people.

Two sets of conclusions emerge from the stories of the civil and national conflicts of the mid-nineteenth century. The first is in terms of the American experience. The Confederacy faced a harder challenge than the Union. Most Civil War historians would probably agree—we have long possessed the data on manpower and matériel disparities between the two sides. Add to this financing, the blockade, and the failure of foreign powers to intervene, and the cause seems not so much lost as hopeless. What we have failed to appreciate is the degree to which these elements, especially the economic, diplomatic, and resource questions, hinged on the attitude that foreign powers brought to the war. As insurgents against an established power, the Confederacy had to overcome serious global impediments. On the other side, the ways that the Union leveraged its position as the natural sovereign in the middle of North America (if not all of it—Seward had his eye on Canada, which confederated immediately after the Civil War) altered the nature of the state.

Historians have argued over the degree of change that the Civil War brought to the American state. The easy, traditional answer—that war made the modern American state by consolidating power in Washington—misrepresents the scale and duration of change. There is no question that in terms of organization and public–private partnerships, the war enhanced the administrative capacity of the federal government, but that system was still shackled to Republicans' limited government vision, as black Southerners realized to their dismay during Reconstruction. The war's judgment on the inviolability of the Union enhanced federal authority in the eyes of Americans and of people around the world. It did so partly because the United States acted in concert with other powerful states at the time. As historian Thomas Bender argues, "Nation-making, whether in the United States or in France and in other states, combined seemingly antagonistic but in fact complementary tendencies: a centralization of power and administration, concurrent with the individualization of the national citizenry."[118]

Does this mean that the Civil War created an American empire? In fact, many American historians today regard the process of westward expansion in the mid-nineteenth century as a form of imperial growth.[119] Because it was not a naval empire—like the one Britain built—it has been harder to see, but certainly for indigenous people living west of the Appalachian Mountains, American expansion constituted a military, political, economic, and cultural threat on the same scale as that faced by people subject to the British, Russian, or Chinese empires.[120] Because the United States functioned as a republic in the east, most white Americans believed that expansion was somehow different from empire. Thomas Bender argues that a "semantic sleight of hand" concealed America's territorial interests. "They obscured their actual empire by describing it as 'the westward movement' or the 'westward expansion' of their country."[121] For some of these historians, the Civil War, and the military and administrative power the United States developed during it, cemented this process of imperial growth.

White Southerners identified the North as an imperial power from the beginning of the conflict. In their view, the star of empire was making its way south rather than west, as it had been for the previous several decades. Foreign observers sometimes reached the same conclusion. Lord Russell, the British foreign secretary during the Civil War, famously juxtaposed the North and South as two parties "contending as so many States of the Old World have contended, the one side for empire and the other for power."[122] Lincoln rejected this interpretation. He took great pains during the war to explain the necessity of repudiating secession as an act of democratic politics, a way of preserving the practice of self-government. It was that. At the same time, the United States acted in harmony with the other major powers of the day, empires like Britain, Russia, and China, and this may help us understand the more explicitly imperial postures that the United States assumed later in the century. It also reinforces the conclusion recently drawn by historian Gary Gerstle in his study of American government that "liberty and coercion were bound together from the earliest days of the republic."[123]

Looking at the U.S. Civil War from abroad, or at least within the context of the other similar conflicts occurring at the same time, also reinforces the unexceptionality of the American experience, at least as it pertains to state-building. In two recent books, historian Max Edling has shown that the Americans who crafted the Constitution did so by drawing directly on the traditions of European fiscal-military states of the eighteenth century. The demands of functioning in a world of ambitious empires and of holding together a polyglot republic compelled the Framers to build a strong yet flexible state.[124] In Edling's memorable use of the Greek myth, the United States at its founding was a "Hercules in the cradle." In the period between 1789 and 1861, as westward expansion demanded military, fiscal, and administrative resources, the state matured.[125] By the end of the Civil War, European empires confronted Hercules risen. At the same time, it is worth noting that American power in the Civil War came partly from emulating not western European fiscal-military states, but Euro-Asian empires like those of Russia and China. The Americans who led the United States through the Civil War were even more polyamorous than the original founders and took inspiration from even more diverse sources.

The second conclusion that can be drawn concerns the global significance of the failed rebellions. The revolutions of the late eighteenth century troubled the global order but did not inaugurate the era of popular sovereignty that reformers imagined. This could be seen clearly in the counterrevolutions of 1848 in Europe, which represented a victory for the forces of empire and conservatism.[126] In Europe, moderates recognized the need for controlling the pace and direction of change. As one historian notes, "European governments of all political colourings undertook reform in order to preserve the existing order. . . . Reform was undertaken to strengthen the establishment."[127] Historian Robert Tombs argues that after 1848, especially in central Europe, "men prepared to exploit new historical forces, including democracy and nationalism. As Napoleon III put it: 'March at the head of the ideas of your century, and they will sustain you . . . march against them and they will overthrow you.' And Bismarck, more tersely: 'If there has to be revolution, we would rather make it than suffer it.'"[128] The failed revolutions of the 1850s and 1860s—in India, Poland, China, and the United States—are a part of this narrative. They embody the curious mix of liberal and conservative elements that characterized the third quarter of the nineteenth century.

The victory of centralized authority, whether it took the form of empires or republics, reinforced the power of established states and of organized, aggressive defense of that order. Liberalism, in the form of free trade, the promotion of Western cultural values and institutions, and a dedication to majority rule in politics, played a role in this story as well, although sometimes more as window-dressing than as genuine cause. It was, in most places, the triumph of the moderates, not the radicals. The outcomes of these failed enterprises helped establish the model for what would work in terms of state-building in the decades to come. Unifying rather than dividing, culturally coherent, dedicated to gradual liberal reform, and drawing on clear popular support—these were the ground rules within the international system that enabled Germany, Bulgaria, and others to organize new states in the coming decades. For thinkers of the era, the presumption of central power often went unstated. When the military strategist Antoine-Henri Jomini wrote about "Civil Wars, and Wars of Religion" (which he considered the same thing), he denounced them as "the most deplorable," and then off-handedly admitted, "We can understand how a government may find it necessary to use force against its own subjects in order to crush out factions which would weaken the authority of the throne and the national strength."[129]

As historians, we must recognize that ideas did not move in one direction only. Many historians of the revolutionary era at the turn of the nineteenth century write as though ideas moved out from America to the world, from the new liberal order to the old conservative one. But ideas entered the stream from all points, and they circulated. When Americans used words like "rebel" and "sovereignty," they did so in the context of how those words had been and were being used by other people around the globe. And the content of the ideas in circulation were not all liberal. Many of the recent global histories of the early nineteenth century describe it as an emancipatory era. The experiences of midcentury are not so clear cut. The ideas and practices generated in the U.S. conflict and those in India, China, and Poland contained both liberal and conservative elements. In this sense, they anticipate the slow resurgence of reform in Europe in the 1860s and 1870s, as the old guard, in places like Germany and France, made peace with moderate reformers in an effort to forestall a more radical outcome led by the working class. The Republicans who led the Union to victory in the Civil War occupied the same ideological space by the 1870s.[130] They viewed Northern success in the war as evidence of order and the rule of law over the irrationality and chaos of secession. The similarities that emerge in this portrait situate the United States in the mainstream of world history among industrializing powers in the second half of the nineteenth century, one that included many European nations but also Asian ones like Japan, which reformed itself without the trauma of a civil conflict. It contradicts the argument that the United States occupied the leading edge of liberal reform in the Western world and that the United States engineered a hybrid liberal nationalism.[131] But if such a perspective denies the United States its traditional role as exemplar for the world, it has the virtue of moving our past from the realm of myth back to history.

EPILOGUE

Ghost Nations of the Nineteenth Century

MOST SCHOLARS TELL US THAT the modern world took its shape from the nationalist movements of the nineteenth century. This seminal period for the nation-state birthed the Latin American republics, European powers like Germany and Italy, and new incarnations of Japan and China. Lingering among these successes were a host of national failures—political communities that coalesced briefly and then sputtered out. But they rarely disappeared definitively. As William Howard Russell, the great British war correspondent who observed the Civil War's first battle from Charleston, South Carolina, reported, "even the flag of a rebellion leaves indelible colors in the political atmosphere."[1] As it was for the Confederates, so it was for the Sepoy, the Taiping, and the Poles. These rebellions hoisted their colors but could not maintain them, yet they left an imprint on both history and memory. Their traces today remain as ghost nations, which float through history, shaping the nature of the empires and states from which they tried to emerge. In some places, they reemerged later and succeeded. In other places, the people who formed them pursued their political or economic or social goals through alternative means. They also served as cautionary tales, warning would-be secessionists or unifiers to avoid certain tactics or rhetoric.

These episodes of rebellion are typically situated within their own national historiographies, with an eye to antecedents or to paths not taken. Positioning the stories together, as they occurred in real time, allows us to see across national boundaries and changes how we view the nineteenth century. The political liabilities, both domestic and foreign, produced by adopting irregular warfare limited the options for insurgents. The effectiveness of guerrilla warfare in the twentieth century, where many different actors made effective use of it, stands out more clearly as a shift in military history. Nineteenth-century insurgents who adopted it impeded their efforts to achieve autonomy. It would be too much to say that irregular warfare always failed, but the ability of established states to marshal industrial and manpower resources into counterinsurgency campaigns gave them a strong hand. The nascent communication networks of the nineteenth century carried reports of the counterinsurgencies waged by dominant powers, but they did not achieve the political resonance that occurred in the twentieth century when democratic nations lost wars in part because of declining public support fueled by reports of atrocities committed by their armies.[2] In the nineteenth century, such reporting could generate unintended consequences, as when Northerners defended their conduct toward Confederates by republishing stories of British excesses in India.

The simultaneous nature of the midcentury rebellions produced a global conversation about the legitimacy and nature of political authority. Although each conflict followed its own unique path, all the major actors were entangled with one another in ways that meant what happened in one place shaped the experience in another. Sometimes this happened explicitly—Northerners rejected the right of secession at home and refused to support nationalist movements abroad that, under other conditions they would have supported, like the Polish rebellion of 1863. In other cases, influences operated more unconsciously. Both insurgents and established powers experienced the difficulty of creating a rhetoric of sovereignty and authority that reconciled ethnonational aspirations, liberalism, and global power politics. European powers hoped to retain imperial control of far-flung colonies while also encouraging the process of political disintegration in North America that would weaken a rival. Confederates tried to establish their own political autonomy while denying the right of people of color and other minority communities to do the same. In all these cases, actors struggled with the historical meanings of words like rebel and insurgent and changed the connotations of those terms for the future.

The failure of the midcentury rebellions also reinforced the importance of central authority in a rapidly modernizing world.[3] The U.S. government demobilized its army with remarkable speed and shrank the federal budget, but the infrastructure established during the war, especially the public–private partnerships and the supremacy of the federal government, created a new political landscape in the postwar world. Similarly, Britain and Russia's successes at curtailing resistance to their imperial projects emboldened their expansion in the 1870s and beyond. The Qing suppression of the Taiping did not end the problem of rebellions in the Chinese empire, although nothing on that scale recurred. We can also see how other states, those that did not experience their own rebellions, interpreted the lessons of midcentury. The movement toward Canadian confederation in 1867 and reform in Japan, launched in 1868, both derived from internal forces, but their leaders clearly saw that maintaining autonomy and managing the transition toward free trade and an industrial economy could be more effectively directed from the center.

Northerners, the British, Russians, and Qing all celebrated their successful bids to retain sovereignty over territory. The people on the losing side of these wars, the national failures of the nineteenth century, saw only the sovereignty's evil twin: dominion.[4] In the wake of the failed rebellions, Indians, white Southerners, Poles, and Taiping fell under the control of political powers they regarded as foreign and malign. Confederates expressed little surprise. Having condemned Northerners as Yankees and, worse still, Roundheads and Puritans throughout the conflict, they expected that the real goal of the war was their subjugation.[5] Indeed, "dominion" over the new world had been an original goal of the Puritans who settled Massachusetts and the formal name of the New England colonies when they unified in 1686. Sovereignty gave established powers authority over not just territory but the people within it. Native Americans had long suffered under this aspect of dominion, but white Americans rarely felt its burden. With the transfer of authority from the East India Company to the British government, Indians felt the power of empire in more manifest ways throughout the rest of the nineteenth century.

As the Japanese and Canadians recognized, what emerged from the failed rebellions of the mid-nineteenth century was the triumph of moderate reform. Despite the boldness of emancipation in Russia and the United States, Lincoln and the tsar short-circuited more radical change. Lincoln and Alexander II aligned themselves with Bismarck, who declared he would "rather make [a revolution] than suffer it."[6] During the Civil War, Northerners celebrated this measured approach in both places. "The analogies between the American and the Russian peoples have too often been described to need further explanation here," *Harper's Weekly* announced in 1863. "Russia, like the United States, is a nation of the future. Its capabilities are only just being developed. Its national destiny is barely shaped. Its very institutions are in their cradle, and have yet to be modeled to fit advancing civilization and the spread of intelligence." The end of slavery and serfdom and the gradual shift to free labor economies marked a pivotal moment for both countries. "Like the United States, Russia is in the agonies of a terrible transition: the Russian serfs, like the American negroes, are receiving their liberty; and the Russian boiars, like the Southern slave-owners, are mutinous at the loss of their property."[7] Similarly, the British victory in India enabled them to bring their version of liberal reform to a continent they believed was stuck in the past. These outcomes are less encouraging than the liberatory politics of the Age of Revolution, which may account for why nationalistic historiographies have obscured the common reactions to the crises of midcentury. Separating these stories ensures that we only read them in the context of their unique histories rather than recognizing commonalities that reflect the limits of liberalism.

In contrast to the uniform response of established powers, the midcentury rebels did not share common ideological or political motives. The tide of revolutionary enthusiasm that carried so many liberals at the turn of the nineteenth century had no counterrevolutionary analogue. If anything, the riptides that pulled back in response to that liberalism coursed into nationalistic eddies and whorls that spun in different directions. In the United States and Poland, the insurgents trumpeted their counterrevolutionary posture. In both places rebels pursued territorial independence to ensure greater control for elite landholders. In India rebels hoped to expel an imperial power and establish indigenous control over their region. The Sepoy coalition encompassed people holding a wide variety of religious, ideological, and economic perspectives, a diversity that inhibited the independence movement in India for decades. The Taiping claimed a similar anti-imperial stance although they pursued a more radical cultural and social restructuring. Unlike the Marxist rebellions of the twentieth century, which shared an ideological orientation, the midcentury rebels did not derive energy or support from a global wave in their favor.

The conclusions of the midcentury rebellions reveal further the isolation of those people pursuing autonomy at the time. Each faced different fates, none enviable. The United States offered the gentlest treatment of its rebels. Abraham Lincoln promised in his Second Inaugural Address "charity for all and malice toward none." His apparent intent, and the policy his successor, Andrew Johnson, followed, granted generous terms to former Confederates. Lincoln saw no value in punishing rebels; ending the rebellion sufficed. The British and the Manchu, in contrast, believed in punishing people to deter future problems. The British executions of Sepoys and the Qing execution of Taipings reveal the importance of violence to imperial control. The Russians exiled Polish leaders, suppressed Polish history in schools, and tried to Russify the region. Insurrections of the sort waged by Indians, Poles, and Taiping did not challenge the idea of an empire, which is predicated on forceful control of foreign peoples. As Lincoln saw, however, secessionist rebellions make the very idea of self-government impossible. Despite the lethality of the threat, leaders of republics relied less on violence and more on coercion and incentives to encourage respect for the state, particularly after active resistance had ended. Whatever their faults, liberal republics proved durable. White Southerners never again mounted a secessionist effort. In India and Poland, meanwhile, insurgent forces eventually achieved the autonomy sought in the nineteenth century, although this did not happen until the twentieth century and only after tumultuous and unpredictable conflicts in each place.

Regardless of the immediate conclusions, the legacies of the midcentury rebellions lived on long after their failures. The war in 1857 convinced British politicians that they could not entrust administration of this most valuable territory to the British East India Company. Within a year, the British crown had assumed control of the colony and would retain it for the next ninety years. It is hard to overstate the significance of the war and its outcome for the history of modern India. The British used memories of the rebellion as an important part of the cultural apparatus of imperialism. In 1903 the British administrator, Lord Curzon, hosted a Delhi Durban, a commemorative ceremony, in this case honoring the coronation of Edward VII as first king-emperor of India. For the event, Curzon brought in British veterans of 1857. One scholarly reading of this event sees the Durban as method of legitimating imperial rule, in this case by celebrating 1857 in "terms of glory and pride," with the rebellion presented "as a national epic of the British race, where Victorian masculine heroes displayed the progressive qualities of duty, honour, and sacrifice."[8]

For Indians, 1857 possessed even more importance. It occupied a central part of the anticolonial narrative and evidence of the barbarity of British rule against which Indians struggled for nearly a century. Historians played a role in the nationalist movement, writing against the heroic British imperial history. "When the battle was joined by Indian nationalists," one scholar notes, "the meaning of the conflict underwent a radical change. It was now symbolic of the love of liberty and the resentment against oppression that burned in the heart of every Indian."[9] What the British called a "mutiny" or, when pressed, a "rebellion," twentieth-century Indians took to calling the War for Independence. A recent study offers a fair index for current attitudes: "In India, the year 1857 marked the beginning of the processes that reached fruition in 1947, when Indians finally overthrew colonial domination and became free citizens of the largest democratic nation in the world."[10]

In 1863 the Russian Empire engaged in "Russification," an attempt "to expand the use of Russian and conversely restricted the prerogatives of local non-Russian languages and cultures."[11] Although scholars today see a more nuanced and less absolute process than did those writing during the Cold War, the effort of Russians to forestall another Polish rebellion are clear. Traditionally, one historian writes, "Polish universities were seen as hotbeds of Polish nationalism and anti-Russian, anti-imperial conspiracies that came to the fore in 1830 and 1863. For sound raison d'etat, these subversive centers had to be shut down."[12] From a purely theoretical perspective, this policy makes sense, but it had the effect of victimizing Poles within the empire. Polish nationalism already contained a healthy admixture of nostalgia for a vanished past. The opening lines of Poland's epic *Pan Tadeusz* recall the glories of the Polish-Lithuanian Commonwealth:

> O Lithuania, my country, thou
> Are like good health; I never knew till now
> How precious, till I lost thee. Now I see
> Thy beauty whole, because I yearn for thee.[13]

Published in 1834, in the wake of Russia's suppression of the 1831 Polish Uprising, the poem anticipates the central role that stories of repression and loss played in Polish national life. White Southerners adopted a similarly tragic tone in their postwar memorialization, ennobling the lost world of the plantation South as an idyll. "The Conquered Banner," by Catholic priest Abram Joseph Ryan, adopts a similarly elegiac tone:

Furl that Banner, softly, slowly!
Treat it gently—it is holy,
For it droops above the dead.
Touch it not—unfold it never;
Let it droop there, furled forever,—
For its people's hopes are fled![14]

The Poles crafted an identity of unjust suffering and national victimhood at the hands of Russians that persisted long enough into the twentieth century to blend into their postwar resentment of Soviet domination. The Russian practice had its own American parallel. Just as officials in Moscow felt that the way to peace and stability was to reduce the Polishness of the region, some white Northerners felt that exporting their model of free labor republicanism to the South would ensure both peace and prosperity.[15]

The Qing did not undertake an equivalent to Russification, but the war helped secure their rule. As Philip Kuhn argues, "the powerful conservative coalition thus forged between the Manchu monarchy and the leading elements of the Han elite was to prolong the dynasty's life into the twentieth century."[16] Alongside this structural aspect, memories of the failed rebellions have been central to several competing schools of Chinese historiography. In the late nineteenth century, imperial scholars focused on the "righteousness and heroism of the martyred dead," in this case Qing loyalists who gave their lives for the regime.[17] In the effort to build a republican China in the early twentieth century, "Chinese politicians and scholars identified the Taiping as a proto-nationalist antecedent to their own revolutionary ambitions."[18] After World War II, a new regime emerged, but the trauma of Taiping remained central. Tobie Meyer-Fong, an astute historian of this process, explains: "The Taiping took on tremendous explanatory power as the origin point for the revolutionary trajectory leading to Communist victory in 1949 and onward to the future."[19] The variety of interpretive uses to which the Taiping Heavenly Kingdom has been put suggests a fundamental disconnect between the actual past and its political uses as history or memory. If the past can mean anything, perhaps it means nothing? Meyer-Fong's careful study of the human reaction to the conflict's death and destruction rejects this nihilism and insists that we acknowledge the personal as well as the political dimensions of war.

In the United States, the Confederacy lived on culturally and politically. White Southerners promulgated the Lost Cause, an interpretive memory of the war that emphasized Confederate valor and moral virtue to conceal the terroristic violence used by veterans in Reconstruction and beyond. The American South, alone among the midcentury rebels, never achieved autonomy, although the home rule secured by Democrats in the 1870s enabled them to limit the scope of emancipation and maintain the racial control that lay at the heart of the Confederate enterprise. The civil wars of the midcentury created a cultural politics of grievance that could sometimes be turned toward genuine independence. But in this cause, like in the wars themselves, the Confederates stood alone. Refusing to abandon slavery, the Confederacy alienated its potential allies and isolated itself outside the Whiggish stream of modern history. Although the Lost Cause performed important political work for white Southerners, the cause itself had little of the adaptability to which Indian, Polish, and Chinese activists bent their past.

From the vantage point of the early twentieth century, the classic Age of Revolution in the late eighteenth century offers an inspiring history. The failed revolutions of the mid-nineteenth century offer a more sober lesson. The pursuit of autonomy in the late eighteenth century shifted sovereignty from monarchs to the people and in the process demonstrably advanced human freedom, but it did not generate an irresistible tide. Within decades, white Southerners, Britons, and others around the world saw the importance of slowing down or reversing that trajectory. Northern victory in the Civil War halted the Confederate counterrevolution but also emboldened the American state to organize and use power in ways that did not always lead toward peace and liberty. The British, Russian, and Chinese learned even more clearly the importance of central authority buttressed by military power and a rhetoric of imperial legitimacy. Their success at stifling the midcentury rebellions encouraged them to enhance the scope and control exercised by their empires. The struggles of the nineteenth century's ghost nations remind us that the political history of the modern world followed an unpredictable not inevitable route.

NOTES

INTRODUCTION

1. Seward to W. Preston and others, March 9, 1861, in George Baker, ed., *The Collected Works of William H. Seward*, vol. 5 (Boston: Houghton Mifflin, 1884), 191.

2. In this, my argument resonates with Edward Ayers's notion of "deep contingency," which emphasizes the "dense and intricate connections in which lives and events are embedded." Ayers advanced this concept in his study of two counties in Civil War America. Here I argue that those connections knitted not only Northerners and Southerners together but people around the world. Edward L. Ayers, *In the Presence of Mine Enemies: War in the Heart of America, 1859–1863* (New York: Norton, 2003), xix.

3. Don H. Doyle, *Nations Divided: America, Italy, and the Southern Question* (Athens: University of Georgia Press, 2002); and Stig Forster and Jörg Nagler, *On the Road to Total War: The American Civil War and the German Wars of Unification, 1861–1871* (Cambridge: Cambridge University Press, 2002).

4. Norman Davies, *God's Playground: A History of Poland*, vol. 2, *1795 to the Present* (New York: Columbia University Press, 2005).

5. The fullest English-language account of the insurrection and its antecedents can be found in R. F. Leslie, *Reform and Insurrection in Russian Poland, 1856–1865* (London: Athalone Press, 1963).

6. Paul A. Kramer, "Power and Connection: Imperial Histories of the United States in the World," *American Historical Review* 116, no. 5 (December 2011): 1366. doi:10.1086/ahr.116.5.1348.

7. Greg Downs's recent book is one of these exceptions and shows how a global framing allows us to see the war's political meaning more clearly. Gregory P. Downs, *The Second American Revolution* (Chapel Hill: University of North Carolina Press, 2019). See also Paul Quigley and James Hawdon, eds. *Reconciliation after Civil Wars: Global Perspectives* (New York: Routledge, 2018).

8. Don H. Doyle, *The Cause of All Nations: An International History of the American Civil War* (New York: Basic Books, 2014).

9. Excellent recent examples of how a global perspective can be integrated into histories of the conflict can be found in Aaron Sheehan-Dean, ed., *Cambridge History of the American Civil War* (Cambridge: Cambridge University Press, 2019), particularly the chapters by Brian Schoen, "The Civil War in Europe," 342–65; Andre Fleche, "The Civil War in the Americas," 319–41; and David K. Thomson, "Financing the War," 174–92; and in Howard Jones, *Union in Peril: The Crisis over British Intervention in the Civil War* (Chapel Hill: University of North Carolina Press, 1992); Howard Jones, *Blue and Gray Diplomacy: A History of Union and Confederate Foreign Relations* (Chapel Hill: University of North Carolina Press, 2010); and Richard J. M. Blackett, *Divided Hearts: Britain and the American Civil War* (Baton Rouge: Louisiana State University Press, 2001).

10. Edward B. Rugemer, *The Problem of Emancipation the Caribbean Roots of the American Civil War* (Baton Rouge: Louisiana State University Press, 2008); Matthew J. Clavin, *Toussaint Louverture and the American Civil War: The Promise and Peril of a Second Haitian Revolution* (Philadelphia: University of Pennsylvania Press, 2009); Andre M. Fleche, *The Revolution of 1861: The American Civil War in the Age of Nationalist Conflict* (Chapel Hill: University of North Carolina Press. 2012); and Doyle, *The Cause of All Nations*.

11. This shibboleth of the field has been challenged in a forthcoming work by Nathan Kalmoe, *With Ballots and Bullets: Partisanship and Violence in the American Civil War*, unpublished manuscript under review, https://nathankalmoe.com/with-ballots-bullets-partisanship-violence-in-the-american-civil-war/.

12. An admirable version of this approach can be found in Daniel T. Rodgers, *Atlantic Crossings: Social Politics in a Progressive Age* (Cambridge, Mass.: Harvard University Press, 2000).

13. Eric Hobsbawm, *The Age of Capital: 1848–1875* (1975; New York: Vintage, 1996), 13, 15.

14. Janet Polasky, *Revolutions without Borders: The Call to Liberty in the Atlantic World* (New Haven, Conn.: Yale University Press, 2015), 8. "Between 1776 and 1804, the possibility of revolution loomed large over four continents" (2).

15. Polasky, *Revolutions without Borders*, 13.

16. Jonathan Israel, *The Expanding Blaze: How the American Revolution Ignited the World, 1775–1848* (Princeton, N.J.: Princeton University Press, 2017), 601, 7. Polasky, Israel, and others writing in this vein can trace their lineage back to R. R. Palmer's two-volume *The Age of the Democratic Revolution: A Political History of Europe and America, 1760–1800* (Princeton, N.J.: Princeton University Press, 1959, 1964). Palmer organized a wide array of "agitations, upheavals, intrigues, and

conspiracies" under the heading of democratic revolution in the late eighteenth century, although he was also alert to the reversals that dominate this period.

17. Richard Stites, *The Four Horsemen: Riding to Liberty in Post-Napoleonic Europe* (New York: Oxford University Press, 2014), 16.

18. Abraham Lincoln, *Collected Works of Abraham Lincoln*, vol. 4, *1860–1861*, edited by Roy Prentice Basler, Marion Dolores Pratt, Lloyd A. Dunlap (New Brunswick, NJ: Rutgers University Press, 1953), 426.

19. Federalist No. 51, available at the Avalon Project, Lillian Goldman Law Library, Yale Law School, http://avalon.law.yale.edu/18th_century/fed51.asp.

20. Charles Maier, *Leviathan 2.0: Inventing Modern Statehood* (Cambridge, Mass.: Harvard University Press, 2012), 9.

21. Benedict Anderson, *Imagined Communities: Reflections on the Origin and Spread of Nationalism*, rev. ed. (London: Verso, 1998); Ernest Gellner, *Nations and Nationalism*, 2nd ed. (Ithaca, NY: Cornell University Press, 2009); and Eric Hobsbawm, *Nations and Nationalism since 1780*, 2nd ed. (Cambridge University Press, 1992).

22. Stephen R. Platt, *Autumn in the Heavenly Kingdom: China, the West, and the Epic Story of the Taiping Civil War* (New York: Vintage, 2012), 320. All emphasis, misspellings, and unusual syntax in quotes derives from the original primary sources. In addition, I have not modernized Indian or Chinese place or personal names that may have changed in response to post-nineteenth-century translation practices.

CHAPTER 1. WHAT KIND OF WAR IS THIS? INSURGENCIES AND THE CHALLENGE OF LEGITIMACY IN WAR

1. Carol Reardon, *With a Sword in One Hand & Jomini in the Other: The Problem of Military Thought in the Civil War North* (Chapel Hill: University of North Carolina Press, 2012), 13.

2. Baron de Jomini, *The Art of War* (1862; Westport, Conn.: Greenwood Press, 1971), 29.

3. Jomini, *The Art of War*, 35.

4. Henry Wager Halleck, *Elements of Military Art and Science*, 3rd ed. (New York: Appleton, 1862).

5. D. H. Mahan, *An Elementary Treatise on Advanced-Guard, Out-Post, and Detachment Service of Troops* (New York: John Wiley, 1862).

6. Jon Tetsuro Sumida, *Decoding Clausewitz: A New Approach to On War* (Lawrence: University Press, of Kansas, 2008), 87.

7. Sumida, *Decoding Clausewitz.*

8. Peter Paret and John W. Shy, *Guerrillas in the 1960s* (New York: Praeger, 1962), 9.

9. Peter S. Carmichael, *The War for the Common Soldier: How Men Thought, Fought, and Survived in Civil War Armies* (Chapel Hill: University of North Carolina Press, 2018).

10. Brian Schoen, *The Fragile Fabric of Union: Cotton, Federal Politics, and the Global Origins of the Civil War* (Baltimore: Johns Hopkins University Press, 2009); and Matthew Karp, *This Vast Southern Empire: Slaveholders at the Helm of American Foreign Policy* (Cambridge, Mass.: Harvard University Press, 2016).

11. Carl von Clausewitz, *On War*, translated by Michael Howard and Peter Paret (Princeton, N.J.: Princeton University Press, 1976), 479. According to Paret and Shy, Clausewitz analyzed the nature of guerrilla war "solely on its operational merits, as a means of fighting." Paret and Shy, *Guerrillas in the 1960s*, 12.

12. Walter Laqueur, *Guerrilla Warfare: A Historical and Critical Study* (1976; New Brunswick, N.J.: Transaction, 1998), xvi–xvii.

13. Laqueur, *Guerrilla Warfare*, 76.

14. Laqueur, *Guerrilla Warfare*, 65.

15. Robert Asprey, whose global history touches only lightly on the Indian conflict, believes the Sepoy did use guerrilla tactics against European imperialists (the British and the Dutch and French). Robert B. Asprey, *War in the Shadows: The Guerrilla in History* (New York: William Morrow, 1994), 72–73. Max Boot's more recent and capacious definition emphasizes "the use of hit-and-run tactics by an armed group directed primarily against a government and its security forces for political and religious reasons." Boot's history excludes those large-scale actors, like the Indians, Poles, Confederates, and Taiping who incorporated guerrilla units or tactics alongside more regular modes of warfare. Max Boot, *Invisible Armies: An Epic History of Guerrilla Warfare from Ancient Times to the Present* (New York: Norton, 2013), xxii.

16. Robert R. Mackey, *The Uncivil War: Irregular Warfare in the Upper South, 1861–1865* (Norman: University of Oklahoma Press, 2004), 6.

17. Sun Tzu, *Art of War*, edited by Ralph D. Sawyer (New York: Perseus, 1994), 61–62, 79.

18. Sun, *Art of War*, 177.

19. Mahan, *An Elementary Treatise*, 31.

20. Sun, *Art of War*, 188.

21. Chris Fraser, "The *Mozi* and Just War Theory in Pre-Han Thought," *Journal of Chinese Military History* 5, no. 2 (November 2016), 142. On the difficulty faced by nineteenth century translators who sought to communicate these abstract philosophical between East and West, see Hungdah Chiu, "The Development of

Chinese International Law Terms and the Problem of their Translation into English," *Journal of Asian Studies* 27 (May 1968): 485–501.

22. David A. Graff, "The Chinese Concept of Righteous War," in *The Prism of Just War: Asian and Western Perspectives on the Legitimate Use of Military Force*, edited by Howard M. Hensel, 195–216 (Surrey, U.K.: Ashgate, 2010), 207.

23. In fact, as Roger Thompson has shown, Chinese and European military officials confronted similar issues in similar ways. See Roger Thompson, "Military Dimensions of the 'Boxer Uprising' in Shanxi, 1898–1901," in *Warfare in Chinese History*, edited by Hans van de Ven, 288–320 (Leiden: Brill, 2000).

24. Joanna Waley-Cohen, *The Culture of War in China: Empire and the Military under the Qing Dynasty* (London: I. B. Tauris, 2006), 1. For a similar argument about the integration of military and political affairs well before the Qing dynasty, see Yuri Pines, "A 'Total War'? Rethinking Military Ideology in the *Book of Lord Shang*," *Journal of Chinese Military History* 5, no. 2 (November 2016): 97–134.

25. William T. Rowe, *China's Last Empire: The Great Qing* (Cambridge, Mass.: Harvard University Press, 2009), 15.

26. Rowe, *China's Last Empire*, 23.

27. Further complicating the situation in China, imperial troops often copied Taiping practices. Europeans exercised quite selective judgment—they often condemned what they regarded as the savagery of the Taiping while ignoring the same actions when committed by imperial troops.

28. *American Annual Cyclopedia and Register of Important Events of the Year 1863* (New York: Appleton & Co., 1866), 747.

29. "Particulars of the Revolt," *Daily Evening Bulletin* (San Francisco), March 17, 1863.

30. "Later from Poland—Revolution Progressing," *Daily Cleveland Herald*, April 24, 1863.

31. "The Reaction in North Carolina," *New Haven* (Connecticut) *Daily Palladium*, August 12, 1863.

32. Aaron Sheehan-Dean, *The Calculus of Violence: How Americans Fought the Civil War* (Cambridge, Mass.: Harvard University Press, 2018).

33. Mackey, *The Uncivil War*, 5.

34. Andrew Lang, *In the Wake of War: Military Occupation, Emancipation, and Civil War America* (Baton Rouge: Louisiana State University, 2017), 24.

35. Daniel Sutherland, *A Savage Conflict: The Decisive Role of Guerrillas in the American Civil War* (Chapel Hill: University of North Carolina Press, 2009), ix, 277.

36. Thomas Rosser to Robert E. Lee, January 11, 1864, in United States War Department, *The War of the Rebellion: A Compilation of the Official Records of the*

Union and Confederate Armies, 128 vols. (Washington, D.C.: Government Printing Office, 1880–1901), I, 33: 1081–82 (hereafter *OR*).

37. Lee to Secretary of War, January 25, 1864, *OR*, I, 33: 1120–21.

38. Davis, Message to Congress, May 2, 1864, in Jefferson Davis, *Papers of Jefferson Davis*, Vol. 10: *October 1863–August 1864*, edited by Lynda Crist, Kenneth M. Williams, and Peggy L. Dillard (Baton Rouge: Louisiana State University Press, 1999), 378.

39. "The Civil War in America," *Cork Examiner*, July 11, 1861; "Foreign Intelligence," *Bristol Mercury*, August 31, 1861; "Virginia Irregulars," *Illustrated Times* (London), September 14, 1861.

40. *Illustrated Times* (London), August 29, 1863; "The War in America," *Western Daily Press*, August 22, 1862; "Latest General Intelligence," *Royal Cornwall Gazette, Falmouth Packet, and General Advertiser*, September 4, 1863; and "America," *Daily News* (London), September 8, 1863.

41. Stuart to Russell, July 21, 1862, in *The American Civil War through British Eyes: Dispatches from British Diplomats, Volume 2, April 1862–February 1863*, edited by James J. Barnes and Patience P. Barnes (Kent, Ohio: Kent State University Press, 2005), 140.

42. "American Affairs," March 18, 1862, *London Times*.

43. Kenneth Noe, "Exterminating Savages: The Union Army and Mountain Guerrillas in Southern West Virginia, 1861–1862," in *The Civil War in Appalachia: Collected Essays*, edited by Kenneth W. Noe and Shannon H. Wilson, 104–127 (Knoxville: University of Tennessee Press, 1997); and Andrew Fialka, "Captain Harry Truman: A Case Study of the Union Military's Use of Guerrilla Tactics against the Civilian Population in Civil War Missouri" (Honors thesis, University of Missouri, 2010).

44. Sutherland, *A Savage Conflict*, 277.

45. Eric Stokes, *The Peasant Armed: The Indian Revolt of 1857*, edited by, C. A. Bayly (Oxford: Clarendon, 1986), 3; see also C. A. Bayly, *Empire and Information: Intelligence Gathering and Social Communication in India, 1780–1870* (Cambridge: Cambridge University Press, 1996), 317.

46. Rudrangshu Mukherjee, *Awadh in Revolt 1857–1858: A Study of Popular Resistance* (Delhi: Oxford University Press, 1984), 135–47.

47. Stokes, *The Peasant Armed*, 19.

48. Pramod K. Nayar, *The Great Uprising: India 1857* (New Delhi: Penguin, 2007), 77, 82, 86–87.

49. Bruce Watson, *The Great Indian Mutiny: Colin Campbell and the Campaign at Lucknow* (Westport, Conn.: Praeger, 1991), 20–21.

50. "The Sepoy Mutiny," *New Englander and Yale Review* 17 (May 1859): 357–58.

51. Sangeeta Mediratta, "The Affair of the Greased Cartridge: Traveling Stories,

Unraveling Empires, and the Sepoy Revolt of 1857," *Harvard Asia Quarterly* 14, no. 3 (Fall 2012): 11–12.

52. "The Bengal Terror," *Leader and Saturday Analyst*, August 8, 1857, 756.

53. Isidor Loewenthal, *Revolt of the Sepoys* (New York: Edward O. Jenkins, 1858), 4.

54. *Correspondence Relating to the Civil War in the United States of North America*, Great Britain Foreign Office and Parliament, North America No. 1 series (London: Harrison and Sons, 1862), 125.

55. Nayar, *The Great Uprising*, 127.

56. Stokes, *The Peasant Armed*, 92.

57. Nayar, *The Great Uprising*, 92.

58. C. A. Bayly, *Indian Society and the Making of the British Empire* (Cambridge: Cambridge University Press, 1998), 194.

59. "What Shall We Do with Them?" *Atlantic Monthly* 9 (April 1862): 470.

60. "What Shall We Do with Them?," 471.

61. "What Shall We Do with Them?," 471; see also Merchant of Philadelphia, *The End of the Irrepressible Conflict* (Philadelphia: King & Baird, 1860), 18–19.

62. "The Magazines," *New York Times*, September 30, 1862.

63. Megan Kate Nelson, *Ruin Nation: Destruction and the American Civil War* (Athens: University of Georgia Press, 2012), 107–8.

64. From the *London Times*, December 19, 1861, quoted in "A New Cause of War—The Stone Fleet," *Newark Advocate*, January 10, 1862. Emphasis original.

65. "Blowing Sepoys from the Guns: The Severities of the English in India," *New York Evangelist*, September 24, 1863.

66. "Will Phosphorus Set Wood on Fire," *Scientific American* 11 (December 24, 1862): 407.

67. Edward J. Thompson, "British Atrocities," in *India in 1857: The Revolt against Foreign Rule*, edited by Ainslie T. Embree (Delhi: Chanakaya, 1987), 105–11; and Nayar, *The Great Uprising*, 143.

68. "The British Methods in War," *Harper's Weekly*, February 15, 1862.

69. "J. Bull's 'Stone Blockades,'" *Frank Leslie's Illustrated Newspaper*, February 1, 1862.

70. James Davey, *In Nelson's Wake: The Navy and the Napoleonic Wars* (New Haven, Conn.: Yale University Press, 2015), 71–72.

71. "Two Lessons in Christianity," *Vanity Fair*, February 15, 1862. The British minister to the United States, Lord Lyons, raised the "Stone Fleet" with Secretary of State Seward, who rebuffed the criticism on the grounds that the practice was visibly insufficient, a steady stream of blockade-runners entering and leaving the port regardless of the stones. Brian Jenkins, *Lord Lyons: A Diplomat in an Age of Nationalism and War* (Montreal: McGill-Queen's University Press, 2014), 186.

72. "The Treatment of the Union Prisoners by the Rebel Chivalry," *New York Herald*, November 11, 1863; and "Our Foreign Friends," *Saturday Evening Post*, July 5, 1862.

73. Quoted in Stephen Platt, *Autumn in the Heavenly Kingdom: China, the West, and the Epic Story of the Taiping Civil War* (New York: Vintage, 2012), 288–89.

74. *Richmond Daily Dispatch*, February 17, 1865.

75. *Daily Telegraph*, November 15, 1862.

76. John Bright, "Seizure of the Southern Commissioners," delivered December 4, 1861, in *Speeches on the Public Affairs of the Last Twenty Years by the Rt. Hon. John Bright M.P.*, 2nd ed. (London: John Camden Hotten, 1869), 126.

77. John Kutolowski argues that the Polish crisis played an important role in Civil War diplomacy because, at several key points in 1863, problems in Central Europe distracted European powers from the North American conflict. Both Union and Confederate diplomats observed this phenomenon. John Kutolowski, "The Effect of the Polish Insurrection of 1863 on American Civil War Diplomacy," *Historian* 27, no. 4 (August 1965): 563, 568.

78. "Insurrection in Poland," *New York Times*, February 14, 1863; and "The Uprising in Poland," *New York Times*, February 17, 1863.

79. *Petersburg Daily Express*, April 3, 1863, as quoted in Joseph W. Wieczerzak, *A Polish Chapter in Civil War America: The Effects of the January Insurrection on American Diplomacy and Opinion* (New York: Twayne, 1967), 57–58.

80. Michael Rapport, *Nineteenth-Century Europe* (New York: Palgrave Macmillan), 205.

81. Jerzy Lukowski and Hubert Zawadzki, *A Concise History of Poland* (Cambridge: Cambridge University Press, 2001), 150–52.

82. Rapport, *Nineteenth-Century Europe*, 206; see also Theodore R. Weeks, *Nation and State in Late Imerial Russia: Nationalism and Russification on the Western Frontier, 1863–1914* (Dekalb: Northern Illinois University Press, 1996), 96–97.

83. Liam [?] Balluzreek to Anson Burlingame, November 15, 1865, Anson Burlingame and Edward L. Burlingame Family Papers [MSS14373], Library of Congress, MMC 3190, Box 2.

84. "Poland as It Is," *National Review* (October 1863): 381.

85. "The Insurrection in Poland," *Telegraph*, February 27, 1863.

86. Viscount Stratford de Redcliffe, July 24, 1863 in *Great Britain: Foreign Policy and the Span of Empire, 1689–1971: A Documentary History*, edited by Joel H. Wiener (New York: Chelsea House, 1972), 397.

87. "Russian Atrocities in Poland," *New Hampshire Statesman*, September 30, 1864.

88. "Foreign Correspondence," *Index*, March 12, 1863.

89. Leslie Leavall, "Just War Theory and the Polish Insurrection of 1863"

(unpublished seminar paper, University of North Florida, 2011; in author's possession).

90. "The Russian Ultimatum: The Polish Insurrection," *New York Times*, October 11, 1863.

91. "The Revolution in Poland," *Richmond Daily Dispatch*, September 16, 1863; and "The Polish Insurrection—Barbarous Doings—An Incident," *Richmond Daily Dispatch*, April 4, 1863.

92. "Alexander II and Abraham I," *Richmond Daily Dispatch*, September 16, 1863; see also "Poland," *Richmond Daily Dispatch*, March 2, 1863.

93. Quoted in Warren Reed West, "Contemporary French Opinion on the American Civil War" (PhD dissertation, Johns Hopkins University, Baltimore, 1922), 136–37.

94. Watson, *The Great Indian Mutiny*, 105.

95. Recent Chinese estimates put the death total at 57 million. Platt, *Autumn in the Heavenly Kingdom*, 358–59; Tobie Meyer-Fong, *What Remains: Coming to Terms with Civil War in 19th Century China* (Stanford, Calif.: Stanford University Press, 2013), 1–2.

96. James Buchanan, *Message of the President of the United States to the Two Houses of Congress at the Commencement of the 35th Congress*, 2nd Session, Ex. Doc. No. 22 (Washington, D.C.: House of Representatives, 1858), 84–85.

97. Eric Setzekorn, "Chinese Imperialism, Ethnic Cleansing, and Military History, 1850–1877," *Journal of Chinese Military History* 4 (2015): 91.

98. J. Callery and M. Yvan, "History of the Insurrection in China," in *Western Reports on the Taiping: A Selection of Documents*, edited by Prescott Clarke and J. S. Gregory (Honolulu: University Press of Hawaii, 1982), 117.

99. Platt, *Autumn in the Heavenly Kingdom*, 51.

100. Platt, *Autumn in the Heavenly Kingdom*, 267.

101. W. H. Medhurst and Lewin Bowring, in Clarke and Gregory, *Western Reports*, 159.

102. Mgr. E. Danicourt, in Clarke and Gregory, *Western Reports*, 177.

103. Burlingame to Seward, January 23, 1862, in U.S. Department of State, *Message of the President to the Two Houses of Congress at the Commencement of the 37th Congress, 3rd Session, Ex. Doc. No. 1* (Washington, D.C.: Government Printing Office, 1862), 833.

104. Most of the Western observers who wrote about the revolution emphasized the brutality of both sides. See, for instance, John Scarth, *Twelve Years in China: The People, the Rebels, and the Mandarins, by a British Resident* (Edinburgh: Thomas Constable, 1860).

105. Meyer-Fong, *What Remains*, 7.

106. Rowe, *China's Last Empire*, 184.

107. Arthur Evans Moule, *Personal Recollections of the T'ai-p'ing Rebellion, 1861–1863* (Shanghai: Shanghai Mercury, 1898), 24.

108. Platt, *Autumn in the Heavenly Kingdom*, 51.

109. Diary entry, February 20, 1864, William B. Allen Papers, Library of Congress.

110. Platt, *Autumn in the Heavenly Kingdom*, 21, 211, 215.

111. January 17, 1854, Robert Nelson Diary, vol. 2, Nelson Family Papers, Virginia Museum of History and Culture, Richmond, Virginia.

112. Paul Horton, "Submitting to the 'Shadow of Slavery': The Secession Crisis and Civil War in Alabama's Lawrence County," *Civil War History* 44, no. 2 (June 1998): 111–36; and Rand Dotson, "'The Grave and Scandalous Evil Infected to Your People': The Erosion of Confederate Loyalty in Floyd County, Virginia," *Virginia Magazine of History and Biography* 108 (September 2000): 393–434.

113. Jeffry D. Wert, *Mosby's Rangers: The True Adventures of the Most Famous Command of the Civil War* (New York: Touchstone, 1990); and Charles Wells Russell, ed. *The Memoirs of Colonel John S. Mosby*, reprint (1917; Gaithersburg, Md.: Olde Soldier Books, 1987).

114. Christopher Phillips, *The Rivers Ran Backward: The Civil War and the Remaking of the American Middle Border* (New York: Oxford University Press, 2016), 261.

115. Matthew M. Stith, *Extreme Civil War: Guerrilla Warfare, Environment, and Race on the Trans-Mississippi Frontier* (Baton Rouge: Louisiana State University Press, 2015), 133.

116. Clay Mountcastle, *Punitive War: Confederate Guerrillas and Union Reprisals* (Lawrence: University Press of Kansas, 2009); Sutherland, *A Savage Conflict*; and Noe, "Exterminating Savages."

117. David Kilcullen, *The Accidental Guerrilla: Fighting Small Wars in the Midst of a Big One* (New York: Oxford University Press, 2009), xv.

118. Timothy Snyder, *The Reconstruction of Nations: Poland, Ukraine, Lithuania, Belarus, 1569–1999*. New Haven, Conn.: Yale University Press, 2003), 30.

119. J. N. Westwood, *Endurance and Endeavour: Russian History 1812–1986*, 3rd ed. New York: Oxford University Press, 1987), 80–83.

120. Rapport, *Nineteenth-Century Europe*, 206.

121. Richard J. Evans, *The Pursuit of Power: Europe, 1815–1914* (New York: Viking, 2016), 247.

122. Sutherland, *A Savage War*, 278.

123. Lawrence N. Powell and Michael S. Wayne, "Self Interest and the Decline of Confederate Nationalism," in *The Old South in the Crucible of War*, edited by Harry P. Owen and James J. Cooke, 29–45 (Jackson: University of Mississippi Press, 1983).

124. Preston Pond Jr. to General Franklin, August 20, 1863, Entry #1756, Letters Received 1863 (Box #4), Department of the Gulf, U.S. Provost Marshal Records, RG 393, Part 1, NARA.

125. Philip A. Kuhn, *Rebellion and Its Enemies in Late Imperial China: Militarization and Social Structure, 1796–1864.* (Cambridge, Mass.: Harvard University Press, 1970), 203.

126. Bao quoted in James H. Cole, *The People Versus the Taipings: Bao Lisheng's "Righteous Army of Dongan"* (Berkeley, Calif.: Center for Chinese Studies, 1981), 14–15.

127. Cole, *The People Versus the Taipings*, 18.

128. An important part of this would have been the fact that once they conquered an area, the Taiping imposed a dramatic reorganization of social practices, including new gender norms, all under the aegis of a devout Christianity. S. Y. Teng, *The Taiping Rebellion and the Western Powers: A Comprehensive Survey* (London: Oxford University Press, 1971), 111–24.

129. Rowe, *China's Last Empire*, 193.

130. William Dalrymple, *The Last Mughal: The Fall of a Dynasty: Delhi, 1857* (New York: Vintage, 2006), 20.

131. "The Different Views of the Indian Revolt," *London Examiner*, August 15, 1857.

132. Harry Hearder, *Italy in the Age of the Risorgimento, 1790–1870* (1983; New York: Routledge, 2013), 230–32.

133. Mazzini, "Rules for the Conduct of a Guerrilla War," in *A Cosmopolitanism of Nations: Giuseppe Mazzini's Writings on Democracy, Nation Building, and International Relations*, edited by Stefano Recchia and Nadia Urbinati (Princeton, N.J.: Princeton University Press, 2009), 111.

134. Eliga H. Gould, *Among the Powers of the Earth: The American Revolution and the Making of a New World Empire* (Cambridge, Mass.: Harvard University Press, 2012), 17.

135. Platt, *Autumn in the Heavenly Kingdom*, 149.

136. Quoted in Teng, *The Taiping Rebellion and the Western Powers*, 296.

137. "The Present Condition of Mexico," *Telegraph*, May 5, 1864.

138. Adam Gurowski, *Diary: 1863–'64–'65* (Washington, D.C.: W. H.& O. H. Morrison, 1866), 300.

139. "The Massacre at Fort Pillow," *New York Herald*, April 16, 1864.

140. Washburn to Rawlins, April 23, 1864, *OR*, I, 32(3): 463; see also E. D. Townsend to Edwin Stanton, February 27, 1864, *OR*, I, 34(2): 443.

141. Curtis to Citizens of Kansas City, March 4, 1864, *OR*, I, 34(2): 500.

142. "Jefferson Davis," *Daily Cleveland Herald*, June 5, 1861, reprinted in *Lowell Daily Citizen and News* (Massachusetts), July 20, 1861.

143. "The Massacre in Kansas," *Independent*, August 27, 1863.

144. "The Lawrence Massacre," *New York Herald*, August 24, 1863; and "Feelings of Americans Abroad," *Liberator*, October 4, 1861.

145. "The Rebel Leaders," *Christian Advocate and Journal*, April 10, 1862.

146. "In a Position to be Recognized," *Vanity Fair*, August 24, 1861: 91–92.

147. "Mind Your Eye," *Vanity Fair*, August 10, 1861, 67–68.

148. "To the Public," *Vanity Fair*, August 31, 1861, 201.

CHAPTER 2. ALL WARS ARE WORLD WARS: FOREIGN IMAGINATION AND THE FATE OF NATIONS

1. "The United States and Europe," *Atlantic Monthly* 45 (July 1861): 97.

2. Eric Hobsbawm, *The Age of Capital: 1848–1875* (1975; New York: Vintage, 1996), 47.

3. Tobias Wolff, *In Pharaoh's Army: Memories of the Lost War* (New York: Vintage, 1994), 96.

4. Hugo Grotius, *The Rights of War and Peace* (1625), edited by Richard Tuck and Jean Barbeyrac (Indianapolis: Liberty Fund, 2005), book 2, chap. 1, p. 393. Emphasis original.

5. Grotius, *Rights*, book 1, chap. 2, p. 189. Emphasis original.

6. Grotius, *Rights*, book 1, chap. 4, p. 337.

7. Emer de Vattel, *The Law of Nations* (1758), edited by Béla Kapossy and Richard Whatmore (Indianapolis: Liberty Fund, 2008), book 3, chap. 3, p. 483.

8. Eliga H. Gould, *Among the Powers of the Earth: The American Revolution and the Making of a New World Empire* (Cambridge, Mass.: Harvard University Press, 2012).

9. George L. Prentiss, *The National Crisis: Being and Address, Delivered before the Phi Beta Kappa Society in Dartmouth College*, July 30, 1862 (New York: W. H. Bidwell, 1862), 3, in Civil War Pamphlets, 1861–71, Newberry Library, Chicago.

10. David Armitage, *Civil Wars: A History in Ideas* (New Haven, Conn.: Yale University Press, 2017), 13.

11. Drew Gilpin Faust, *The Creation of Confederate Nationalism: Ideology and Identity in the Civil War South* (Baton Rouge: Louisiana State University Press, 1988), 14–15.

12. Lee to George Washington Custis Lee, January 23, 1861, in *The Civil War: The First Year Told by Those Who Lived It*, edited by Brooks D. Simpson, Stephen W. Sear, and Aaron Sheehan-Dean (New York: Library of America, 2011), 200.

13. Anne Sarah Rubin, *A Shattered Nation: The Rise and Fall of the Confederacy, 186–868* (Chapel Hill: University of North Carolina Press, 2005), 19.

14. Gould, *Among the Powers*, 114.

15. Dennis C. Grube, "Sticky Words? Towards a Theory of Rhetorical Path Dependency," *Australian Journal of Political Science* 51, no. 3 (April 2016): 535.

16. Kay Ryan, "Bait Goat," in *The Best of It: New and Selected Poems* (New York: Grove Press, 2010), 5.

17. Stephanie McCurry, *Confederate Reckoning: Power and Politics in the Civil War South* (Cambridge, Mass.: Harvard University Press, 2010); and Michael Johnson, *Toward a Patriarchal Republic: The Secession of Georgia* (Baton Rouge: Louisiana State University Press, 1999).

18. Adam Gurowski, *Diary, from March 4, 1861, to November 12, 1862* (Boston: Lee & Shepard, 1862), 254.

19. Timothy Roberts, *Distant Revolutions: 1848 and the Challenge to American Exceptionalism* (Charlottesville: University of Virginia Press, 2009), 14–15.

20. Adam I. P. Smith, *The Stormy Present: Conservatism and the Problem of Slavery in Northern Politics, 1846–1865* (Chapel Hill: University of North Carolina Press, 2017), 28.

21. Amy Greenberg, *Manifest Manhood and the Antebellum American Empire* (Cambridge: Cambridge University Press, 2005), 100. This was true after the Civil War as well. Gregory P. Downs, "The Mexicanization of American Politics: The United States' Transnational Path from Civil War to Stabilization," *American Historical Review* 117, no. 2 (April 2012): 387–409.

22. Timothy J. Henderson, *A Glorious Defeat: Mexico and Its War with the United States* (New York: Hill & Wang, 2007), 22. See also Amy S. Greenberg, *A Wicked War: Polk, Clay, Lincoln, and the 1846 U.S. Invasion of Mexico* (New York: Knopf, 2012), 56–57.

23. Peter Guardino, *The Dead March: A History of the Mexican-American War* (Cambridge, Mass.: Harvard University Press, 2017), 12–13.

24. Brian Hamnett, "Benito Juárez, Early Liberalism, and the Regional Politics of Oaxaca, 1828–1853," *Bulletin of Latin American Research* 10, no. 1 (1991): 9.

25. Henderson, *A Glorious Defeat*, 144–45; and "The Revolution in Mexico," *New Orleans Daily Creole*, November 24, 1856.

26. "Latest from Yucatan," *Tri-Weekly Flag & Advertiser* (Montgomery, Alabama), June 13, 1848; see also "Intelligence from Mexico," *New York Herald*, June 21, 1848; "Latest from Mexico," *Weekly Raleigh Register and North Carolina Gazette*, June 28, 1848; and "Later from Mexico," *The Press* (Philadelphia), December 28, 1857.

27. "Late from Mexico," *National Anti-Slavery Standard*, January 9, 1845; see also Guardino, *The Dead March*, 25–28.

28. Nelson A. Reed, *The Caste War of the Yucatán*, rev. ed. (Stanford, Calif.: Stanford University Press, 2001), 114–15, 122–23; and "Latest from Mexico," *Macon Weekly Telegraph*, April 29, 1853.

29. "Later from Yucatan," *Baltimore Sun*, April 17, 1848.

30. Hugh Dubrulle, *Ambivalent Nation: How Britain Imagined the American Civil War* (Baton Rouge: Louisiana State University Press, 2018), 220.

31. "It Is Now about Six Months," *London Times*, December 6, 1861.

32. "Late from Mexico," *New Orleans Picayune*, January 12, 1849; "From Mexico," *New Orleans Picayune*, September 8, 1849; and *San Antonio Ledger and Texan*, April 24, 1858.

33. Terry Rugeley, *Yucatán's Maya Peasantry and the Origins of the Caste War* (Austin: University of Texas Press, 1996); Reed, *The Caste War of Yucatán*; and Terry Rugeley, *Rebellion Now and Forever: Mayas, Hispanics, and Caste War Violence in Yucatán, 1800–1880* (Stanford, Calif.: Stanford University Press, 2009).

34. Quoted in Smith, *The Stormy Present*, 168. The speaker was referring to all the regional challenges that Mexico City faced, not just the Caste War.

35. "The Decadence of the Tartars," *Daily Ohio Statesman*, December 7, 1865.

36. "Ningpo: Letter from Dr. MacGowan," *Missionary Magazine* 35 (August 1854): 354. See also "The Chinese Rebellion," *Philadelphia Inquirer*, October 21, 1861.

37. "From China," *Boston Daily Advertiser*, September 22, 1856.

38. Elizabeth J. Perry, *Challenging the Mandate of Heaven: Social Protest and State Power in China* (New York: Routledge, 2015), ix.

39. William T. Rowe, *China's Last Empire: The Great Qing* (Cambridge, Mass.: Harvard University Press, 2009).

40. Stephen R. Platt, *Imperial Twilight: The Opium War and the End of China's Last Golden Age* (New York: Knopf, 2018), xxiv.

41. Rowe, *China's Last Empire*, 173.

42. Wetmore & Co. to Robert McLane, July 15, 1865, in James Buchanan, *Message of the President of the United States to the Two Houses of Congress at the Commencement of the 35th Congress*, 2nd Session, Ex. Doc. No. 22 (Washington, D.C.: House of Representatives, 1858), 371.

43. Philip A. Kuhn, "The Taiping Rebellion," in *The Cambridge History of China*, vol. 10: *Late Ch'ing, 1800–1911*, part 1, edited by John K. Fairbank, 264–317 (Cambridge: Cambridge University Press, 1978), 301.

44. "Later from China," *San Francisco Bulletin*, June 25, 1861.

45. "Later from China," *San Francisco Bulletin*, February 12, 1862. See also "Later from China," *San Francisco Bulletin*, March 25, 1862; and "Present State of the Rebellion in China," *New York Evangelist*, July 3, 1862.

46. "Letter from Mr. Williams," *Missionary Herald* 51 (June 1855): 167.

47. Robert McClune, quoted in Prescott Clarke and J. S. Gregory, eds., *Western Reports on the Taiping: A Selection of Documents*, (Honolulu: University Press of Hawai'i, 1982), 133.

48. "The English and French Troubles in China," *Philadelphia Inquirer*, August 15, 1862.

49. Cemil Aydin, "Regions and Empires in the Political History of the Long Nineteenth Century," in *An Emerging Modern World, 1750–1870*, edited by Sebastian Conrad and Jürgen Osterhammel (Cambridge, Mass.: Belknap Press, 2018), 112. This sort of thinking was not necessarily confined to the West. Peter C. Perdue argues that the Qing oscillated between a racialist approach to the diverse peoples that came within the empire's power, which excluded and marginalized them, and a culturalist approach, which recognized the possibility of acculturating foreign people into the empire provided they made the change. Peter C. Perdue, "Erasing the Empire, Re-Racing the Nation: Racialism and Culturalism in Imperial China," in *Imperial Formations*, edited by Laura Ann Stoler, Carole McGranahan, and Peter C. Perdue (Santa Fe, N.M.: School for Advanced Research Press, 2007), 141–69.

50. Aaron Sheehan-Dean, *The Calculus of Violence: How Americans Fought the Civil War* (Cambridge, Mass.: Harvard University Press, 2018), 223.

51. Michel-Rolph Trouillot, *Silencing the Past: Power and the Production of History* (Boston: Beacon, 1995), 73.

52. McCurry, *Confederate Reckoning*; and Steven Hahn, *The Political Worlds of Slavery and Freedom* (Cambridge, Mass.: Harvard University Press, 2009).

53. Steven Hahn, *A Nation under Our Feet: Black Political Struggles in the Rural South from Slavery to the Great Migration* (Cambridge, Mass.: Belknap Press, 2003), 15.

54. Julius Scott, *The Common Wind: Afro-American Currents in the Age of the Haitian Revolution* (London: Verso, 2018), 118.

55. Hahn, *Political Worlds*, 98.

56. Hahn, *Political Worlds*, 94; and Carolyn E. Fick, *The Making of Haiti: The Saint Domingue Revolution from Below* (Knoxville: University of Tennessee Press, 1990), 1.

57. Caitlin Fitz, *Our Sister Republics: The United States in an Age of American Revolutions* (New York: Norton, 2016), 9–10, 13.

58. Quoted in Fitz, *Our Sister Republics*, 208.

59. "The Chinese Rebels," *New York Observer and Chronicle* 37 (April 14, 1859): 114.

60. Only Hong Xiuquan, the Taiping leader, and his cousin and advisor, Hong Rengan, studied with missionaries, so the question of how this language permeated Taiping writings remains unclear.

61. "Manifesto on the Right to the Throne," in *The Taiping Rebellion: History and Documents*, vol. 2, *Documents and Comments*, edited by Michael Franz and Chung-li Chang (Seattle: University of Washington Press, 1971), 78–79.

62. Historians have been equally unsure of what to call the event. Wong Ching Him Felix, "The Images of the Taiping Heavenly Kingdom as Shown in the Publications in France, Germany, and Italy during the Second Half of the Nineteenth Century," *Journal of Chinese Studies* 55 (July 2012): 148–49. Both Stephen Platt and Tobie Meyer-Fong have called on scholars to rename this conflict the Taiping Civil War. I find their argument persuasive, although in much of what follows I use "rebellion" because that was the language of Western observers at the time. Stephen R. Platt, *Autumn in the Heavenly Kingdom: China, the West, and the Epic Story of the Taiping Civil War* (New York: Vintage, 2012), xxvii–xxviii.

63. Seward to Burlingame, March 6, 1862, in U.S. Department of State, *Message of the President of the United States to the two houses of Congress at the Commencement of the 37th Congress, Third Session, Ex. Doc. No. 1* (Washington, D.C.: Government Printing Office, 1862), 839.

64. Walter Stahr, *Seward: Lincoln's Indispensable Man* (New York: Simon and Schuster, 2012), 430.

65. "The Revolution in China," *Daily National Intelligencer*, December 29, 1857.

66. Abraham Lincoln, "A Proclamation," April 15, 1861, in *Papers of Abraham Lincoln*, vol. 4, edited by Roy P. Basler (New Brunswick, N.J.: Rutgers University Press), 332.

67. Gaines Foster, "What's Not in a Name: The Naming of the American Civil War," *Journal of the Civil War Era* 8, no. 3 (September 2018): 416–54.

68. *Morning Post* (London), January 7, 1861.

69. "Tremendous Effects to Britain of the American Break-Up," *Dundee Courier*, January 23, 1861.

70. "England's Duty to America," *Dundee (U.K.) Courier*, April 29, 1861.

71. Robert Zaller, "What Does the English Revolution Mean? Recent Historiographical Interpretations of Seventeenth Century England," *Albion: A Quarterly Journal Concerned with British Studies* 18, no. 4 (Winter 1986): 621; see also Blair Worden, *The English Civil Wars, 1640–1660* (London: Weidenfeld & Nicolson, 2009), 2.

72. Christopher Hill, "The Word 'Revolution' in Seventeenth-Century England," in *For Veronica Wedgewood These: Studies in Seventeenth-Century History*, edited by Richard Ollard and Panela Tudor-Craig (London: William Collins, 1986), 139.

73. Quoted in Hill, "The Word 'Revolution,'" 144.

74. Hill, "The Word 'Revolution,'" 148.

75. Timothy Lang, *The Victorians and the Stuart Heritage: Interpretations of a Discordant Past* (New York: Cambridge University Press, 1995), 3.

76. Lang, *The Victorians and the Stuart Heritage*, 51.

77. Lang, *The Victorians and the Stuart Heritage*, 124. See also William MacDonald, "English Historians Repeating Themselves: The Refining of the Whig Interpretation of the English Revolution and Civil War," *Journal of Thought* 7, no. 3 (July 1972): 167.

78. *Daily Telegraph*, May 16, 1861.

79. *Daily Telegraph*, September 28, 1863.

80. *Daily Telegraph*, December 10, 1863.

81. Seward to Lyons, May 1, 1861, *Correspondence Relating to the Civil War in the United States of North America*, Great Britain Foreign Office and Parliament, North America No. 1 series (London: Harrison and Sons, 1862), 32.

82. Lyons to Russell, May 2, 1861, in *Correspondence Relating to the Civil War*, 30.

83. Russell to Lyons, August 2, 1861, in *Correspondence Relating to the Civil War*, 161.

84. Armitage, *Civil Wars*, 131–32.

85. Armitage, *Civil Wars*, 133–34.

86. *Daily Telegraph*, June 16, 1864.

87. Stève Sainlaude, *France and the American Civil War: A Diplomatic History* (Chapel Hill: University of North Carolina Press, 2018), 108.

88. "Letter from New York," *San Francisco Bulletin*, July 28, 1862.

89. "Public Executions in China," *The Friend* (Honolulu), May 1, 1865.

90. "The Lounger," *Harper's Weekly*, October 24, 1863.

91. *Third Annual Address of President Jefferson Davis*, 1864 (London: Saunders, Otley, 1864), 33.

92. *Southern Historical Society Papers* 52 (1930): 172.

93. "Progress of the War," *Richmond Daily Dispatch*, January 23, 1863.

94. Alexander Stephens, "Cornerstone" Speech, March 21, 1861, available at http://teachingamericanhistory.org/library/document/cornerstone-speech/.

95. Faust, *The Creation of Confederate Nationalism*, 13.

96. Augustus F. Lindley, *Ti-ping tien-kwoh: The History of the Ti-Ping Revolution* (London: Day & Son, 1866), 95–96.

97. "The Emperor Napoleon's American Proposals," *Richmond Daily Dispatch*, February 20, 1863.

98. Theodore R. Weeks, *Nation and State in Late Imperial Russia: Nationalism and Russification on the Western Frontier, 1863–1914* (Dekalb: Northern Illinois University Press, 1996), 93–94.

99. "Poland," *Richmond Daily Dispatch*, March 25, 1863. See also "The Polish Insurrection," *Richmond Daily Dispatch*, April 4, 1863.

100. "Certified Vanity," *Richmond Daily Dispatch*, April 4, 1863.

101. "The Revolution in Poland," *Richmond Daily Dispatch*, April 6, 1863.

102. Quoted in Albert Woldman, *Lincoln and the Russians* (Cleveland, Ohio: World Publishing, 1952), 65.

103. "The Executive Departments," *Richmond Daily Dispatch*, December 15, 1863.

104. An excellent illustration of this dilemma can be found in Yonatan Eyal, "A Romantic Realist: George Nicholas Sanders and the Dilemmas of Southern International Engagement," *Journal of Southern History* 78 (February 2012): 107–30, where the author addresses the tension between a "chauvinistic proslavery ideology and [a] cosmopolitan commitment to worldwide republican revolution" (19).

105. Richard Stites, *The Four Horsemen: Riding to Liberty in Post-Napoleonic Europe* (New York: Oxford University Press, 2014), 10.

106. Stites, *The Four Horsemen*, 11.

107. Stites, *The Four Horsemen*, 16.

108. Stites, *The Four Horsemen*, 19.

109. Leo Tolstoy, *Anna Karenina*, trans., Richard Pevear and Larissa Volokhonsky (New York: Penguin, 2004), 1.

110. Vattel, *Law of Nations*, book 2, chap. 3, p. 489.

111. Warren Reed West, "Contemporary French Opinion on the American Civil War" (PhD dissertation, Johns Hopkins University, Baltimore, 1922), vii.

112. Stites, *The Four Horsemen*, 224.

113. Stites, *The Four Horsemen*, 239.

114. Platt, *Autumn in the Heavenly Kingdom*, 29–38.

115. Platt, *Autumn in the Heavenly Kingdom*, 45–49.

116. Nearly all the reports are in "The Early Years," in *Western Reports on the Taiping: A Selection of Documents*, edited by Prescott Clarke and J. S. Gregory, 40–55 (Honolulu: University Press of Hawaii, 1982).

117. "Report by T. T. Meadows," in *Western Reports on the Taiping*, 9. See also John Scarth, *Twelve Years in China: The People, the Rebels, and the Mandarins, by a British Resident* (Edinburgh: Thomas Constable, 1860), 132.

118. "Report from the *Chinese Repository*, vol. XX," in *Western Reports on the Taiping*, 9.

119. Thomas Taylor Meadows, *The Chinese and their Rebellions* (London: Smith, Elder, 1856), 118. Emphasis original.

120. My effort here responds partly to the call of historian of China Tobie Meyer-Fong, who argues that "terming these events [the Taiping conflict] a 'civil war' rather a rebellion or a revolutionary movement allows the historian to think outside these inevitable timelines, to engage with other regional histories comparatively and beyond the strictures imposed by Chinese (or American) exceptionalism. It facilitates attention to the war's global context and to the human suffering it caused." Tobie Meyer-Fong, "Where the War Ended: Violence, Community, and

Commemoration in China's Nineteenth-Century Civil War," *American Historical Review* 120 (December 2015): 1724.

121. "Report by A de Bourboulon," in *Western Reports on the Taiping*, 90.

122. General Correspondence, 1852–1853, Box 1, Humphrey Marshall Papers, Library of Congress.

123. Marshall to Perry, Shanghai, May 13, 1853, Box 1, Humphrey Marshall Papers, Library of Congress.

124. Scarth, *Twelve Years in China*, 277.

125. Platt, *Autumn in the Heavenly Kingdom*, 277.

126. Beth Lew-Williams, *The Chinese Must Go: Violence, Exclusion, and the Making of the Alien in America* (Cambridge, Mass.: Harvard University Press, 2018), 172.

127. Rowe, *China's Last Empire*, 202.

128. Gould, *Among the Powers*, 113.

129. S. Y. Teng, *The Taiping Rebellion and the Western Powers: A Comprehensive Survey* (London: Oxford University Press, 1971), 182–83, 201.

130. Teng, *The Taiping Rebellion*, 283.

131. Platt, *Autumn in the Heavenly Kingdom*, 170–73.

132. Teng, *The Taiping Rebellion*, 173. See also Platt, *Autumn in the Heavenly Kingdom*, xxvi; and Kuhn, "The Taiping Rebellion," 304.

133. Orlando Figes, *The Crimean War: A History* (New York: Metropolitan, 2010), 80.

134. "What Can Be Done for Poland," *Telegraph*, March 17, 1863. Emphasis original.

135. Adam Gurowski, *Diary, from November 18, 1862 to October 18, 1863*, vol. 2 (New York: Carleton, 1864), 201.

136. Richard Cobden to Charles Sumner, August 7, 1863, in "Letters of Richard Cobden to Charles Sumner, 1862–1865," *American Historical Review* 2 (January 1897): 312–13.

137. Rev. Joshua Leavitt, "Poland," *New Englander*, April 1864, 12, Massachusetts Historical Society, Boston.

138. The Polish émigré Adam Gurowski, who served as a translator in the State Department, tracked European opinion carefully. See, for instance, Gurowski, *Diary, from March 4, 1861, to November 12, 1862*, 26–27.

139. Howard Jones, *Union in Peril: The Crisis over British Intervention in the Civil War* (Chapel Hill: University of North Carolina Press, 1992); and Howard Jones, *Blue and Gray Diplomacy: A History of Union and Confederate Foreign Relations* (Chapel Hill: University of North Carolina Press, 2010).

140. Richard J. M. Blackett, *Divided Hearts: Britain and the American Civil War* (Baton Rouge: Louisiana State University Press, 2001).

141. Don H. Doyle, *The Cause of all the World: An International History of the American Civil War* (New York: Basic Books, 2014); see also James M. McPherson, "'The Whole Family of Man:' Lincoln and the Last Best Hope Abroad," in *The Union, the Confederacy, and the Atlantic Rim*, edited by Robert E. May, 131–58 (West Lafayette, Ind.: Purdue University Press, 1995).

142. Letter to the *London Morning Post*, February 22, 1862, in *Henry Hotze, Confederate Propagandist: Selected Writings on Revolution Recognition, and Race*, edited by Lonnie A. Burnett (Tuscaloosa: University of Alabama Press, 2008), 117.

143. *The Union, the Constitution, and the Laws. Secession, A National Crime and Curse: A Discourse Delivered in The Tabernacle Church, Philadelphia*. National Fast Day April 30, 1863. Daniel C. Eddy. Philadelphia: American Baptist Publication Society, 1863), 15. In *Civil War Pamphlets*, vol. 1, Newberry Library, Chicago.

144. William E. Gienapp and Erica L. Gienapp, eds., *The Civil War Diary of Gideon Welles, Lincoln's Secretary of the Navy* (Urbana: University of Illinois Press, 2014), 298.

145. Gienapp and Gienapp, *Diary of Gideon Welles*, 317, 320.

146. Woldman, *Lincoln and the Russians*, 157.

147. Arthur Jaffray, "European View of our Great Struggle A Candid and Generous Englishman," *London Daily News*, June 11, 1862, reprinted in *New York Times*, July 10, 1862.

CHAPTER 3. THE CENTER HOLDS: AUTHORITY IN THE NINETEENTH CENTURY

1. C. A. Bayly, *The Birth of the Modern World, 1780–1914* (Malden, Mass.: Blackwell, 2004), 41.

2. Jürgen Osterhammel, *The Transformation of the World: A Global History of the World* (Princeton, N.J.: Princeton University Press, 2014), 466; see also Jane Burbank and Mark von Hagen, "Coming in the Territory: Uncertainty and Empire," in *Russian Empire: Space, People, Power, 1700–1930*, edited by Jane Burbank, Mark von Hagen, and Anatolyi Remnev (Bloomington: Indiana University Press, 2007), 1–2.

3. Osterhammel, *The Transformation of the World*, 392, 405, 427, 466. This perspective had earlier advocates—in 1982 V. G. Kiernan argued that "Europe's 19th century is known as the Age of Nationalism, but might better be called that of Imperialism"—but Osterhammel offers the fullest reformulation of the argument. V. G. Kiernan, *Colonial Empires and Armies, 1815–1960* (1982; Montreal, CA: McGill-Queen's University Press, 1998), xi.

4. Cemil Aydin, "Regions and Empires in the Political History of the Long Nineteenth Century," in *An Emerging Modern World, 1750–1870*, edited by Sebas-

tian Conrad and Jürgen Osterhammel, 35–247 (Cambridge, Mass.: Belknap Press, 2018).

5. Tony Ballentyne and Antoinette Burton, "Empires and the Reach of the Global," in *A World Connecting, 1879–1945*, edited by Emily Rosenberg, 285–434 (Cambridge, Mass.: Harvard University Press, 2012), 294.

6. Peter J. Taylor, "The State as Container: Territoriality in the Modern World-System," *Progress in Human Geography* 18, no. 2 (June 1994): 151–62.

7. Anthony Pagden, *Lords of All the World: Ideologies of Empire in Spain, Britain, and France, c. 1500–c.1800* (New Haven, Conn.: Yale University Press, 1995).

8. Timothy Lang, *The Victorians and the Stuart Heritage: Interpretations of a Discordant Past* (New York: Cambridge University Press, 1995), 218.

9. Norman Etherington, *Theories of Imperialism: War, Conquest and Capital* (London: Croom Helm, 1984), 2.

10. Paul A. Kramer, "Power and Connections: Imperial Histories of the United States in the World," *American Historical Review* 116, no. 5(December 2011): 1359.

11. Michael W. Doyle, *Empires* (Ithaca, N.Y.: Cornell University Press, 1986), 21.

12. Eric Stokes, *The Peasant Armed: The Indian Revolt of 1857*, ed. C. A. Bayly (Oxford: Clarendon, 1986), 3.

13. April 19, 1858; quoted in Rudrangshu Mukherjee, *Awadh in Revolt 1857–1858: A Study of Popular Resistance* (New Delhi: Permanent Black, 2002), 170.

14. "The Rev. J. P. Mursell on British Sovereignty in India," *Leicestershire Mercury and General Advertiser for the Midland Counties*, December 18, 1858.

15. "The Sepoy Mutiny," *New Englander and Yale Review* 17 (May 1859): 358.

16. Francis F. Stockwell diary, September 29, 1857, Massachusetts Historical Society, Boston.

17. Francis F. Stockwell diary, December 31, 1857, Massachusetts Historical Society, Boston.

18. Quoted in Pramod K. Nayar, *The Great Uprising: India, 1857* (New Delhi: Penguin, 2007), 196.

19. C. A. Bayly, *Indian Society and the Making of the British Empire* (Cambridge: Cambridge University Press, 1998), 181.

20. William Dalrymple, *The Last Mughal: The Fall of a Dynasty: Delhi, 1857* (New York: Vintage, 2006), 19.

21. Thavolia Glymph, "Rose's War and the Gendered Politics of a Slave Insurgency in the Civil War," *Journal of the Civil War Era* 3 (December 2013): 520.

22. It is also true that actions like enslaved people's efforts to achieve freedom could aggregate and take on importance within the larger context. Beth Lew-Williams makes a similar point regarding the ways that the efforts of Chinese immigrants in the United States who resisted their forcible expulsion from northwestern communities in the 1860s and 1870s compelled changes in U.S.–China

diplomacy. She calls this a "trans-scalar" process. Beth Lew-Williams, *The Chinese Must Go: Violence, Exclusion, and the Making of the Alien in America* (Cambridge, Mass.: Harvard University Press, 2018), 10–11.

23. Jonathan Spence, *God's Heavenly Kingdom: The Taiping Heavenly Kingdom of Hong Xiuquan* (New York: Norton, 1996).

24. Platt, *Autumn in the Heavenly Kingdom*, 161.

25. Platt, *Autumn in the Heavenly Kingdom*, xxvii; see also Wong Ching Him Felix, "The Images of the Taiping Heavenly Kingdom as Shown in the Publications in France, Germany, and Italy during the Second Half of the Nineteenth Century," *Journal of Chinese Studies* 55 (July 2012), 152.

26. JB to "my dear sister," Peking, June 2, 1863, Anson Burlingame and Edward L. Burlingame Family Papers [MSS14373], Library of Congress, MMC 3190, Box 3.

27. Augustus F. Lindley, *Ti-ping tien-kwoh: The History of the Ti-Ping Revolution* (London: Day & Son, 1866). Lindley shared this attitude, writing, "at length, during the reign of the last emperor, the national feeling could no longer be controlled, and in the year 1850 the great Ti-ping rebellion burst forth" (101).

28. Philip A. Kuhn, "The Taiping Rebellion," in *The Cambridge History of China*, vol. 10, *Late Ch'ing, 1800–1911*, part 1, edited by John K. Fairbank (Cambridge: Cambridge University Press, 1978), 276; see also Tobie Meyer-Fong, *What Remains: Coming to Terms With Civil War in 19th Century Chin* (Stanford, Calif.: Stanford University Press, 2013), 5.

29. Arthur Evans Moule, *Personal Recollections of the T'ai-p'ing Rebellion, 1861–1863* (Shanghai: Shanghai Mercury, 1898), 4.

30. "Report from the North China Herald," in *Western Reports on the Taiping: A Selection of Documents*, edited by Prescott Clarke and J. S. Gregory (Honolulu: University Press of Hawaii, 1982), 27.

31. Quoted in Platt, *Autumn in the Heavenly Kingdom*, 179.

32. Platt, *Autumn in the Heavenly Kingdom*, 181.

33. "Letter from I. J. Roberts," in *Western Reports on the Taiping*, 20.

34. Diary entry, June 13, 1854, William B. Allen Papers, Library of Congress.

35. Quoted in Platt, *Autumn in the Heavenly Kingdom*, 320. In 1860, when British forces compelled the royal family and court to abandon Beijing and burned the summer palace as punishment, the Qing signed the Beijing Convention, giving Westerners much greater trading access. In their absence, Prince Gong was left in charge. William T. Rowe notes, "Prince Gong had shown unanticipated competence under the circumstances and gained the respect of the terrifying Westerners with whom he dealt." The conversation between Gong and Burlingame is a good example of his diplomatic skill. William T. Rowe, *China's Last Empire: The Great Qing* (Cambridge, Mass.: Harvard University Press, 2009), 201–2.

36. William Minns Tileston to Mary Tree Tileston, May 13, 1864, William Minns Tileston II Papers, Massachusetts Historical Society, Boston.

37. Platt, *Autumn in the Heavenly Kingdom*, 89.

38. Peter Parker, "Proclamation to All U.S. Citizens in China," January 5, 1855, in James Buchanan, *Message of the President of the United States to the Two Houses of Congress at the Commencement of the 35th Congress*, 2nd Session, Ex. Doc. No. 22 (Washington, D.C.: House of Representatives, 1858).

39. *N.C. Herald*, November 12, 1864, in S. Y. Teng, *The Taiping Rebellion and the Western Powers: A Comprehensive Survey* (London: Oxford University Press, 1971), 339.

40. Burlingame's Speech in New York City, June 23, 1868, in *Official Papers of the Chinese Legation* (Berlin: S. Calvary & Co., n.d.), Correspondence covers 1867–1869, 23, Anson Burlingame and Edward L. Burlingame Family Papers [MSS14373], Library of Congress, MMC 3190, Boxes 2.

41. John Pomfret, *The Beautiful Country and the Middle Kingdom: America and China, 1776 to the Present* (New York: Picador, 2016), 48.

42. Burlingame to Seward, December 24, 1861, *Papers Relating to Foreign Affairs*, part 2 (Washington, D.C.: Government Printing Office, 1862), 826.

43. Adam Gurowski, *Diary: 1863–'64–'65* (Washington, D.C.: W. H.& O. H. Morrison, 1866), 66.

44. Stephen V. Ash, *When the Yankees Came: Conflict and Chaos in the Occupied South* (Chapel Hill: University of North Carolina Press, 1995); Gary W. Gallagher, *The Confederate War* (Cambridge: Harvard University Press, 1997); Anne Sarah Rubin, *A Shattered Nation: The Rise and Fall of the Confederacy, 1861–1868* (Chapel Hill: University of North Carolina Press, 2005); Aaron Sheehan-Dean, *Why Confederates Fought: Family and Nation in Civil War Virginia* (Chapel Hill: University of North Carolina Press, 2007); and Michael T. Bernath, *Confederate Minds: The Struggle for Intellectual Independence in the Civil War South* (Chapel Hill: University of North Carolina Press, 2010).

45. William Freehling, *The South vs. The South: How Anti-Confederate Southerners Shaped the Course of the Civil War* (New York: Oxford University Press, 2002); and Armistead Robinson, *Bitter Fruits of Bondage: The Demise of Slavery and the Collapse of the Confederacy, 1861–1865* (Charlottesville: University Press of Virginia, 2005).

46. Lorien Foote, *The Yankee Plague: Escaped Union Prisoners and the Collapse of the Confederacy* (Chapel Hill: University of North Carolina Press, 2016).

47. Joseph W. Wieczerzak, *A Polish Chapter in Civil War America: The Effects of the January Insurrection on American Opinion and Diplomacy* (New York: Twyane, 1967), 15.

48. R. R. Palmer, *The Age of the Democratic Revolution: A Political History of*

Europe and America, 1760–1800, vol. 1 (Princeton, N.J.: Princeton University Press, 1959), 411–35.

49. "Poland," *New York Times*, April 24, 1861; "Arrival of the Asia," *New York Times*, April 26, 1861; "Poland," *New York Times*, April 30, 1861; "Affairs in Poland," *New York Times*, May 12, 1861; "Poland," *New York Times*, October 31, 1861; and "General News," *New York Times*, November 28, 1861.

50. "The Revolt at Cracow," *New York Times*, March 25, 1861. See also "Poland and Russia," *New York Times*, March 29, 1861.

51. "Henry Ward Beecher on the Crisis," *New York Times*, April 15, 1861; "Great Britain," *New York Times*, May 10, 1861; "A Cry of Life from Poland," *New York Times*, May 15, 1861; "The Camp and Country," *New York Times*, November 19, 1861; and "Poland," *New York Times*, March 29, 1863.

52. "Amusements," *New York Times*, May 22, 1863. See also Joshua Leavitt, "Poland," *New Englander*, April 1864, 20.

53. "The Rebellion as Opposed to the Nationality of Race," *New York Times*, June 3, 1863.

54. Thomas Bender, *A Nation among Nations: America's Place in World History* (New York: Hill and Wang, 2006), 127; see also Helena Rosenblatt, *The Lost History of Liberalism: From Ancient Rome to the Twenty-First Century* (Princeton, N.J.: Princeton University Press, 2018), 168–75.

55. David Morris Potter, "The Civil War in the History of the Modern World: A Comparative View," in *The South and the Sectional Conflict* (Baton Rouge: Louisiana State University Press, 1968), 296.

56. "Certified Vanity," *Richmond Daily Dispatch*, April 4, 1863.

57. "The Polish Exiles," *Daily South Carolinian*, September 25, 1864.

58. Abraham Lincoln to Roscoe Conkling, August 26, 1863, in *Collected Works of Abraham Lincoln*, vol. 6, edited by Roy T, Basler (New Brunswick, N.J.: Rutgers University Press, 1953), 410.

59. W. H. Seward to C. M. Clay, May 6, 1861, *Message of the President of the United States to the Two Houses of Congress at the Commencement of the 37th Congress*, Second Session (Washington, D.C.: Government Printing Office, 1861), 293. Seward's statement is a good example of what inspired persistent criticism from Adam Gurowksi. "O, why cannot Mr. Seward learn . . . how not to put gas in such weighty documents? Could Seward learn how to be earnest, precise and clear, without spread-eagleism." Adam Gurowski, *Diary, from November 18, 1862 to October 18, 1863*, vol. 2 (New York: Carleton, 1864), 320. See also Cassius M. Clay to Abraham Lincoln, July 25, 1861, Series I, Lincoln Papers, Library of Congress, Washington, D.C.; "The Empire of the North," *New York Times*, April 8, 1861; and "The Rebellion Necessarily a Failure," *New York Times*, April 25, 1863.

60. Albert Woldman, *Lincoln and the Russians* (Cleveland, Ohio: World Publishing, 1952), 58.

61. Harold E. Blinn, "Seward and the Polish Rebellion of 1863," *American Historical Review* 45 (July 1940): 828–29.

62. William H. Seward to William L. Dayton, May 11, 1863, in *Papers Relating to Foreign Affairs, 1863*, part 1 (Washington, D.C.: Government Printing Office, 1864), 667–68.

63. "The Polish Insurrection and American Opinion," *New York Times*, August 19, 1863.

64. Gurowski, *Diary, from November 18, 1862 to October 18, 1863*, 320.

65. "The Polish Insurrection and American Opinion," *New York Times*, August 19, 1863.

66. "How Poland Is to Be Pacified," *New York Times*, July 26, 1863. See also "The War A War of the People Against the Aristocracy," *New York Times*, May 1, 1862.

67. Woldman, *Lincoln and the Russians*, 64.

68. "A Precedent for Intervention in America," *New York Times*, July 19, 1863.

69. A. N. Sakharov, "The Main Phases and Distinctive Features of Russian Nationalism," in *Russia Nationalism: Past and Present*, edited by Geoffrey Hosking and Robert Service (New York: St. Martin's, 1998), 8.

70. Alexander Polunov, *Russia in the Nineteenth Century: Autocracy, Reform, and Social Change, 1814–1914* (2005; New York: Routledge, 2015), 73.

71. Aileen M. Kelly, *The Discovery of Chance: The Life and Thought of Alexander Herzen* (Cambridge, Mass.: Harvard University Press, 2016), 464.

72. Muraviev quoted in Theodore R. Weeks, *Nation and State in Late Imperial Russia: Nationalism and Russification on the Western Frontier, 1863–1914* (Dekalb: Northern Illinois University Press, 1996), 97.

73. Frederick Walker Lincoln, quoted in "Russia and the Emancipation of the Serfs," *Liberator*, June 17, 1864.

74. Jane Burlingame to "My Dear Father," January 23, 1864, Anson Burlingame and Edward L. Burlingame Family Papers [MSS14373], Library of Congress, MMC 3190, Box 3.

75. "Russia and the Emancipation of the Serfs," *Liberator*, June 17, 1864.

76. Astute observers at the time (and generations of historians since) have harbored no illusions about Russia as a liberal regime. Michael Rapport explains the Russian reforms (mostly serf emancipation but some educational changes as well) as a result of defeat in the Crimean War along with social and economic changes that would be necessary to make Russia a leading power. "The young Tsar was, in fact, a reluctant reformer; he had no desire either to relinquish any power as an autocrat or to unravel Russia's hierarchical society. . . . Those who put the freedom of the serfs on to the statue book were conservative officials, appointed by Nicholas,

who less likely to be influenced by progressive currents." Michael Rapport, *Nineteenth-Century Europe* (New York: Palgrave Macmillan, 2005), 201.

77. Leavitt, "Poland," 22.

78. Woody Holton, *Unruly Americans and the Origins of the Constitution* (New York: Hill & Wang, 2008); and Max Edling, *A Hercules in the Cradle: War, Money, and the American State, 1783–1867* (Chicago: University of Chicago Press, 2014).

79. Philip Paludan, "The Civil War Considered as a Crisis in Law and Order," *American Historical Review* 77 (October 1972): 1013–34.

80. George L. Prentiss, *The National Crisis: Being and Address, Delivered before the Phi Beta Kappa Society in Dartmouth College* (New York: W. H. Bidwell, 1862), 24, in Civil War Pamphlets, 1861–71, Newberry Library.

81. "America Backing Russia against Poland," *Hereford Times*, June 6, 1863.

82. "The American Poland," *New York Times*, December 25, 1864. See also "Tubling Bogus Thunderbolts at Us," *Daily Evening Bulleting* (San Francisco), December 26, 1863; and "The Reform Struggle in Russia," *New York Times*, March 9, 1865. In fact, in the postwar period, white Southerners made exactly that argument—that when the federal government chose a path of vindictive peace, it created another Poland or Ireland. Ann L. Tucker, "To 'Heal the Wounded Spirit': Former Confederates' International Perspective on Reconstruction and Reconciliation," in *Reconciliation After Civil Wars: Global Perspectives*, edited by Paul Quigley and James Hawdon, 187–202 (New York: Routledge, 2018).

83. Writing about why conservative Polish landowners eventually endorsed land reform, Stefan Kieniewicz argues that they "they simply could not run the risk of being considered antinational in a moment of social tension." Stefan Kieniewicz, *The Emancipation of the Polish Peasantry* (Chicago: University of Chicago Press, 1969), 164. Contrast this behavior with that of Southern land- and slaveowners who did not consider being "national" (in the sense of unifying the region's full population) during the U.S. Civil War.

84. "The Tsar's Proclamation of Emancipation in Poland The Epoch of Liberty," *New York Times*, April 12, 1864. See also "Late Reforms in Russia," *New York Times*, April 26, 1864.

85. Bender, *A Nation among Nations*, 177.

86. Gregory P. Downs, "Mapping Power: The Shape of the State in the Post-Civil War American South," in *State Formations: Global Histories and Cultures of Statehood*, edited by John L. Brooke, Julia C. Strauss, and Greg Anderson, 202–14 (Cambridge: Cambridge University Press, 2018).

87. Lincoln to Taylor, December 25, 1863, in Abraham Lincoln, *Collected Works of Abraham Lincoln*, edited by Roy P. Basler (New Brunswick, N.J.: Rutgers University Press, 1953), VII: 93.

88. "Side-lights," *Harper's Weekly*, November 2, 1861.

89. Joanne Melish, *Disowning Slavery: Gradual Emancipation and "Race" in New England, 1780–1860* (Ithaca, N.Y.: Cornell University Press, 2000).

90. William C. Harris, *Lincoln and the Border States: Preserving the Union* (Lawrence: University Press of Kansas, 2011), esp. chap. 5.

91. Glenn D. Brasher, *The Peninsula Campaign and the Necessity of Emancipation: African Americans and the Fight for Freedom* (Chapel Hill: University of North Carolina Press, 2012); Scott Nesbitt and Edward L. Ayers, "Seeing Emancipation: Scale and Freedom in the American South," *Journal of the Civil War Era* 1, no. 1 (March 2011): 3–24; Amy Taylor, *Embattled Freedom: Journeys through the Civil War's Slave Refugee Camps* (Chapel Hill: University of North Carolina Press, 2018); and Joseph P. Reidy, *Illusions of Emancipation: The Pursuit of Freedom & Equality in the Twilight of Slavery* (Chapel Hill: University of North Carolina Press, 2019).

92. Seymour Drescher, *The Mighty Experiment: Free Labor versus Slavery in British Emancipation* (New York: Oxford University Press, 2002); and David Brion Davis, *Inhuman Bondage: The Rise and Fall of Slavery in the New World* (New York: Oxford University Press, 2006).

93. David Baronov, *The Abolition of Slavery in Brazil: The "Liberation" of Africans Through the Emancipation of Capital* (Westport, Conn.: Greenwood Press, 2000); Robert Edgar Conrad, *The Destruction of Brazilian Slavery, 1850–1888* (Berkeley: University of California Press, 1972); and Rebecca Jarvis Scott, *Slave Emancipation in Cuba: The Transition to Free Labor, 1860–1899* (Princeton, N.J.: Princeton University Press, 1985).

94. Cassius Clay, *The Life of Cassius Marcellus Clay: Memoirs, Writings, and Speeches*, vol. 1 (Cincinnati, Ohio: Fletcher Brennan, 1886), 333–34.

95. "The Rebellion," *New York Times*, October 18, 1861. William T. Sherman famously phrased his war goals in very similar language. "I would not coax them, or even meet them half-way, but make them so sick of war that generations would pass away before they would again appeal to it." William T. Sherman to H. W. Halleck, September 17, 1863, in William T. Sherman, *Memoirs of William Tecumseh Sherman*, vol. 1 (New York: Appleton, 1875), 340.

96. "Commissioners from Poland," *Daily Richmond Examiner*, August 31, 1864.

97. Edward Everett, *An Address Delivered at the Inauguration of the Union Club* (Boston: Little Brown, 1863), 34, in Civil War Pamphlets, vol. 1, Newberry Library, Chicago.

98. John Bright, "America——I. The 'Trent' Affair," delivered December 4, 1861, in John Bright, *Selected Speeches of the Right Hon. John Bright, M.P., on Public Questions* (New York: E. P. Dutton, 1914), 61, 68. By "represented in excess," Bright referred to the effect of the three-fifths clause on Southern congressional representation.

99. John Bright, "On the American Question," delivered August 1, 1861, in John Bright, *Speeches of John Bright, M.P. on the American Question* (Boston: Little, Brown, 1865), 7.

100. Howell, March 26, 1863, Trades Union meeting, in Bright, *Speeches of John Bright, M.P. on the American Question*, 188.

101. Charles Drake, "The Rebellion, Its Character, Motive, and Aim: Oration of Charles D. Drake, Delivered at Washington, Missouri, July 4, 1862," in *Civil War Politics*, vol. 1, Newberry Library, Chicago, 3.

102. Francis Lieber, *No Party Now but All for Our Country*, rev. ed. [No. 16] (New York: Loyal Publication Society, 1863), 3.

103. Lieber, *No Party Now but All for Our Country*, 3.

104. Leavitt, "Poland," 16.

105. Dispatch 244, Lyons to Russell, April 11, 1862, in *The American Civil War through British Eyes: Dispatches from British Diplomats*, vol. 2, *April 1862–February 1863*, edited by James J. Barnes and Patience P. Barnes (Kent, Ohio: Kent State University Press, 2005), 8.

106. Gorchakov to Cassius Clay, February 14, 1862, in Clay, *The Life of Cassius Marcellus Clay*, 338.

107. Gortschakoff [Gorchakov] to Baron de Stoeckl, July 10, 1861 in Frank Moore, ed. *The Rebellion Record: A Diary of American Events*, first supplemental vol. (1865; New York: Arno, 1977), 81.

108. "The Work Done by Congress," *Harper's Weekly*, March 14, 1863.

109. Adam Gurowski, *Diary, from March 4, 1861, to November 12, 1862* (Boston: Lee & Shepard, 1862), 108.

110. Thomas R. Metcalf, *Ideologies of the Raj* (Cambridge: Cambridge University Press, 1995), 42.

111. Edward B. Rugemer, *The Problem of Emancipation the Caribbean Roots of the American Civil War* (Baton Rouge: Louisiana State University Press, 2008), 291–301.

112. Metcalf, *Ideologies of the Raj*, 57.

113. Warren Reed West, "Contemporary French Opinion on the American Civil War" (PhD dissertation, Johns Hopkins University, Baltimore, 1922), 25. See also Stève Sainlaude, *France and the American Civil War: A Diplomatic History* (Chapel Hill: University of North Carolina Press, 2019), 166.

114. "What Shall We Do with Them?" *Atlantic Monthly* 9 (April 1862): 472.

115. Elizabeth Varon, *Disunion! The Coming of the American Civil War, 1789–1859* (Chapel Hill: University of North Carolina Press, 2008); and Gallagher, *The Union War*.

116. As it had at the time of the American founding, when, as historian Peter Onuf explains, "America's survival in a dangerous world depended on a strong

central government capable of exercising sovereign authority." Peter S. Onuf, "Epilogue," in *Between Sovereignty and Anarchy: The Politics of Violence in the American Revolutionary Era*, eds. Patrick Griffin, Robert G. Ingram, Peter S. Onuf, and Brian Schoen (Charlottesville: University of Virginia Press, 2015), 289.

117. "The Principle of Centralization," April 13, 1861, *Harper's Weekly*.

118. Bender, *A Nation among Nations*, 170.

119. Amy Greenberg, *Manifest Manhood and the Antebellum American Empire* (Cambridge: Cambridge University Press, 2005), 18–19; A. G. Hopkins, *American Empire: A Global History* (Princeton, N.J.: Princeton University Press 2018); Daniel Immerwahr, *How to Hide an Empire: A History of the Greater United States* (New York: Farrar Strauss and Giroux, 2019); and Kathleen Burk, *The Lion & The Eagle: The Interaction of the British and American Empires, 1783–1972* (London: Bloomsbury, 2018), 1–6.

120. Paul Frymer offers the clearest recent argument on this front: "The imperial aspirations and geographic expansion of the United States over the long nineteenth century represents one of the nation's earliest and most foundational political projects." Paul Frymer, *Building an American Empire: The Era of Territorial and Political Expansion* (Princeton, N.J.: Princeton University Press, 2017), 6.

121. Bender, *Nation among Nations*, 183; see also Charles S. Maier, *Among Empires: America Ascendancy and Its* Predecessors (Cambridge, Mass.: Harvard University Press, 2006), 26.

122. Quoted in Hugh Dubrulle, *Ambivalent Nation: How Britain Imagined the American Civil War* (Baton Rouge: Louisiana State University Press, 2018), 226.

123. Gary Gerstle, *Liberty and Coercion: The Paradox of American Government from the Founding to the Present* (Princeton, N.J.: Princeton University Press, 2015), 4. Gerstle's main objective is to explain the balance of authority between the federal and state governments and how those powers have changed over time, but the story I tell here resonates with the ironies and contradictions he emphasizes in his account.

124. Max Edling, *A Revolution in Favor of Government: Origins of the U.S. Constitution and the Making of the American State* (New York: Oxford University Press, 2003).

125. Edling, *A Hercules in the Cradle*, 246–48.

126. Michael Rappaport, *1848: Year of Revolution* (New York: Basic Books, 2008).

127. Rapport, *Nineteenth-Century Europe*, 200.

128. Robert Tombs, "Politics," in *The Nineteenth Century, Europe, 1789–1914*, ed. T.C.W. Blanning (Oxford: Oxford University Press, 2000), 41.

129. Baron de Jomini, *The Art of War*, translated by G. H. Mendell and W. P. Craighill (1862; Westport, Conn.: Greenwood Press, 1971), 35.

130. For instance, Greg Downs shows that, despite changes wrought by the war, the federal government exercised its authority mostly to remake the structure of the federal system rather than to promote racial justice. Gregory P. Downs, *After Appomattox: Military Occupation and the Ends of War* (Cambridge, Mass.: Harvard University Press, 2015).

131. Don H. Doyle, *The Cause of All Nations: An International History of the Civil War* (New York: Basic Books, 2014); and Bender, *A Nation Among Nations*, 144–46, 178.

EPILOGUE: GHOST NATIONS OF THE NINETEENTH CENTURY

1. William Howard Russell, *My Diary North and South* (Boston: T.O.H.P. Burnham, 1863), 216.

2. Andrew Mack, "Why Big Nations Lose Small Wars: The Politics of Asymmetric Conflicts," *World Politics* 27 (January 1975): 175–200.

3. My emphasis on "failure" should not convey a sense of inevitability. Jeremy Adelman's analysis of the eighteenth-century revolutions against Iberian empires in the Western hemisphere flips the traditional interpretation. Wary of putting the nationalist cart before the independent horse, he argues "the revolutions that made the world anew were the consequence, not the cause, of the end of imperial sovereignty." In midcentury, the only serious "crisis at the core" was in the United States. The British, Russian, and Chinese empires (and, ultimately, the Americans too) remained strong. Adelman identifies the eighteenth-century imperial weakness stemming from imperial rivalries. "Social revolutions transpired when international pressures of competing sovereignties broke down state systems." This never happens at midcentury. Instead, the Americans and Russians cooperated as did the Americans, British, and Russians with the Chinese. Jeremy Adelman, *Sovereignty and Revolution in the Iberian Atlantic World* (Princeton, N.J.: Princeton University Press, 2006), 395, 5.

4. My thinking here owes a debt to Eliga H. Gould's argument about the nature of North American life after the Revolution. *Among the Powers of the Earth: The American Revolution and the Making of a New World Empire* (Cambridge, Mass.: Harvard University Press, 2012), 213–14.

5. William R. Taylor, *Cavalier and Yankee: The Old South and American National Character* (New York: G. Braziller, 1961).

6. Robert Tombs, "Politics," in *The Nineteenth Century, Europe, 1789–1914*, ed. T. C. W. Blanning (Oxford: Oxford University Press, 2000), 41.

7. "A Russian Alliance," *Harper's Weekly*, October 17, 1863.

8. Sonakshi Goyle, "Tracing a Cultural Memory: Commemoration of 1857 in

the Delhi Durbars, 1877, 1903, and 1911," in *The Historical Journal* 59, no. 3(September 2016): 805–6.

9. Darshan Perusek, "Subaltern Consciousness and the Historiography of the Indian Rebellion of 1857," *Novel: A Forum on Fiction* 25, no. 3 (Spring 1992): 286–301.

10. Rattan Lal Hangloo, "1857: A Literary-Historical Perspective," *Icfai University Journal of English Studies* 3, no. 3 (September 2008), 21.

11. Theodore R. Weeks, *Nation and State in Late Imperial Russia: Nationalism and Russification on the Western Frontier, 1863–1914* (Dekalb: Northern Illinois University Press, 1996), 12.

12. Weeks, *Nation and State in Late Imperial Russia*, 13. See also Timothy Snyder, *The Reconstruction of Nations: Poland, Ukraine, Lithuania, Belarus, 1569–1999* (New Haven, Conn.: Yale University Press, 2003), 33, 49.

13. Adam Mickiewicz, *Pan Tadeusz*, translated by Kenneth R. Mackenzie (1834, New York: Hippocrene, 1992), 2.

14. "The Conquered Banner," *New York Freemen*, June 24, 1865.

15. Heather Cox Richardson, *The Death of Reconstruction: Race, Labor and Politics in the Post-Civil War North, 1865–1901* (Cambridge, Mass.: Harvard University Press, 2004).

16. Philip A. Kuhn, "The Taiping Rebellion," in *The Cambridge History of China*, vol. 10: *Late Ch'ing, 1800–1911*, part 1, edited by John K. Fairbank (Cambridge: Cambridge University Press, 1978), 298.

17. Tobie Meyer-Fong, *What Remains: Coming to Terms with Civil War in 19th Century China* (Stanford, Calif.: Stanford University Press, 2013), 3.

18. Meyer-Fong, *What Remains*, 12.

19. Meyer-Fong, *What Remains*, 13; and William T. Rowe, *China's Last Empire: The Great Qing* (Cambridge, Mass.: Harvard University Press, 2009), 185.

BIBLIOGRAPHY

PRIMARY SOURCES

MANUSCRIPT SOURCES

Library of Congress
- William B. Allen Papers
- Anson Burlingame and Edward L. Burlingame Family Papers
- Humphrey Marshall Papers
- Abraham Lincoln Papers

Massachusetts Historical Society, Boston
- Rev. Joshua Leavitt, "Poland," *New Englander*, April 1864
- Francis F. Stockwell Diary
- William Minns Tileston II Papers

National Archives and Records Administration (NARA)
- U.S. Provost Marshal Records, RG 393

Newberry Library, Chicago, Illinois
- Civil War Pamphlets, 1861–71

Virginia Museum of History and Culture, Richmond, Virginia
- Nelson Family Papers

PUBLISHED PRIMARY SOURCES

Baker, George, ed. *The Collected Works of William H. Seward*, Vol. 5. Boston: Houghton Mifflin, 1884.

Barnes, James J., and Patience P. Barnes, eds. *The American Civil War through British Eyes: Dispatches from British Diplomats*, 3 vols. Kent, Ohio: Kent State University Press, 2005.

Bright, John. *Selected Speeches of the Right Hon. John Bright, M.P., on Public Questions*. New York: E. P. Dutton, 1914.

———. *Speeches of John Bright, M.P. on the American Question*. Boston: Little, Brown, 1865.

———. *Speeches on the Public Affairs of the Last Twenty Years by the Rt. Hon. John Bright M.P.*, 2nd ed. London: John Camden Hotten, 1869.

Buchanan, James. *Message of the President of the United States to the Two Houses of Congress at the Commencement of the 35th Congress*, 2nd Session, Ex. Doc. No. 22. Washington, D.C.: House of Representatives, 1858.

Callery, J., and M. Yvan. "History of the Insurrection in China." In *Western Reports on the Taiping: A Selection of Documents*, edited by Prescott Clarke and J. S. Gregory. Honolulu: University Press of Hawaii, 1982.

Clarke, Prescott, and J. S. Gregory, eds. *Western Reports on the Taiping: A Selection of Documents*. Honolulu: University Press of Hawai'i, 1982.

Clausewitz, Carl von. *On War*. Translated by Michael Howard and Peter Paret. 1832. New York: Oxford University Press, 2007.

Clay, Cassisus. *The Life of Cassius Marcellus Clay: Memoirs, Writings, and Speeches*, Vol. 1. Cincinnati, Ohio: Fletcher Brennan, 1886.

Correspondence Relating to the Civil War in the United States of North America. Great Britain Foreign Office and Parliament, North America No. 1 series. London: Harrison and Sons, 1862.

Davis, Jefferson. *Papers of Jefferson Davis*. Vol. 10: *October 1863–August 1864*, edited by Lynda Crist, Kenneth M. Williams, and Peggy L. Dillard. Baton Rouge: Louisiana State University Press, 1999.

Everett, Edward. *An Address Delivered at the Inauguration of the Union Club*. Boston: Little Brown, 1863, 34, in Civil War Pamphlets, vol. 1, Newberry Library, Chicago.

Franz, Michael, and Chung-li Chang, ed. *The Taiping Rebellion: History and Documents*, 3 vols. Seattle: University of Washington Press, 1971.

Gienapp, William E., and Erica L. Gienapp, eds. *The Civil War Diary of Gideon Welles, Lincoln's Secretary of the Navy*. Urbana: University of Illinois Press, 2014.

Grotius, Hugo. *The Rights of War and Peace*. 1625. Edited by Richard Tuck and Jean Barbeyrac. Indianapolis: Liberty Fund, 2005.

Gurowski, Adam. *Diary, from March 4, 1861, to November 12, 1862*. Boston: Lee & Shepard, 1862.

———. *Diary, from November 18, 1862 to October 18, 1863*, Vol. 2. New York: Carleton, 1864.

———, Adam. *Diary: 1863–'64–'65*. Washington, D.C.: W. H. & O. H. Morrison, 1866.

Halleck, H. Wager. *Elements of Military Art and Science*, 3rd ed. New York: D. Appleton, 1862.

Jomini, Baron de. *The Art of War*. Translated by G. H. Mendell and W. P. Craighill. 1862. Westport, Conn.: Greenwood, 1977.

"Letters of Richard Cobden to Charles Sumner, 1862–1865," *American Historical Review* 2 (January 1897): 306–19.

Lieber, Francis. *No Party Now but All for Our Country*, rev. ed. New York: Loyal Publication Society, 1863.

Lincoln, Abraham. *Collected Works of Abraham Lincoln*, Vol. 4, *1860–1861*. Edited by Roy Prentice Basler, Marion Dolores Pratt, Lloyd A. Dunlap. New Brunswick, NJ: Rutgers University Press, 1953.

Lindley, Augustus F. *Ti-ping tien-kwoh: The History of the Ti-Ping Revolution*. London: Day & Son, 1866.

Loewenthal, Isidor. *Revolt of the Sepoys*. New York: Edward O. Jenkins, 1858.

Mahan, D. H. *An Elementary Treatise on Advanced-Guard, Out-Post, and Detachment Service of Troops*. New York: John Wiley, 1862.

Meadows, Thomas Taylor. *The Chinese and Their Rebellions*. London: Smith, Elder, 1856.

Merchant of Philadelphia. *The End of the Irrepressible Conflict*. Philadelphia: King & Baird, 1860.

Mickiewicz, Adam. *Pan Tadeusz*, translated by Kenneth R. Mackenzie. 1834. New York: Hippocrene, 1992.

Moore, Frank, ed. *The Rebellion Record: A Diary of American Events*, first supplemental vol. 1865. New York: Arno, 1977.

Moule, Arthur Evans. *Personal Recollections of the T'ai-p'ing Rebellion, 1861–1863*. Shanghai: Shanghai Mercury, 1898.

Newton, Thomas Wodehouse Legh, ed. *Lord Lyons: A Record of British Diplomacy*, Vol. 1. London: Edward Arnold, 1913.

Prentiss, George L. *The National Crisis: Being and Address, Delivered before the Phi Beta Kappa Society in Dartmouth College*. New York: W. H. Bidwell, 1862. In Civil War Pamphlets, 1861–71, Newberry Library, Chicago.

Recchia, Stefano, and Nadia Urbinati, eds. *A Cosmopolitanism of Nations: Giuseppe Mazzini's Writings on Democracy, Nation Building, and International Relations*. Princeton, N.J.: Princeton University Press, 2009.

Russell, Charles Wells, ed. *The Memoirs of Colonel John S. Mosby*. 1917. Gaithersburg, Md.: Olde Soldier Books, 1987.

Russell, William Howard. *My Diary North and South*. Boston: T.O.H.P. Burnham, 1863.

Scarth, John. *Twelve Years in China: The People, the Rebels, and the Mandarins, by a British Resident*. Edinburgh: Thomas Constable, 1860.

Sherman, William T. *Memoirs of William Tecumseh Sherman*, Vol. 1 (New York: Appleton, 1875.

Sun Tzu. *Art of War*. Edited by Ralph D. Sawyer. New York: Perseus, 1994.

U.S. Department of State, *Message of the President to the Two Houses of Congress at the Commencement of the 37th Congress, 3rd Session, Ex. Doc. No. 1*. Washington, D.C.: Government Printing Office, 1862.

U.S. War Department. *War of the Rebellion: Official Records of the Union and Confederate Armies*. 128 vols. Washington, D.C.: Government Printing Office, 1880–1901.

Vattel, Emer de. *The Law of Nations*. Edited by Béla Kapossy and Richard Whatmore. 1758. Indianapolis: Liberty Fund, 2008.

Wiener, Joel H., ed. *Great Britain: Foreign Policy and the Span of Empire, 1689–1971: A Documentary History*. New York: Chelsea House, 1972.

SECONDARY SOURCES

Adelman, Jeremy. "An Age of Imperial Revolutions." *American Historical Review* (April 2008): 319–40.

———. *Sovereignty and Revolution in the Iberian Atlantic World*. Princeton, N.J.: Princeton University Press, 2006.

American Annual Cyclopedia and Register of Important Events of the Year 1863. New York: Appleton & Co., 1866.

Anderson, Benedict. *Imagined Communities: Reflections on the Origin and Spread of Nationalism*, rev. ed. London: Verso, 1998.

Armitage, David. *Civil Wars: A History in Ideas*. New Haven, Conn.: Yale University Press, 2017.

———. *The Declaration of Independence: A Global History*. Cambridge, Mass.: Harvard University Press, 2008.

Ash, Stephen V. *When the Yankees Came: Conflict and Chaos in the Occupied South*. Chapel Hill: University of North Carolina Press, 1995.

Asprey, Robert B. *War in the Shadows: The Guerrilla in History*. New York: William Morrow, 1994.

Aydin, Cemil. "Regions and Empires in the Political History of the Long Nineteenth Century." In *An Emerging Modern World, 1750–1870*, edited by Sebastian Conrad and Jürgen Osterhammel, 35–247. Cambridge, Mass.: Belknap Press, 2018.

Ayers, Edward L. *In the Presence of Mine Enemies: War in the Heart of America, 1859–1863*. New York: Norton, 2003.

Ballentyne, Tony, and Antoinette Burton. "Empires and the Reach of the Global." In *A World Connecting, 1879–1945*, edited by Emily Rosenberg, 285–434. Cambridge, Mass.: Harvard University Press, 2012.

Balogh, Brian. *A Government Out of Sight: The Mystery of National Authority in the Nineteenth Century*. Cambridge: Cambridge University Press, 2009.

Baronov, David. *The Abolition of Slavery in Brazil: The "Liberation" of Africans through the Emancipation of Capital*. Westport, Conn.: Greenwood Press, 2000.

Bayly, C. A. *The Birth of the Modern World, 1780–1914: Global Connections and Comparisons*. Malden, Mass.: Blackwell, 2004.

———. *Empire and Information: Intelligence Gathering and Social Communication in India, 1780–1870*. Cambridge: Cambridge University Press, 1996.

———. *Indian Society and the Making of the British Empire*. Cambridge: Cambridge University Press, 1998.

Beilein, Joseph M., and Matthew C. Hulbert, eds. *The Civil War Guerrilla: Unfolding the Black Flag in History, Memory, and Myth*. Lexington: University Press of Kentucky, 2015.

Bell, David A. *The First Total War: Napoleon's Europe and the Birth of Warfare as We Know It*. Boston: Houghton Mifflin, 2007.

Bender, Thomas. *A Nation among Nations: America's Place in World History*. New York: Hill and Wang, 2006.

Bensel, Richard Franklin. *Yankee Leviathan: The Origins of Central State Authority in America, 1859–1877*. Cambridge: Cambridge University Press, 1990.

Bernath, Michael T. *Confederate Minds: The Struggle for Intellectual Independence in the Civil War South*. Chapel Hill: University of North Carolina Press, 2010.

Blackett, Richard J. M. *Divided Hearts: Britain and the American Civil War*. Baton Rouge: Louisiana State University Press, 2001.

Blanning, T. C. W., ed. *The Nineteenth Century: Europe, 1789–1914*. Oxford, UK: Oxford University Press, 2000.

Blinn, Harold E. "Seward and the Polish Rebellion of 1863." *American Historical Review* 45 (July 1940): 828–33.

Boot, Max. *Invisible Armies: An Epic History of Guerrilla Warfare from Ancient Times to the Present*. New York: Liveright, 2013.

Brasher, Glenn D. *The Peninsula Campaign and the Necessity of Emancipation: African Americans and the Fight for Freedom*. Chapel Hill: University of North Carolina Press, 2012.

Brooke, John L., Julia C. Strauss, and Greg Anderson. *State Formations: Global Histories and Cultures of Statehood*. Cambridge: Cambridge University Press, 2018.

Burbank, Jane, and Frederick Cooper. *Empires in World History: Power and the Politics of Difference*. Princeton, N.J.: Princeton University Press, 2010.

Burbank, Jane, and Mark von Hagen. "Coming in the Territory: Uncertainty and Empire." In *Russian Empire: Space, People, Power, 1700–1930*, edited by Jane Burbank, Mark von Hagen, and Anatolyi Remnev, 1–29. Bloomington: Indiana University Press, 2007.

Burk, Kathleen. *The Lion & The Eagle: The Interaction of the British and American Empires, 1783–1972*. London: Bloomsbury, 2018.

Burkhardt, George S. *Confederate Rage, Yankee Wrath: No Quarter in the Civil War*. Carbondale: Southern Illinois University Press, 2007.

Burbank, Jane, Mark Von Hagen, and Anatolyi Remnev, eds. *Russian Empire: Space, People, Power, 1700–1930*. Bloomington: Indiana University Press, 2007.

Bushnell, David, and Neill Macaulay. *The Emergence of Latin America in the Nineteenth Century*. New York: Oxford University Press. 1988.

Carmichael, Peter S. *The War for the Common Soldier: How Men Thought, Fought, and Survived in Civil War Armies*. Chapel Hill: University of North Carolina Press, 2018.

Chiu, Hungdah. "The Development of Chinese International Law Terms and the Problem of their Translation into English." *Journal of Asian Studies* 27 (May 1968): 485–501. doi:10.4159/harvard.9780674594838.

Clavin, Matthew J. *Toussaint Louverture and the American Civil War: The Promise and Peril of a Second Haitian Revolution*. 2009: Philadelphia: University of Pennsylvania Press, 2009.

Cole, James H. *The People Versus the Taipings: Bao Lisheng's "Righteous Army of Dongan."* Berkeley, Calif.: Center for Chinese Studies, 1981.

Colley, Linda. *Britons: Forging the Nation, 1707–1837*, rev. ed. New Haven, Conn.: Yale University Press, 2012.

Collier, Richard. *The Great Indian Mutiny: A Dramatic Account of the Sepoy Rebellion*. New York: Dutton, 1964.

Conrad, Robert Edgar. *The Destruction of Brazilian Slavery, 1850–1888*. Berkeley: University of California Press, 1972.

Conrad, Sebastian, and Jürgen Osterhammel, eds. *An Emerging Modern World: 1750–1870*. Cambridge, Mass.: Belknap Press of Harvard University Press, 2018).

Cooper, Frederick, and Ann Laura Stoler, eds. *Tensions of Empire: Colonial Cultures in a Bourgeois World*. Berkeley: University of California Press, 1997.

Dalrymple, William. *The Last Mughal: The Fall of a Dynasty: Delhi, 1857*. New York: Vintage, 2006.

Davey, James. *In Nelson's Wake: The Navy and the Napoleonic Wars*. New Haven, Conn.: Yale University Press, 2015.

Davies, Norman. *God's Playground: A History of Poland*. Vol. 2, *1795 to the Present*. New York: Columbia University Press, 2005.

Davis, David Brion. *Inhuman Bondage: The Rise and Fall of Slavery in the New World*. New York: Oxford University Press, 2006.

Dotson, Rand. "'The Grave and Scandalous Evil Infected to Your People': The

Erosion of Confederate Loyalty in Floyd County, Virginia." *Virginia Magazine of History and Biography* 108 (September 2000): 393–434.

Downs, Gregory P. *After Appomattox: Military Occupation and the Ends of War.* Cambridge, Mass.: Harvard University Press, 2015.

———. "Mapping Power: The Shape of the State in the Post-Civil War American South," in *State Formations: Global Histories and Cultures of Statehood,* edited by John L. Brooke, Julia C. Strauss, and Greg Anderson, 202–14. Cambridge: Cambridge University Press, 2018.

———. "The Mexicanization of American Politics: The United States' Transnational Path from Civil War to Stabilization." *American Historical Review* 117, no. 2 (April 2012): 387–409.

———. *The Second American Revolution.* Chapel Hill: University of North Carolina Press, 2019.

Doyle, Don H. *The Cause of All Nations: An International History of the American Civil War.* New York: Basic Books, 2014.

———. *Empires.* Ithaca, N.Y.: Cornell University Press, 1986.

———. *Nations Divided: America, Italy, and the Southern Question.* Athens: University of Georgia Press, 2002.

Drescher, Seymour. *The Mighty Experiment: Free Labor versus Slavery in British Emancipation.* New York: Oxford University Press, 2002.

Dubrulle, Hugh. *Ambivalent Nation: How Britain Imagined the American Civil War.* Baton Rouge: Louisiana State University Press, 2018.

Duggan, Christopher. *The Force of Destiny: A History of Italy Since 1796.* London: Allen Lane, 2007.

Edling, Max. *A Hercules in the Cradle: War, Money, and the American State, 1783–1867.* Chicago: University of Chicago Press, 2014.

———. *A Revolution in Favor of Government: Origins of the U.S. Constitution and the Making of the American State.* New York: Oxford University Press, 2003.

Embree, Ainslie T., ed. *India in 1857: The Revolt against Foreign Rule.* Delhi: Chanakaya, 1987.

Engelstein, Laura. *Slavophile Empire: Imperial Russia's Illiberal Path.* Ithaca, N.Y.: Cornell University Press, 2009.

Esdaile, Charles J. *Fighting Napoleon: Guerrillas, Bandits, and Adventurers in Spain, 1808–1814.* New Haven, Conn.: Yale University Press, 2004.

Etherington, Norman. *Theories of Imperialism: War, Conquest and Capital.* London: Croom Helm, 1984.

Evans, Richard J. *The Pursuit of Power: Europe 1815–1914.* New York: Viking, 2016.

Eyal, Yonatan. "A Romantic Realist: George Nicholas Sanders and the Dilemmas of Southern International Engagement." *Journal of Southern History* 78 (February 2012): 107–30.

Fairbank, John K. "Introduction: Varieties of Chinese Miltiary Experience." In *Chinese Ways in Warfare*, edited by Frank A. Kierman Jr. and John K. Fairbank, 1–26. Cambridge, MA: Harvard University Press, 1974.

Faust, Drew Gilpin. *The Creation of Confederate Nationalism: Ideology and Identity in the Civil War South*. Baton Rouge: Louisiana State University Press, 1988.

Felix, Wong Ching Him. "The Images of the Taiping Heavenly Kingdom as Shown in the Publications in France, Germany, and Italy during the Second Half of the Nineteenth Century." *Journal of Chinese Studies* 55 (July 2012): 139–74.

Fialka, Andrew. "Captain Harry Truman: A Case Study of the Union Military's Use of Guerrilla Tactics against the Civilian Population in Civil War Missouri." Honors thesis, University of Missouri, 2010.

Fick, Carolyn E. *The Making of Haiti: The Saint Domingue Revolution from Below*. Knoxville: University of Tennessee Press, 1990.

Figes, Orlando. *The Crimean War: A History*. New York: Metropolitan, 2010.

Fitz, Caitlin. *Our Sister Republics: The United States in an Age of American Revolutions*. New York: Norton, 2016.

Fleche, Andre M. "The Civil War in the Americas." In *Cambridge History of the American Civil War* (Cambridge: Cambridge University Press, 2019), edited by Aaron Sheehan-Dean, 319–41. Cambridge: Cambridge University Press, 2019.

———. *The Revolution of 1861: The American Civil War in the Age of Nationalist Conflict*. Chapel Hill: University of North Carolina Press, 2012.

Foote, Lorien. *The Yankee Plague: Escaped Union Prisoners and the Collapse of the Confederacy*. Chapel Hill: University of North Carolina Press, 2016.

Forster, Stig, and Jörg Nagler. *On the Road to Total War: The American Civil War and the German Wars of Unification, 1861–1871*. Cambridge: Cambridge University Press, 2002.

Foster, Gaines. "What's Not in a Name: The Naming of the American Civil War." *Journal of the Civil War Era* 8, no. 3 (September 2018): 416–54.

Fraser, Chris. "The *Mozi* and Just War Theory in Pre-Han Thought." *Journal of Chinese Military History* 5, no. 2 (November 2016): 135–75.

Freehling, William. *The South vs. The South: How Anti-Confederate Southerners Shaped the Course of the Civil War*. New York: Oxford University Press, 2002.

Frymer, Paul. *Building an American Empire: The Era of Territorial and Political Expansion*. Princeton, N.J.: Princeton University Press, 2017.

Fuller, A. James. *Oliver P. Morton and the Politics of the Civil War and Reconstruction*. Kent, Ohio: Kent State University Press, 2017.

Gabbert, Wolfgang. "Of Friends and Foes: The Caste War and Ethnicity in Yucatan." *Journal of Latin American Anthropology* 9 (May 2008): 90–118.

Gallagher, Gary W. *The Confederate War*. Cambridge, Mass.: Harvard University Press, 1999.

Gandhi, Rajmohan. *A Tale of Two Revolts: India's Mutiny and the American Civil War*. London: Haus, 2011.

Gellner, Ernest. *Nations and Nationalism*, 2nd ed. Ithaca, N.Y.: Cornell University Press, 2009.

Gerstle, Gary. *Liberty and Coercion: The Paradox of American Government*. Princeton, N.J.: Princeton University Press, 2015.

Geyer, Michael, and Charles Bright. "Global Violence and Nationalizing Wars in Eurasia and America: The Geopolitics of War in the Mid-Nineteenth Century." *Society for Comparative Studies in Society and History* 38 (October 1996): 619–57.

Gilmour, David. *The British in India: A Social History of the Raj*. New York: Farrar, Strauss and Giroux, 2018.

Glymph, Thavolia. "Rose's War and the Gendered Politics of a Slave Insurgency in the Civil War." *Journal of the Civil War Era* 3 (December 2013): 501–32.

Gould, Eliga H. *Among the Powers of the Earth: The American Revolution and the Making of a New World Empire*. Cambridge, Mass.: Harvard University Press, 2012.

Goyle, Sonakshi. "Tracing a Cultural Memory: Commemoration of 1857 in the Delhi Durbars, 1877, 1903, and 1911." In *The Historical Journal* 59, no. 3 (September 2016): 799–815.

Graff, David A. "The Chinese Concept of Righteous War." In *The Prism of Just War: Asian and Western Perspectives on the Legitimate Use of Military Force*, edited by Howard M. Hensel, 195–216. Surrey, U.K.: Ashgate, 2010.

Greenberg, Amy S. *Manifest Manhood and the Antebellum American Empire*. Cambridge: Cambridge University Press, 2005.

———. *A Wicked War: Polk, Clay, Lincoln, and the 1846 U.S. Invasion of Mexico*. New York: Knopf, 2012.

Greenfeld, Liah. *Nationalism: Five Roads to Modernity*. Cambridge, Mass.: Harvard University Press, 1992.

Grube, Dennis C. "Sticky Words? Towards a Theory of Rhetorical Path Dependency," *Australian Journal of Political Science* 51, no. 3 (April 2016): 530–45.

Guardino, Peter. *The Dead March: A History of the Mexican-American War*. Cambridge, Mass.: Harvard University Press, 2017.

Hahn, Steven. *A Nation under Our Feet: Black Political Struggles in the Rural South from Slavery to the Great Migration*. Cambridge, Mass.: Belknap Press, 2003.

———. *The Political Worlds of Slavery and Freedom*. Cambridge, Mass.: Harvard University Press, 2009.

Halsey, Stephen R. *Quest for Power: European Imperialism and the Making of Chinese Statecraft*. Cambridge, Mass.: Harvard University Press, 2005.

Hamnett, Brian R. "Benito Juárez, Early Liberalism, and the Regional Politics of Oaxaca, 1828–1853." *Bulletin of Latin American Research* 10, no. 1 (1991): 3–21.

———. *A Concise History of Mexico*. New York: Cambridge University Press, 1999.

———. "Mexican Conservatives, Clericals, and Soldiers: The 'Traitor' Tomás Mejía through Reform and Empire, 1855–1867." *Bulletin of Latin American Research* 20 (April 2001): 187–209.

Hangloo, Rattan Lal. "1857: A Literary-Historical Perspective." *Icfai University Journal of English Studies* 3, no. 3 (September 2008): 20–35.

Harris, William C. *Lincoln and the Border States: Preserving the Union*. Lawrence: University Press of Kansas, 2011.

Hearder, Harry. *Italy in the Age of the Risorgimento, 1790–1870*. 1983. New York: Routledge, 2013.

Henderson, Timothy J. *A Glorious Defeat: Mexico and Its War with the United States*. New York: Hill & Wang, 2007.

Hibbert, Christopher. *The Great Mutiny: India 1857*. London: Penguin, 2000.

Hill, Christopher. "The Word 'Revolution' in Seventeenth-Century England." In *For Veronica Wedgwood These: Studies in Seventeenth-Century History*, edited by Richard Ollard and Panela Tudor-Craig, 134–51. London: William Collins, 1986, 134–51.

Hobsbawm, Eric. *The Age of Capital: 1848–1875*. 1975. New York: Vintage, 1996.

———. *Nations and Nationalism since 1780*, 2nd ed. Cambridge University Press, 1992.

Holton, Woody. *Unruly Americans and the Origins of the Constitution*. New York: Hill & Wang, 2008.

Hopkins, A. G. *American Empire: A Global History*. Princeton, N.J.: Princeton University Press, 2018.

Horton, Paul. "Submitting to the 'Shadow of Slavery': The Secession Crisis and Civil War in Alabama's Lawrence County." *Civil War History* 44, no. 2 (June 1998): 111–36.

Immerwahr, Daniel. *How to Hide an Empire: A History of the Greater United States*. New York: Farrar, Strauss and Giroux, 2019.

Israel, Jonathan. *The Expanding Blaze: How the American Revolution Ignited the World, 1775–1848*. Princeton, N.J.: Princeton University Press, 2017.

Janda, Lance. "Shutting the Gates of Mercy: The American Origins of Total War, 1860–1880." *Journal of Military History* 59, no. 1 (January 1995): 7–26.

Jenkins, Brian. *Lord Lyons: A Diplomat in an Age of Nationalism and War*. Montreal: McGill-Queen's University Press, 2014.

Johnson, Michael. *Toward a Patriarchal Republic: The Secession of Georgia*. Baton Rouge: Louisiana State University Press, 1999.

Jones, Howard. *Blue and Gray Diplomacy: A History of Union and Confederate Foreign Relations*. Chapel Hill: University of North Carolina Press, 2010.

———. *Union in Peril: The Crisis over British Intervention in the Civil War.* Chapel Hill: University of North Carolina Press, 1992.

Kalmoe, Nathan. *With Ballots and Bullets: Partisanship and Violence in the American Civil War.* Unpublished manuscript under review. https://nathankalmoe.com/with-ballots-bullets-partisanship-violence-in-the-american-civil-war/.

Kalyvas, Stathis N. *The Logic of Violence in Civil War.* Cambridge: Cambridge University Press, 2006.

Kaplan, Amy. "'Left Alone with America:' The Absence of Empire in the Study of American Culture." In *Cultures of United States Imperialism*, edited by Amy Kaplan and Donald E. Pease, 3–21. Durham, N.C.: Duke University Press, 1993.

Karp, Matthew. *This Vast Southern Empire: Slaveholders at the Helm of American Foreign Policy.* Cambridge, Mass.: Harvard University Press, 2016.

Kelly, Aileen M. *The Discovery of Chance: The Life and Thought of Alexander Herzen.* Cambridge, Mass.: Harvard University Press, 2016.

Kieniewicz, Stefan. *The Emancipation of the Polish Peasantry.* Chicago: University of Chicago Press, 1969.

Kiernan, V. G. *Colonial Empires and Armies, 1815–1960.* 1982. Montreal: McGill-Queen's University Press, 1998.

Kilcullen, David. *The Accidental Guerrilla: Fighting Small Wars in the Midst of a Big One.* New York: Oxford University Press, 2009.

Kinsley, D. A. *The Fight Like Devils: Stories from Lucknow During the Great Indian Mutiny, 1857–58.* New York: Sarpedon, 2001.

Kramer, Paul A. "Power and Connection: Imperial Histories of the United States in the World." *American Historical Review* 116, no. 5 (December 2011): 1348–91. doi:10.1086/ahr.116.5.1348.

Kuhn, Philip A. *Rebellion at Its Enemies in Late Imperial China: Militarization and Social Structure, 1796–1864.* Cambridge, Mass.: Harvard University Press, 1970.

———. "The Taiping Rebellion," in *The Cambridge History of China.* Vol. 10: *Late Ch'ing, 1800–1911*, Part 1, edited by John K. Fairbank, 264–317 (Cambridge: Cambridge University Press, 1978).

Kutolowski, John. "The Effect of the Polish Insurrection of 1863 on American Civil War Diplomacy." *Historian* 27, no. 4 (August 1965): 560–77. doi:10.1111/j.1540-6563.1965.tb00302.x.

Lang, Andrew. *In the Wake of War: Military Occupation, Emancipation, and Civil War America.* Baton Rouge: Louisiana State University, 2017.

Lang, Timothy. *The Victorians and the Stuart Heritage: Interpretations of a Discordant Past.* New York: Cambridge University Press, 1995.

Laqueur, Walter. *Guerrilla Warfare: A Historical & Critical Study.* 1976. New Brunswick, N.J.: Transaction, 2010.

Leslie, R. F. *Reform and Insurrection in Russian Poland*. London: University of London/Athlone, 1963.

Lew-Williams, Beth. *The Chinese Must Go: Violence, Exclusion, and the Making of the Alien in America*. Cambridge, Mass.: Harvard University Press, 2018.

Lukowski, Jerzy, and Hubert Zawadzki. *A Concise History of Poland*. Cambridge: Cambridge University Press, 2001.

MacDonald, William. "English Historians Repeating Themselves: The Refining of the Whig Interpretation of the English Revolution and Civil War." *Journal of Thought* 7, no. 3 (July 1972): 166–75.

Mack, Andrew. "Why Big Nations Lose Small Wars: The Politics of Asymmetric Conflicts." *World Politics* 27 (January 1975): 175–200.

Mackey, Robert. *The Uncivil War: Irregular Warfare in the Upper South, 1861–1865*. Norman: University of Oklahoma Press, 2004.

Maier, Charles S. *Among Empires: America Ascendancy and Its* Predecessors. Cambridge, Mass.: Harvard University Press, 2006.

———. *Leviathan 2.0: Inventing Modern Statehood*. Cambridge, Mass.: Harvard University Press, 2012.

McCurry, Stephanie. *Confederate Reckoning: Power and Politics in the Civil War South*. Cambridge, Mass.: Harvard University Press, 2010.

McKnight, Brian D., and Barton A. Myers, eds. *The Guerrilla Hunters: Irregular Conflicts during the Civil War*. Baton Rouge: Louisiana State University Press, 2017.

McPherson, James M. "'The Whole Family of Man:' Lincoln and the Last Best Hope Abroad." In *The Union, the Confederacy, and the Atlantic Rim*, edited by Robert E. May, 131–58. West Lafayette, Ind.: Purdue University Press, 1995.

Mediratta, Sangeeta. "The Affair of the Greased Cartridge: Traveling Stories, Unraveling Empires, and the Sepoy Revolt of 1857." *Harvard Asia Quarterly* 14, no. 3 (Fall 2012): 8–16.

Mehta, Uday Singh. *Liberalism and Empire: A Study in Nineteenth-Century British Liberal Thought*. Chicago: University of Chicago Press, 1999.

Melish, Joanne. *Disowning Slavery: Gradual Emancipation and "Race" in New England, 1780–1860*. Ithaca, N.Y.: Cornell University Press, 2000.

Metcalf, Thomas R. *Ideologies of the Raj*. Cambridge: Cambridge University Press, 1995.

Meyer-Fong, Tobie. *What Remains: Coming to Terms with Civil War in 19th Century China*. Stanford, Calif.: Stanford University Press, 2013.

———. "Where the War Ended: Violence, Community, and Commemoration in China's Nineteenth-Century Civil War." *American Historical Review* 120, no. 5 (December 2015): 1724–38.

Mountcastle, Clay. *Punitive War: Confederate Guerrillas and Union Reprisals*. Lawrence: University Press of Kansas, 2009.

Mukherjee, Rudrangshu. *Awadh in Revolt, 1857–1858: A Study of Popular Resistance*. New Delhi: Permanent Black, 2002.

Naquin, Susan. *Millenarian Rebellion in China: The Eight Trigrams Uprising of 1813*. New Haven, Conn.: Yale University Press, 1976.

Nayar, Pramod K. *The Great Uprising: India, 1857*. New Delhi: Penguin, 2007.

Nelson, Megan Kate. *Ruin Nation: Destruction and the American Civil War*. Athens: University of Georgia Press, 2012.

Nesbitt, Scott, and Edward L. Ayers, "Seeing Emancipation: Scale and Freedom in the American South." *Journal of the Civil War Era* 1, no. 1 (March 2011): 3–24.

Ninkovich, Frank. "The United States and Imperialism." In *Companion to American Foreign Policy*, edited by Robert Schulzinger, 79–102. Malden, Mass.: Wiley-Blackwell, 2003.

Noe, Kenneth. "Exterminating Savages: The Union Army and Mountain Guerrillas in Southern West Virginia, 1861–1862." In *The Civil War in Appalachia: Collected Essays*, edited by Kenneth W. Noe and Shannon H. Wilson, 104–127. Knoxville: University of Tennessee Press, 1997.

Oakes, James. *Freedom National: The Destruction of Slavery in the United States, 1861–1865*. New York: Norton, 2013.

Onuf, Peter S. "Epilogue," in *Between Sovereignty and Anarchy: The Politics of Violence in the American Revolutionary Era*, eds. Patrick Griffin, Robert G. Ingram, Peter S. Onuf, and Brian Schoen. Charlottesville: University of Virginia Press, 2015.

Osterhammel, Jürgen. *The Transformation of the World: A Global History of the Nineteenth Century*. Princeton, N.J.: Princeton University Press, 2015.

Pagden, Anthony. *Lords of All the World: Ideologies of Empire in Spain, Britain, and France, c. 1500–c.1800*. New Haven, Conn.: Yale University Press, 1995.

Palmer, R. R. *The Age of the Democratic Revolution: A Political History of Europe and America, 1760–1800*. Vol. 1. Princeton, N.J.: Princeton University Press, 1959.

Paludan, Phillip S. "The Civil War Considered as a Crisis in Law and Order." *American Historical Review* 77 (October 1972): 1013–34.

Papers Relating to Foreign Affairs, 1863, Part 1. Washington, D.C.: Government Printing Office, 1864.

Paret, Peter, and John W. Shy, *Guerrillas in the 1960s*. New York: Frederick A. Praeger, 1962.

Pati, Bismawpoy. *The 1857 Mutiny*. Delhi: Oxford University Press, 2010.

Perdue, Peter C. "Erasing the Empire, Re-Racing the Nation: Racialism and Culturalism in Imperial China." In *Imperial Formations*, edited by Laura Ann Stoler, Carole McGranahan, and Peter C. Perdue, 141–69. Santa Fe, N.M.: School for Advanced Research Press, 2007.

Perusek, Darshan. "Subaltern Consciousness and the Historiography of the Indian Rebellion of 1857." *Novel: A Forum on Fiction* 25, no. 3 (Spring 1992): 286–301.

Perry, Elizabeth J. *Challenging the Mandate of Heaven: Social Protest and State Power in China*. New York: Routledge, 2015.

Phillips, Christopher. *The Rivers Ran Backward: The Civil War and the Remaking of the American Middle Border*. New York: Oxford University Press, 2016.

Pines, Yuri. "A 'Total War'? Rethinking Military Ideology in the *Book of Lord Shang*." *Journal of Chinese Military History* 5, no. 2 (November 2016): 97–134.

Platt, Stephen R. *Autumn in the Heavenly Kingdom: China, the West, and the Epic Story of the Taiping Civil War*. New York: Vintage, 2012.

———. *Imperial Twlight: The Opium War and the End of China's Last Golden Age*. New York: Knopf, 2018.

Polasky, Janet. *Revolutions without Borders: The Call to Liberty in the Atlantic World*. New Haven, Conn.: Yale University Press, 2015.

Polunov, Alexander. *Russia in the Nineteenth Century: Autocracy, Reform, and Social Change, 1814–1914*. 2005. New York: Routledge, 2015.

Pomfret, John. *The Beautiful Country and the Middle Kingdom: America and China, 1776 to the Present*. New York: Picador, 2016.

Potter, David Morris. "The Civil War in the History of the Modern World: A Comparative View." In *The South and the Sectional Conflict*. Baton Rouge: Louisiana State University Press, 1968, 287–300.

Powell, Lawrence N., and Michael S. Wayne. "Self Interest and the Decline of Confederate Nationalism." In *The Old South in the Crucible of War*, edited by Harry P. Owen and James J. Cooke, 29–45. Jackson: University of Mississippi Press, 1983.

Rapport, Michael. *1848: The Year of Revolution*. New York: Basic Books, 2009.

———. *Nineteenth-Century Europe*. New York: Palgrave Macmillan, 2005.

Quigley, Paul, and James Hawdon, eds. *Reconciliation after Civil Wars: Global Perspectives*. New York: Routledge, 2018.

Reardon, Carol. *With a Sword in One Hand and Jomini in the Other: The Problem of Military Thought in the Civil War North*. Chapel Hill: University of North Carolina Press, 2012.

Reed, Nelson A. *The Caste War of Yucatán*, rev. ed. Stanford, Calif.: Stanford University Press, 2001.

Reidy, Joseph P. *Illusions of Emancipation: The Pursuit of Freedom & Equality in the Twilight of Slavery*. Chapel Hill: University of North Carolina Press, 2019.

Riall, Lucy. *Risorgimento: The History of Italy from Napoleon to Nation State*. London: Palgrave Macmillan, 2009.

Richardson, Heather Cox. *The Death of Reconstruction: Race, Labor and Politics in the Post-Civil War North, 1865–1901*. Cambridge, Mass.: Harvard University Press, 2004.

Richmond, Douglas W. *Conflict and Carnage in the Yucatán: Liberals, the Second Empire, and Maya Revolutionaries, 1855–1876*. Tuscaloosa: University of Alabama Press, 2015.

Roberts, Timothy. *Distant Revolutions: 1848 and the Challenge to American Exceptionalism*. Charlottesville: University of Virginia Press, 2009.

Robinson, Armistead. *Bitter Fruits of Bondage: The Demise of Slavery and the Collapse of the Confederacy, 1861–1865*. Charlottesville: University Press of Virginia, 2005.

Rodgers, Daniel T. *Atlantic Crossings: Social Politics in a Progressive Age*. Cambridge, Mass.: Harvard University Press, 2000.

Rodriguez O., Jaime E. "The Emancipation of America." *American Historical Review* 105, no. 1 (February 2000): 131–52.

Rosenblatt, Helena. *The Lost History of Liberalism: From Ancient Rome to the Twenty-First Century*. Princeton, N.J.: Princeton University Press, 2018.

Rowe, William T. *China's Last Empire: The Great Qing*. Cambridge, Mass.: Harvard University Press, 2009.

Royster, Charles. *The Destructive War: William Tecumseh Sherman, Stonewall Jackson, and the Americans*. New York: Knopf, 1991.

Rubin, Anne Sarah. *A Shattered Nation: The Rise and Fall of the Confederacy, 1861–1868*. Chapel Hill: University of North Carolina Press, 2005.

Rugeley, Terry. "The Caste War: Rural Insurgency in Nineteenth-Century Yucatán." In *Revolution and Revolutionaries: Guerrilla Movements in Latin America*, edited by Daniel Castro, 11–22. Lanham, Md.: Scholarly Resource, 2006.

———. ed. *Maya Wars. Ethnographic Accounts from Nineteenth-Century Yucatán*. Norman: University of Oklahoma Press, 2001.

———. *Rebellion Now and Forever: Mayas, Hispanics, and Caste War Violence in Yucatan, 1800–1880*. Stanford, Calif.: Stanford University Press, 2009.

———. "Rural Political Violence and the Origins of the Caste War." *Americas* 53 (April 1997): 469–96.

———. *Yucatán's Maya Peasantry and the Origins of the Caste War*. Austin: University of Texas Press, 1996.

Rugemer, Edward B. *The Problem of Emancipation the Caribbean Roots of the American Civil War*. Baton Rouge: Louisiana State University Press, 2008.

Ryan, Kay. *The Best of It: New and Selected Poems*. New York: Grove Press, 2010.

Sabato, Hilda. *Republics of the New World: The Revolutionary Political Experiment in 19th-Century Latin America*. Princeton, N.J.: Princeton University Press, 2018.

Sainlaude, Stève. *France and the American Civil War: A Diplomatic History.* Chapel Hill: University of North Carolina Press, 2018.

Sakharov, A. N. "The Main Phases and Distinctive Features of Russian Nationalism." In *Russia Nationalism: Past and Present,* edited by Geoffrey Hosking and Robert Service, 7–18. New York: St. Martin's, 1998.

Schoen, Brian. "The Civil War in Europe." In *Cambridge History of the American Civil War,* edited by Aaron Sheehan-Dean, 342–65. Cambridge: Cambridge University Press, 2019.

———. *The Fragile Fabric of Union: Cotton, Federal Politics, and the Global Origins of the Civil War.* Baltimore: Johns Hopkins University Press, 2009.

Scott, Julius. *The Common Wind: Afro-American Currents in the Age of the Haitian Revolution.* London: Verso, 2018.

Scott, Rebecca Jarvis. *Slave Emancipation in Cuba: The Transition to Free Labor, 1860–1899.* Princeton, N.J.: Princeton University Press, 1985.

Setzekorn, Eric. "Chinese Imperialism, Ethnic Cleansing, and Military History, 1850–1877." *Journal of Chinese Military History* 4 (2015): 80–100.

Sexton, Jay. "William H. Seward in the World." *Journal of the Civil War Era* 4, no. 3 (October 2014): 398–430.

Sheehan-Dean, Aaron. *The Calculus of Violence: How Americans Fought the Civil War.* Cambridge, Mass.: Harvard University Press, 2018.

———, ed. *Cambridge History of the American Civil War.* Cambridge: Cambridge University Press, 2019.

———. *Why Confederates Fought: Family and Nation in Civil War Virginia.* Chapel Hill: University of North Carolina Press, 2007.

Showalter, Dennis. *The Wars of German Unification,* 2nd ed. London: Bloomsbury, 2015.

Simpson, Brooks D., Stephen W. Sear, and Aaron Sheehan-Dean, eds. *The Civil War: The First Year Told by Those Who Lived It.* New York: Library of America, 2011.

Sitarman, Ganesh. *The Counterinsurgent's Constitution: Law in the Age of Small Wars.* New York: Oxford University Press, 2010.

Slotkin, Richard. *No Quarter: The Battle of the Crater, 1864.* New York: Random House, 2009.

Smith, Adam I. P. *The Stormy Present: Conservatism and the Problem of Slavery in Northern Politics, 1846–1865.* Chapel Hill: University of North Carolina Press, 2017.

Snyder, Timothy. *The Reconstruction of Nations: Poland, Ukraine, Lithuania, Belarus, 1569–1999.* New Haven, Conn.: Yale University Press, 2003.

Spence, Jonathan. *God's Heavenly Kingdom: The Taiping Heavenly Kingdom of Hong Xiuquan.* New York: Norton, 1996.

Stahr, Walter. *Seward: Lincoln's Indispensable Man*. New York: Simon and Schuster, 2012.

Stites, Richard. *The Four Horsemen: Riding to Liberty in Post-Napoleonic Europe*. New York: Oxford University Press, 2014.

Stith, Matthew M. *Extreme Civil War: Guerrilla Warfare, Environment, and Race on the Trans-Mississippi Frontier*. Baton Rouge: Louisiana State University Press, 2015.

Sumida, Jon Tetsuro. *Decoding Clausewitz: A New Approach to "On War."* Lawrence: University Press of Kansas, 2008.

Sutherland, Daniel. *A Savage Conflict: The Decisive Role of Guerrillas in the American Civil War*. Chapel Hill: University of North Carolina Press, 2009.

Stokes, Eric. *The Peasant Armed: The Indian Revolt of 1857*. Edited by C. A. Bayly. Oxford: Clarendon, 1986.

Taylor, A. J. P. *Bismarck: The Man and Statesman*. New York Vintage, 1967.

Taylor, Amy. *Embattled Freedom: Journeys through the Civil War's Slave Refugee Camps*. Chapel Hill: University of North Carolina Press, 2018.

Taylor, Peter J. "The State as Container: Territoriality in the Modern World-System." *Progress in Human Geography* 18, no. 2 (June 1994): 151–62. doi:10.1177%2F030913259401800202.

Taylor, William R. *Cavalier and Yankee: The Old South and American National Character*. New York: G. Braziller, 1961.

Teng, S. Y. *The Taiping Rebellion and the Western Powers: A Comprehensive Survey*. London: Oxford University Press, 1971.

Thomson, David K. "Financing the War." In *Cambridge History of the American Civil War*, edited by Aaron Sheehan-Dean, 174–92. Cambridge: Cambridge University Press, 2019.

Thompson, Edward J. "British Atrocities." In *India in 1857: The Revolt against Foreign Rule*, edited by Ainslie T. Embree, 105–11. Delhi: Chanakaya, 1987.

Thomson, Roger R. "Military Dimensions of the 'Boxer Uprising' in Shanxi, 1898–1901." In *Warfare in Chinese History*, edited by Hans van de Ven, 288–320. Leiden: Brill, 2000.

Tombs, Robert. "Politics." In *The Nineteenth Century, Europe, 1789–1914*, ed. T.C.W. Blanning. Oxford: Oxford University Press, 2000.

Trouillot, Michel-Rolph. *Silencing the Past: Power and the Production of History*. Boston: Beacon, 1995.

Tucker, Ann L. "To 'Heal the Wounded Spirit': Former Confederates' International Perspective on Reconstruction and Reconciliation." In *Reconciliation After Civil Wars: Global Perspectives*, edited by Paul Quigley and James Hawdon, 187–202. New York: Routledge, 2018.

Urwin, Gregory J. W. *Black Flag over Dixie: Racial Atrocities and Reprisals in the Civil War*. Carbondale: Southern Illinois University Press, 2004.

Varon, Elizabeth. *Disunion! The Coming of the American Civil War, 1789–1859*. Chapel Hill: University of North Carolina Press, 2008.

Waley-Cohen, Joanna. *The Culture of War in China: Empire and the Military under the Qing Dynasty*. London: I. B. Tauris, 2006.

Wandycz, Piotr S. *The Lands of Partitioned Poland, 1795–1918*. Seattle: University of Washington Press, 1974.

Watson, Bruce. *The Great Indian Mutiny: Colin Campbell and the Campaign at Lucknow*. Westport, Conn.: Praeger, 1991.

Wawro, Geoffrey. *The Franco-Prussian War: The German Conquest of France in 1870–1871*. Cambridge: Cambridge University Press, 2003.

Weeks, Theodore R. *Nation and State in Late Imperial Russia: Nationalism and Russification on the Western Frontier, 1863–1914*. Dekalb: Northern Illinois University Press, 1996.

Wert, Jeffry D. *Mosby's Rangers: The True Adventures of the Most Famous Command of the Civil War*. New York: Touchstone, 1990.

West, Warren Reed. "Contemporary French Opinion on the American Civil War." PhD dissertation, Johns Hopkins University, Baltimore, 1922.

Westwood, J. N. *Endurance and Endeavour: Russian History 1812–1986*, 3rd ed. New York: Oxford University Press, 1987.

Wieczerzak, Joseph W. *A Polish Chapter in Civil War America: The Effects of the January Insurrection on American Diplomacy and Opinion*. New York: Twayne, 1967.

Wills, Brian Steel. *Inglorious Passages: Noncombatant Deaths in the American Civil War*. Lawrence: University Press of Kansas, 2017.

Witt, John Fabian. *Lincoln's Code: The Laws of War in American History*. New York: Free Press, 2012.

Woldman, Albert. *Lincoln and the Russians*. Cleveland, Ohio: World, 1952.

Wolfe, Patrick. "History and Imperialism: A Century of Theory, from Marx to Postcolonialism." *American Historical Review* (April 1997): 388–420.

Wolff, Tobias. *In Pharaoh's Army: Memories of the Lost War*. New York: Vintage, 1994.

Worden, Blair. *The English Civil Wars, 1640–1660*. London: Weidenfeld & Nicolson, 2009.

Zaller, Robert. "What Does the English Revolution Mean? Recent Historiographical Interpretations of Seventeenth Century England." *Albion: A Quarterly Journal Concerned with British Studies* 18, no. 4 (Winter 1986): 617–35.

INDEX

Page numbers in *italics* indicate illustrations.

Aaron Sheehan-Dean is the Fred C. Frey Professor of Southern Studies at Louisiana State University and the chairman of the History Department. He is the author of the award-winning *The Calculus of Violence: How Americans Fought the Civil War*; *Why Confederates Fought: Family and Nation in Civil War Virginia*; and *Concise Historical Atlas of the U.S. Civil War* and is the editor of several books.

FRONTIERS OF THE AMERICAN SOUTH

Edited by William A. Link

United States Reconstruction across the Americas, edited by William A. Link (2019)
Reckoning with Rebellion: War and Sovereignty in the Nineteenth Century, by Aaron Sheehan-Dean (2020)

www.ingramcontent.com/pod-product-compliance
Lightning Source LLC
Chambersburg PA
CBHW030306100426
42812CB00002B/591
* 9 7 8 0 8 1 3 0 6 6 4 2 4 *